C0-AWJ-767

RECOLLECTIONS OF THE FRENCH REPUBLIC

(Volume I)

RECOLLECTIONS OF THE FRENCH REPUBLIC is one of the *Makers of History Series*

Other titles in the Series include:

THE ADMIRAL HORTHY MEMOIRS
by Admiral Nicholas Horthy

EDUCATION OF AN HISTORIAN
by Halvdan Koht

SISU
by Oskari Tokoi

SOLDIERING ON
by General Sir Hubert Gough

KHAKI AND GOWN
by Field Marshal Lord Birdwood

A SECOND LOOK AT AMERICA
by General Emilio Aguinaldo & Vicente Albano Pacis

ALWAYS WITH HONOUR
by General Baron Peter N. Wrangel

EAST AFRICAN CAMPAIGNS
by General Paul von Lettow-Vorbeck

FINAL REPORT
by Colonel Jozef Beck

CHANCELLOR BEFORE THE CATACLYSM
by Otto Ender and Hans Huebmer

IN THE STRUGGLE FOR FREEDOM
by Vladko Macek

THE CRETAN DRAMA
by H. R. H. Prince George of Greece

THREE CRITICAL YEARS
by Maurice Paleologue

RECOLLECTIONS OF THE THIRD REPUBLIC

(Volume I)

by

JOSEPH PAUL-BONCOUR

Translated from the French by

GEORGE MARION, JR.

ROBERT SPELLER & SONS, PUBLISHERS, INC.
NEW YORK 36

1957

33 West 42nd Street
New York 36, New York

Library of Congress Catalog Card No. 57-14571

First Edition

PRINTED IN THE UNITED STATES OF AMERICA

Intertype Composition—11/13 Janson
by Arrow Composition, Inc., Worcester, Mass.

Printed and bound by
M. Wolff Book Mfg. Co. Inc., New York

CONTENTS

FOREWORD

These are not *Memoirs*.

I have never thought that, before or after my death, what has happened to me in life, good or bad, could interest others than myself, my family, those close to me, those I have loved and who have loved me.

But, as a child, I grew up in a family and social environment wherein were confronted, as in a microcosm, rendering them all the more easily grasped, the varying opinions awakened by the founding of the Republic, which was then inseparably linked with the recovery of a vanquished France.

As a young man, I took part in the battles into which the young Republic was drawn.

As a man, either by intimate collaboration with those who, at certain hours, have incarnated her with unequalled mastery, or by myself, successively Deputy, Senator, Minister of Labor, Minister of War, Minister of Foreign Affairs, President of the Council, Permanent Delegate of France to the League of Nations, I have been closely associated with some of the events and the negotiations that have oriented her destinies.

And I have displayed the originality of remaining faithful to her, even after she has been immolated on the altar of defeat, for mistakes only in part chargeable to her, and committed by those who, in their cowardice, abandoned her, after having so largely profited from her.

My friends have thought, and I have thought myself, that here was a sheaf of memories lived through, and that it seemed unseemly to wait until one is dead to bind them together.

They are, indeed, of a sort to cast some light on that unlikely adventure which, in one month, brought France to capitulation, the Republic to the tomb, and caused too many Frenchmen to accept too easily the one and the other event.

At every page of these recollections, even those which might appear to have no connection with this preoccupation, it has been mine. It shall remain mine, as long as I have the strength to think and act, in order that, by seeing more clearly the causes of this double disaster, republican France and those who, abroad, in friendly countries and in conquered countries, still accord her their confidence, may find here, as I do, the hope of resurrections.

Moreover, let no one search here for dates, precision, circumstantiated reports.

I have striven to find again, not the details of the events themselves, but my impressions in advance of the events.

Nor should anyone seek in these pages the serenity of an Olympus to which I am not at all entitled to ascend. This is a book of good faith. I say nothing which is inexact. But I do not say it with indifference. There is too much sorrow within me, and too many abandonments have brought us to a point where, reduced too often to the role of an unheeded Cassandra, I had not awaited the effects before denouncing the peril of them.

Without a doubt I, too, have made mistakes. I do not believe I have dissimulated them, when my memory re-encountered them. If I have omitted any, there will be plenty of readers, unburdened with benevolence, ready to remedy this forgetfulness. I have assuredly committed one when, reared in a different atmosphere and dominated by an outmoded passion for courtesy, I failed to denounce with enough brutality those against whom I tried to warn the country.

I belong to a generation that really, and perpetually, lived between two wars: between that of 1870, the memories of which, sufficiently recent, accompanied its childhood, and that of 1914, which it fought and won: and later, between that and the one of 1939, at which debacle it could only look on helplessly.

Is not the picture of this generation, an image of France herself?

Fundamentally peace-loving, France is nevertheless forever

"between two wars" by reason of her equilibrium, her prosperity, her neighbors, and the continuing covetousness directed at her and her Empire. She can only remain herself if she is strong enough, not only to defend herself, but to maintain a Europe where force is not the sole master.

Her history and her geography, her tradition and her safety, condemn her to greatness. It is for having understood this, that the First Republic conquered. For having forgotten it, the last leaders of the Third Republic were conquered.

Why now?

Why not wait to publish these recollections until time has passed, wounds are healed, passions calmed?

I have already answered: because they have a definite goal. To help us *understand*.

To understand what has happened to us. It is all the more necessary because, in misleading us about the causes, as some have contrived to do, we are also misled as to the ways to be followed to repair the damage.

To understand how, and why, a regime which seemed so definitely established, and for which every electoral test, far from raising doubts about it, signified clearly that the Nation intended to go on with it and solidify it, could have collapsed with such rapidity. I am reminded of trees that tower, robust in appearance but inwardly stricken, which the first gale sends crashing to the ground.

To understand what we must do to reestablish it and strengthen it, so that the Fourth Republic may save France, "*la grande vaincue*" of 1940, as the Third Republic restored to vigor "*la grande vaincue*" of 1870.

Later, "when we shall rise again from among the dead."

(Saint Aignan, October 1940, October 1942.)

November 11, 1944.

It will surprise no one that these Recollections were not puublished at the time they were terminated, under the Vichy regime. I would not have found a publisher, and, had I made the attempt, the censor would have reacted vigorously.

I present them now, with France freed, even though the war is not over, and I dedicate them to the dead we commemorate on this day: those of the other war and of this one, those who fell before the firing-squads of the Occupation, and those of the Underground, who contributed so much to our deliverance.

I present them unretouched, though there have been great changes wrought since I set them down, principally our liberation and the fall of the regime I berated so bitterly. It will be observed that I never despaired of these twin blessings, and that many of the views and conjectures I had advanced have now been thoroughly verified. I have indicated some of them by references, in footnote form, to subsequent events confirming them.

I present them, all vibrant with the great sorrow which then held me in its embrace, replaced now by the vast hope of a nation set free, a Republic refound and refurbished.

Ten years have passed since I wrote these pages. I have nothing to add to them, nothing to eliminate from them. Any more than I have anything to add to, or subtract from the volumes this one precedes.

I thank the American publisher, Robert Speller, for presenting the text in a translation, the correctness and comprehension of which I have been able to verify, in order that the American public would be better able to judge what an elder statesman of France thinks of the events that took place immediately after the war of 1870, since the founding of the Third Republic, and during the two wars it had to undergo.

I have stopped immediately following the last one. Although ten years have elapsed, I had no desire to take advantage of this new edition to lengthen it with an appraisal of current events. They are too close. They lack the somewhat remote vantage-point of History, necessary to form an equitable estimate of them.

Not one of them, as a matter of fact, modifies the judgment I have passed on those that preceded them, and which formed the subject of these three volumes. It merely seems, alas, that the same mistakes have recurred, and that the United Nations, which succeeded it, is recommitting and amplifying those of the League of Nations.

This should not be allowed to happen.

By reading these recollections, filled with a faith that still stirs me, may our American friends be fortified in the resolution to prevent the reproduction of these early errors and, on the contrary, to build together, resolutely, a better society and a Peace for which we have struggled and suffered together.

September 20, 1957

JOSEPH PAUL-BONCOUR

Chapter One

THE YOUNGER DAYS OF THE REPUBLIC

A provincial town in the 80's.–Monarchist loyalties.–The new notables.–My family.–Interview at Chambord.–The Sixteenth of May and its consequences.–An unpopular encyclical.–The Republic and the Nation.–A college of 1034.–My future friend.–Boulangism in the rural areas.

"How beautiful she was . . . under the Empire!"

In the 1880's, many a former belle could have heard this comment as she went by. Forain, a decade later, used it as the caption for one of his corrosive cartoons, showing a lady on the decline, excessively fleshy in the popular places, and coiffed raffishly with the Phrygian cap: the Republic.

Never a benevolent man, Forain. Let us admit that the lady was still passable. But how lovely she was in her youth, just after the end of the Empire, the faults of which she sought to mend, along with our disaster, so inconsiderable compared to the one we have just suffered. Toward her soared the hopes that accompany new regimes, when force has not imposed them and the people have given them their hearts.

Lovely and vigorous, for it is a miracle that she was able to withstand the assaults directed against her.

Nothing better, for a clear understanding of this, than to have been reared in our provinces during the years that followed that Sixteenth of May, when the Republic encountered so much hostility from a solid section of the Middle Class. It is nothing to proclaim, from some parliamentary rostrum or the balcony of a city hall, the fall of one regime and the advent of another: it still remains for the new one to establish itself in the hearts, the habits, and the reflexes of the people.

Incontestably, universal suffrage, each time it was consulted, decided in favor of the Republic. But all is not decided by universal suffrage, as we have seen only too often. For the Republic to install herself and remain, she had to gain the adherence of those local mentors whose influence was derived, not so much from their social rank as from the esteem of their compatriots, their services to the community, their family traditions, and on whom, sometimes a bit enviously, the population of our small towns and villages kept their eyes fixed.

It was not easy for her.

It required all the prudence of her first leaders, all their patriotism, to have her progressively accepted by certain circles that took little part in political battles, but wielded a moral and social influence one had to take into account.

To measure it, I have only to remember. . . .

Dominating the little town where I was born, there is an old chateau, where the elegances of the Renaissance have flowered above the solid feudal foundations. A magnificent stairway, constructed by Mansard, connects it with the romanesque church, forming an architectural ensemble which reflects in the waters of the Cher one of the most beautiful pictures of our Touraine.

On the other bank, I can see my old home, transformed into a Kommandantur, and above which floats the swastika flag. The Mansard stairway still ascends toward the clear sky. But the old romanesque steeple has been struck by a shell. Others have damaged the upper windows of the chateau and destroyed some family portraits. The lady who lives there gave her son to the nation in the last war, and her brother in the previous one.

The Cher, until now always preserved from invasion—the Arabs had been halted at Poitiers, the English at Orleans, the armies allied against Napoleon had stayed on the far side of the Loire, the Prussians in 1870 had only sent down a few patrols of uhlans—has become our frontier.

Over the habitually peaceful section of railroad from Tours to Vierzon, where passing trains usually indicated nothing more than the direction of the wind—"you can hear the train tonight; it'll be cold tomorrow"—now, without a pause, I hear them thunderously transporting troops and equipment up and down, connecting the two wings of the army of occupation, through the hitherto inviolate heart of France.

As a child, on the steps of that stairway, in the church on Sunday, in the leafy aisles of a great park, which was then open to a few families of Saint-Aignan, I saw The Emigré pass.

He was a tall old gentleman, or so he appeared to me. However, he could not have been so very old, because I had seen him at the side of his father, who had an ear frozen in the Retreat from Moscow, and was an acquaintance of Chateaubriand. How few generations it takes to journey far back in History!

Sideburns neatly trimmed, long frock-coat, cravat of the Louis Philippe period, gray top-hat, gold-handled cane, but walking erect, head high, this was Elie-Roger-Louis de Talleyrand-Perigord, Prince of Chalais, Duke of Perigord. Death had struck close to him; he had lost his wife when quite young, then his daughter; he lived alone on his property at Saint-Aignan, which was only slightly less extensive than that of his cousins at nearby Valencay, and, like it, one of the finest estates in France.

One saw him only intermittently. He went out very little. Sometimes, riding in his carriage, he was preceded by an outrider, in the manner of the Old Regime. To the saluting peasantry, he would call out, "Put your hat on!" And to the municipal bigwigs who, after passing a law reorganizing the poor-houses, came to tell him they had nominated him for membership on the Council of Administration, he replied, "Messieurs, I am grateful to you for nominating me . . . to a post which belongs to me, nominated or not!" For it was his ancestor, the Duke of Beauvilliers, who had commissioned Mansard to build the charity hosptial, paid for its construction and its upkeep.

But he had the grand manner, our Prince of Chalais!

And not just outwardly! My father was his physician; the

Prince gave him his complete confidence, additionally grateful to our family because, in 1793, my great-grandfather had been delegated by the district of Saint-Aignan to seek a pardon for the Duchess of Beauvilliers, condemned to the guillotine by the revolutionary tribunal. My father—who occasionally dined alone with the Prince, both of them formally attired, in this lonely chateau where etiquette was as strictly observed as when the courtiers of Louis XIV hovered around the Duke of Beauvilliers, preceptor of the king's grandson, the future Philip V of Spain—often regaled us with vivid descriptions of the characteristic traits of this uncompromising representative of a past that was vanishing into the mists of History.

Suffering from an unrelenting malady, the speed of which he quite misjudged, he said one day to my father:

"Doctor, I want you to promise me something. For reasons which I cannot be bothered to go over in detail, it is quite necessary for my death to take place in Paris. Will you promise to give me timely warning, when you see there is no hope for me?"

My father paled, hesitated, then spoke out:

"Prince, you must leave at once!"

"Thank you, Doctor," he said, evenly. And he clasped my father's hand.

At the hour of departure, my father went up to the Prince's room, and found him stretched out on the bed, writhing in pain. After giving him a morphine injection, my father lent him a supporting arm on the slow, spasmodic journey down the long stairway, at the foot of which stands the sarcophagus, adorned with a Grecian bas-relief, in which a former Duke de Beauvilliers, ambassador of France, had brought home the body of his daughter. When my father and his princely patient reached the lower steps, the household staff and the game-keepers in their green velvet uniforms were aligned at the front door; when he saw them, the Prince steadied, straightened, passed through their lines, militarily erect, not a muscle of his face moving. After taking his seat in the coupe, incapable of continuing the effort, he collapsed in my father's arms.

Let us salute him, as he was saluted even by the Reds of those days. Who were, as a matter of fact, still rather pink.

But one could be certain that the influence exerted by men such as this, and which emanated as much from their good deeds as from their fortune and social position, would not precisely be exerted in favor of the Republic.

However, the very distance that separated them from the lower orders, in this era when social hierarchies were still quite strong—for if they no longer existed in law, they were very much alive in fact—weakened their influence to the gain of that wielded by a middle class element: doctors, lawyers, veterinaries, pharmacists, well-to-do merchants, rural landowners, whose profession or business put them in closer contact with the mass of the people. Nearer to it, many of them having come out of it, they were less likely to arouse its distrust. Alfred Capus, momentarily abandoning his satirical studies of Parisian life, wrote a rather unexpected book, *Scenes de la Vie Difficile*, describing admirably the decisive role played by them in the founding and the defense of the Republic. We shall meet them again on that crucial Sixteenth of May, again at the time of the Boulangist episode, and still later, until the "new brood" takes over from them and brings about what Daniel Halevy termed, and I consider the term inexact, "The End of the Notables."

Inexact, because it was more a matter of new notables replacing the old, a changing of the guard rather than a dismissal. It was Gambetta who called them the "new brood." These men, who were the founders of the Third Republic, resembled remarkably a type which the present Vichy regime seems to believe it invented. In reality, and with less verbosity, they practised some of those virtues about which there is so much fuss and fanfare today: the family spirit, roots in the native soil, a taste for parochial patriotism, thrift, the will to work. Middle class for the most part, sheltered from want, spared from adventures, they ran the State, their departments and communes, with the same order and method they used in their private life to strengthen and conserve their patrimony. This is one of the reasons why the people trusted them in a country where, except for revolutionary explosions generally provoked by a hard-headed reluctance of those in command to lighten ship in time, the citizens are rather partial to these qualities and, all things considered, pretty conservative.

The "return to the soil"! They talk enough about it, the Vichyites! Even though, constrained by the obligations of an armistice, the terms and duration of which are unprecedented in History, they harass the cultivator of the soil as no one has ever done before.

The elders of the Republic had no need to return to the soil. They were of it. They were on it. Even the doctors and lawyers. They had all, more or less, inherited fields and vines in the sun. It is intriguing to note that, for a long time, the name of a piece of land, "Mont-Sous-Vaudrey", "la Begude", "le Loupillon", has been attached even to those designated by the regime as Chiefs of State. Chiefs of State too deprived of power, whose moderation and sense of realism could have been put to greater use, if they had been given more authority. But the recruiting of them was sound, and often our Presidents of the Republic have acted with a discretion that was admissible in an era when the violent processes of publicity had not yet numbed the brain, and the moderation that is proper for the government of states continued to be observed.

It was the same with the smaller wheels; even in the remotest corners of the provinces, the Republic had at her disposal such excellent material that, out of the images he retained of that period, the regionalist I was to become remarked to himself what a pity it was that a more complete decentralization had not permitted a further use of them at a local level, which would have been all profit for the community and the country.

Let us not forget, however, that this Republic passed the law of 1871 and 1884, loosened the chains which, under the Empire, bound departments and communes, and gave back to the citizens the right to choose their municipal magistrates. It has needed the latest decrees of the Vichy regime to bring us back to the conditions prevailing at the time of the Empire, and to cause us to imagine, while discussing regionalism, that it can rise from the arbitrary choices of a central power without control.

The eagerness of the bourgeoisie to rally round the Republic was considerably less than unanimous. I only need to point out what happened in my own family. No matter how intimate certain recollections, it is they that give the best impression of the complexity of this period in our national History, and put one on guard against simplifications which are excessive and too chronological.

Free in his thinking and in his beliefs, as well as profoundly tolerant, my father was a republican. He had come to this decision, not so much by family tradition—although his kinsmen, lawyers and doctors, often administrators of their communes, were quite representative of that liberal bourgeoisie of the provinces—but by the dictates of his own mind and heart. His mind persuaded him that there was no longer any other regime possible in France. His heart—his great heart that made him the perfect type of country doctor described in Balzac's *Medecin de Campagne*, and won him an affection the traces of which have not been effaced in the thirty-eight years since his death—inclined him toward a regime whose motto, at that time, still retained its luster and its meaning.

His republicanism was as sincere as it was unobtrusive, for he persistently refused any mandates offered him. And I firmly believe that those I have received from my compatriots were more intended to honor his memory than my person. He was without personal ambition, and proved it well. After intensive medical studies at Tours, then at Paris, and as an interne at hospitals where he had been the companion and the equal of the most illustrious representatives of a great medical generation, he had returned very simply to a practice in the little town where, for two centuries, his family lived, and where I write these lines. He met his well-established colleagues again one day at Tours, where a monument had been erected commemorating three great medical men of Touraine —Bretonneau, Trousseau, and Velpeau—who had been his teachers; and his colleagues voiced their astonishment at the extreme simplicity of his life, and their admiration for his disinterestedness.

My mother was from an old Norman family, whose name appears on the roster of companions of William the Conqueror, inscribed on the wall of the church at Dives. She and her kin were, by tradition, royalist and catholic. For generations, they rarely stirred from their land in Lower Normandy, where they lived meagerly, except to serve in the King's army or in his ships.. A great-uncle had been killed at Quiberon. Her maternal grandfather, M. Duhamel, counsellor at the Law Court of Caen, had been arrested twice during the Terror. Her brother, an attorney general, had been removed from office by the Republic in 1877, following the events of the Sixteenth of May. My grandfather had been propelled to prison at Avranches by two Bonapartist gendarmes in 1851, during Louis Napoleon's *coup d'etat.*

About him, I have my doubts! Later, long after his death, certain remarks made at election time by the republicans of his commune, who spoke of him quite fraternally, would lead me to suspect that—independent, impetuous, generous, a bit of a nonconformist* like his grandson—very possibly it was not as a royalist, but as a republican, that the Empire locked him up. A point on which my mother's family is discreetly and dignifiedly silent.

At certain times in my public life, certain people, who were aware of these family origins, have thought to embarrass me by contrasting them with political stands that a carefully considered conviction had led me to take. I always replied that, not only did I see no reason to disavow some worthy people who had loyally supported ideas and causes which are no longer mine, without ever receiving or expecting any recompense, but they had given me the example of a fidelity that I have maintained toward the cause of my choice, and

* My grandfather had been the first to try to put under cultivation the polders of Mont Saint-Michel. This was profitable to those who followed, but not to him. He then tried to do the same with the marshlands of the Brenne, bordering on Touraine. It was due to this proximity that my Norman mother married my father, doctor at Saint-Aignan.

still maintain, all the stronger since it appears to be momentarily vanquished and persecuted.

Perhaps it was the effect of seeing them live side by side in the bosom of my family, united by the tenderest affection, yet following divergent political paths, that gave me the illusion, still tenacious within me, that it could be the same with the nation, that France could move toward the future while retaining the precious legacies of her past. This may be why I have always loved so much these words of Jaures: "It is in going toward the ocean, that the river remains faithful to its source."

Not that I have ever embraced the hypocritical conception of a France where all divergencies would be hushed. I have heard it too often from the mouths of those who, weary of serving their ideas, would like to find patriotic pretexts to cover an abandonment that was generally to their personal advantage . . . . Whoever says "a free country," means one where political parties dispute, oppose, and succeed each other. The Great Hush is only suited to dictatorships, if one can speak of a hush amid the hubbub of propaganda to which totalitarian countries have conditioned us. The essentials are: that the nation should not be torn apart; that the parties should be in accord on a few common points relating to the nation's vital interests; and, finally, that the parties respect each other and their reciprocal liberties.

Other nations, with quite dissimilar regimes, have achieved it: the parliamentary monarchy of Great Britain, the American republic. Why can't France?

Because the French Republic has lacked a conservative party accepting frankly the institutions which the Nation had freely given itself, conducting its own campaign, playing its part, and which would have come into power when circumstances or the errors of its adversaries caused the people to prefer it. I have always regretted—precisely because I knew, esteemed, and loved them—that these sound forces, with a solid French tradition, had adopted a policy which systematically kept them away from affairs of state and swept them into various adventures from which the Republic always emerged victorious, but weakened by the countermove, and deterred by these struggles from certain constitutional reforms which would have been salutary. Then, the defeated forces, instead of rallying round the perfectly capable and honorable leaders to be found in their own ranks, and looking only to them for revenge—which always comes to those who know how to wait for it—their entire policy has consisted in seeking turncoats among their adversaries, who betrayed each other in turn, trying new and unstable balances of power, alternate concessions, "deals"—an ugly word, but one that says well what it wants to say—preventing any clear-cut program, and clear choice of the electoral body.

The Sixteenth of May was the first of these adventures.

In 1877, at the age of four, I was too young for it to have left any direct imprint on my mind; but, for several years afterward, the memory clung tenaciously in our town of the rancors it had aroused, and the reprisals that had followed. They discussed it in the evening, by lamplight, at the hour when the children go to sleep, and the grown-ups talk politics.

The National Assembly, predominantly conservative, even monarchist, would have undoubtedly restored the monarchy, had it not been for the intransigent attitude of the Count of Chambord, who, all during his voluntary exile in Austria, had been the object of touching manifestations of fidelity in the depths of our provinces, which I was privileged to witness fairly frequently, as a child. They even outlived him. . . . I recall, a few years after his death, going with my mother to visit some elderly cousins, two of them spinsters, one a widow, whose combined ages added up to something like a hundred-and-eighty years. They lived in a corner of Tours that was full of mysticism and empty of tourists, in a cluster of convents and churches. Balzac has described it well in *Le Curé de Tours*, also in *Le Musee des Antiques*, where he has transposed, as he had a habit of doing, to another city, his memories of his native town. Our cousins' house, its peepholed door tight closed against the century, tall candles burning in a room furnished in the style of Louis Philippe and serving as a sanctuary, stood near that of a citizen beatified by the church, M. Dupont. My mother, speaking to them of some recent event of importance, was surprised to learn they had never heard of it.

"Don't you read the newspapers?"

"Oh, you know," they sighed, "now that our poor dear Count of Chambord is dead, what's the use?"

The legitimate pretender gone, they had retired into seclusion, and preferred to ignore the world outside.

Neither the prayers nor the actions of his loyal supporters had sufficed to set him on a throne to which he was obstinately unwilling to ascend without the accompanying restoration of the white banner of the old monarchy. A double drama had taken place at his Austrian residence, the castle of Frohsdorf, and here in our neighborhood, at Chambord. They talked about it a long time in the country, some rejoicing, some saddened by what happened here. At Chambord, purchased by national subscription as a gift for the future Henri V, the hopes of the monarchy were buried. And until its sequestration in 1914, as Austrian property, one could see, in a bare room of the vast and deserted chateau, the tapestry woven by the ladies of Blois for the return of the King.

About ten years ago, I came to Chambord to settle certain differences between the ministries of Domains, Waters and Forests, and Beaux-Arts, who were vying for possession of the chateau. I was informed by the custodian that, the day before, a woman in deep mourning, accompanied by a young boy, had driven up in a hired carriage from Blois. She went to the chapel to pray, then asked permission to visit the private apartments where the meeting of the pretender and his supporters had been held. The two visitors were the Empress Zita and her son, Archduke Otto, to whom I had occasion to recall, at the beginning of the war, this quiet pilgrimage he had made with his mother.

Embittered by its inability to find a solution, paralyzed by the differences between legitimists and orleanists, and blaming him for having more or less tricked them all, the National Assembly had rather shamefully overthrown M. Thiers, who had liberated the country from the Prussians. An aging field-marshal was selected as a very temporary replacement, and a government, known as the government of "Moral Order," was set up under the presidency of a duke, De Broglie. Feeling that the Republic was on the rise, he reacted strongly, very strongly, too strongly, not only in his laws, which seemed to be deliberately designed to run counter to popular sentiment, but in his individual measures: a shifting of personnel, arbitrary removals, resignations demanded, which, far more than the general measures, aroused great secret resentment, although a certain degree of cowardice had seemed to make them apparently accepted without protest.

Useless to say more: the story is known: and much more recent happenings have made them topical. With, however, considerably more brutality. The totalitarian countries have brought such an element of the arbitrary and the violent into political customs, and have trampled on what used to be considered the extreme limit of what is permissible, and what is not, to such a degree that France herself, or, more exactly, the government claiming to represent her, has not wished to lag too far behind the conquerors. It has struck against the institutions and the men of yesterday with an ardor that would have made De Broglie draw back. This what Pierre Laval termed—at a session of the Senate where, supported only by my colleague Astier, I raised my voice in contradiction—"aligning ourselves with the totalitarian nations. . . ."

We know the consequences of De Broglie's decisions, and how universal suffrage replied to the dissolution of the Chamber of Deputies, which had been the final act of the operation.

Unhappily, by one of those lasting prejudices that take hold of institutions and parties, as well as individuals, and make them refuse to use remedies that would save them, the act of dissolution received its death-blow. Because, in 1877, Marshal MacMahon ordered the Chamber dissolved, as a move against the Left—twenty, thirty, forty years later, the Left found this measure repugnant, although it is written in our constitution, and indispensable to the proper functioning of a parliamentary regime, as its judicious use in England attests. Since MacMahon, no government of France, no President of the Republic has ever dared to employ it.

This is a first example—we shall find others—where the

efforts of the Republic to repulse assaults directed against her, have caused her to turn away, not only from reforms necessary to any organism in the process of evolution, but even from the normal application of her own initial statutes.

Another unhappy problem was that the Church had somewhat over-blessed the enterprise: she had brought to bear all her influence, which had remained considerable, to support a "Moral Order" which was more conservative than christian, and which sought to unify a defense of religion and social conservation. The result was that, up to the war of 1914, anticlericalism established itself solidly in the Republic; and the Republic had to expend, in this struggle, forces that would have been better employed elsewhere, if only to make certain structural reforms indispensable in other, more difficult, struggles.

Vainly, some years later, a great Pope, Leo XIII, aware of the injury this antagonism was doing to religion, amplified the echo of Cardinal de Lavigerie's speech in Algiers—when the French prelate advised his listeners to adhere, without reservation, to the republican form of government—and, from the Chair of Peter, recommended to Catholic France a union with the Republic.

His Holiness was widely misunderstood. I know of convents, where nuns of simple soul prayed for the Pope's conversion. *Sancta simplicitas!* But the pontifical instructions encountered far heavier resistance from many distinguished catholics. My personal qualms of conscience were so severe that, many years later, when another pope condemned the royalist newspaper, *L'Action Francaise*, and forbade the faithful to read it, in spite of my lack of tenderness toward a journal which had so savagely attacked my friends and myself, unlike them, I did not find this at all heartening. I had too clear a perception of the mental anguish that can result for catholics who have to choose between their political convictions and the directives of the Sovereign Pontiff. And then, I believe that, neither in one sense, nor the other, should the two domains be unified.

Even those who followed the directive and renounced

their struggle against the regime, did it badly. I must except Count de Mun, whose electors in Brittany made him pay dearly for it for awhile, and those of his particular political group, the Social-Catholics, animated by the ardent words of this tall, elegant royalist, former cuirassier, who had fought to repress the Commune and written *Les Derniers Jours du Drapeau Blanc*, before consecrating his life to an apostleship, the benefits of which were to be reaped by a certain young Minister of Labor in 1911. But, for the most part, this business of giving one's allegiance to the form of a regime, separated from its social aspect, deprived of its substance, failed to have the political consequences the Pope could have hoped for. The same Pope who wrote the magnificent encyclical *Rerum Novarum*.

The old republicans were little inclined to welcome these republicans of the directive. Anticlericalism was in full swing, and one of the companions of Gambetta, M. Spuller, had been brought to task for venturing to speak of the "new spirit." The old guard stood firm in their positions; the young ones, spurred by ambition, never neglected an opportunity to profit from the bitter memories left in the rural districts, where they are long-lived, and in the workers' sections of the cities, where they are violent, by the actions of the clergy in the reprisals following the Sixteenth of May. The Dreyfus Affair helped to revive these passions, which are capable of dividing a nation in quite a different way from mere opposing points of view on customs duties, or even on political or social economy. Briand himself, with all his talent for appeasement, could not succeed. It was only after the Great War—a war in which the catholics, the socialists, the freemasons, the priests, the anticlericals, fought side by side—that these peacetime battles appeared progressively obsolete, in the light of more absorbing problems.

At least, from this adventure of the Sixteenth of May, and the victory of the republicans, the Nation emerged unwounded. Moreover, the Republic, in this conflict, seemed to have the same face as the Nation; and this became the keynote of the campaign waged by the republican political leaders, a campaign that triumphed. In the eyes of all those unblinded by prejudice or unbound by old convictions, this was the regime most capable of reuniting the greatest possible number of citizens in the will to rise from the Prussian defeat and to restore a France, free to face its destiny.

However, the men of the Sixteenth of May were irreproachable from the patriotic point of view. Like the others, they had aided in the rebuilding of our army, some of the organic laws for which date from the National Assembly. Like the others, the conservative deputies did their duty in what the country then called the "Terrible Year," unable to foresee the one in which we live. Many had commanded mobile units from their department. The Papal Zouaves of Charette fought at Patay and Auvours, while the Red Shirts of Garibaldi battled in the east under the command of Bourbaki and D'Aurelle de Paladine, who, it must be admitted, seemed not to know quite what to do with them; a true *union sacree*, such as we found again in 1914, and which 1940 never knew.

And was it not D'Audiffret-Pasquier, another duke in a legislative assembly that included a great many of them, who, turning toward the Bonapartists suddenly seeking to reassert themselves, shouted at them the old Roman cry, just as timely today to those who have lost their armies, "Varus, give us back our legions!"

But the National Assembly of Bordeaux and of Versailles, from which the governments of May 24 and May 16 emanated, bore the stigma of having been elected under the domination of the enemy and of having made a peace which the French people, in the main, did not accept.

On the other hand, it was the Republic which, together with the Commune in Paris, and Gambetta in Bordeaux, had protested against the capitulation and the mutilation of France; and which had, with Thiers, liberated the territory. And even if Thiers had called Gambetta a "mad fool," the clairvoyance of the one and the wisdom of the other, along with their patriotism, had reunited them. Republican propaganda quickly seized upon the party's stand; the campaign was conducted with vigor and a picturesque utilization of every publicity device then known; in addition to public meetings, where the orators of the Left triumphed with their customary ease, opportunities were found to spread the message at country market-days and fairs which, in an era when transportation was still difficult—(often, a great, creaking public conveyance, resembling the Hirondelle in *Madame Bovary*, leaving at dawn and returning at dusk, was our chief link with the principal town of our department)—served as the farmers' forum. The peddler once more took the place he had held during the Restoration and the Reign of Louis Philippe, as a disseminator of Napoleonic and republican propaganda, which went together in those days, and for the benefit of Louis Napoleon, the Prince-President, after 1849.

I have still seen some of those handkerchiefs, with the likenesses of Thiers and Gambetta side by side, and the names of leaders of the Extreme-Left intermingled with those of the more moderate republicans without seeming to cause any surprise. These were enormous handkerchiefs of white cotton, with a wide red border and black lettering, quite like the ones the army issued its soldiers, containing instructions for the care of their rifles or their duties in the field, as well as being useful to tie up and cover their packs. They were long perpetuated in our army, for they continued to be issued when I reported for military service at the barracks at Blois, in 1893.

This military touch pleased the purchaser, who was thus reminded of his soldierly memories, and who read thereon, in the place of army regulations, the proclamations of the battling republicans. It was all very adroitly presented, and the peddlers sold their handkerchiefs under the very noses of the police. I had kept a few in my collection of revolutionary and republican souvenirs; if I can find them now, I shall look at them a bit ironically. How much more dynamic the republicans of 1877 than those of 1940!

And the propaganda had its effects, because it stirred not only the republican fiber deep in people's hearts, but also a patriotic fiber that had never slackened, despite the wounds, the bruises, the battering.

The education of the children was strongly oriented toward this goal. Even before the great law of Jules Ferry, the free schools of the state had multiplied, and their teachers were the servants of a great patriotic cult quite without bluster, its simple lessons finding the way to our young hearts.

It was frequently stated that the German schoolmaster had won the war, just as it is being said today that the French schoolmaster caused us to lose the present one. Like General Bourbaki after one of the battles of 1870, I maintain that it was mainly a matter of their having well-trained reserves, when we had none. And a general staff which, as 1940 showed so convincingly, retained intact, through all the various political manifestations in Germany, its value, its capacity for hard work, and the faculty of adapting itself to changing conditions of technique and strategy.

In any case, the schoolmasters of France in 1877 went to work vigorously. Perhaps it was due to their early training that the teachers of 1914, after many deviations and pacifist illusions, acquitted themselves so admirably in battle, and gave us so many splendid reserve officers, that Colonel Driant, who had denounced them earlier in his books on *La Guerre de Demain*, made an apology to them in the woods at Caures, near Verdun, where he himself was to die; an apology that was as much an honor to the man who made it as to those who received it.

The first schoolbook we had, after the alphabet, was a small volume that lingered so long in my memory, I went from bookshop to bookshop hunting for a copy, in the days that followed the Great War. It was called *Le Tour de France de Deux Enfants*. From it, we learned about the geography, history, physiognomy and resources of our provinces through the impressions gathered by two children from our lost province of Lorraine, who had promised their dying father to seek their future in France and, to earn their living, went to work with a peddler along the highways and byways.

It was a minor masterpiece, and the authors, if they are

still alive, deserve to be spared the reprobation which is now heaped on everything that was done since the Republic. But perhaps this ardent little book would not be admitted to the expurgated list of our current textbooks. Ardent, but discreet, as befitted a nation which needed to be reconstituted, but *refused to accept defeat.*

When we were a bit older, our teachers read to us *La Derniere Classe*, by Alphonse Daudet, and another pretty story, the name of which escapes me, about an aging Alsatian magistrate, who was not quite ready to give up his post and return to France, because his chair in the courtroom was so very comfortable. He was somewhat remorseful, however, and at night, he dreamed he was attending his own funeral, and a great wave of laughter rolled over the cemetery when, instead of a wreath, they placed on his tomb the well-stuffed leather cushion he had preferred to *la patrie!*

It would have been only fitting for Alsace and Lorraine to erect a statue to Alphonse Daudet of Provence, whose touching patriotism charmed our childhood.

The acceptance of compulsory military service furnished ample proof of France's unanimous resolution to rise again and be strong. Not enough thought is given, after the long interval of time, to the great upheaval in our habits, in our conception of civic duty, in our individual lives and that of the Nation, wrought by this idea of conscription without substitution, obligatory for all, and before which the country, where civic spirit is habitually high, had long held back.

It should be remembered that in France, right after 1870, the bulk of the population, imitating the victor, consented to the sacrifice of sending their young, all their young, into the barracks, submitting for several years to a discipline much longer and rougher than it has since become. Five years, at first; then three years; then two; returning to a service of three years on the eve of 1914; each reduction of time being accompanied by a greater equality and a suppression of exemptions. It hit every section of the citizenry; but obviously it was the middle class that was hit hardest by this veritable revolution, not yet called "national," although that is what it was in every sense of the word, without provocation and without hypocrisy.

The leading classes had become accustomed, under the preceding regimes where conscription existed, to escape by hiring a substitute. It was hard for them to renounce this privilege which, after the parenthesis of the Revolution—the real one, the one that is spelled with a capital "R"—and even after the establishment of universal suffrage, had outlived all others. And I am not saying that distant childhood memories do not recall how it wounded the sensibilities of mothers, and other less touching manifestations of egoism. But this never went beyond the intimate family circle and private conversation: the instinctive love of country, and the passion for equality, so permanent and so deep-rooted in a Frenchman's heart, swept all before them.

The "drawing of lots" and the "medical examination" were two military ceremonies which, each year, indicated to the population this great change in their lives. In the rural districts especially, these were events which the prefects and the politicians determinedly enhanced by their presence.

A prefect! In those days, that was something! The prefects of the young Republic managed to retain, but with less arrogance, something of the authority of the hard-hitting prefects of the Empire. In the streets of our town, at the sight of one of the new dignitaries of the government in his silver-braided uniform, the older inhabitants were reminded of the visit of M. de Chambaron, long the prefect of our department. He had married a young girl from an old family of Saint-Aignan, relatives of ours. On his first visit, he went to call on some of the notables, and, coming out of my great-grandfather's house, he saw a group of open-mouthed rustics waiting.

"Do you know the Emperor, my friends?" he asked.

"No, *monsieur le Prefet*."

"Here's what he looks like," he said, tossing them some gold coins bearing the imperial portrait.

Strong governments know how to make good use of secret funds!

As for the deputy, it was interesting to see how the farmers appreciated, in the person of their elected representative, the right to choose him freely, without payment of poll-tax as in the reign of Louis Philippe, and without administrative pressure as under the Empire. They still recalled the election of 1860, where the voters were summoned to come and vote for the "re-election of Monsieur . . . who has well-deserved it." They attached a considerable amount of importance to their ballot, somewhat more than yesterday, but much less than tomorrow, for those who govern us today do not seem to realize that these grandsons of our republican peasants, the same ones I meet every day on my walks, after having grown up with them, have not the slightest intention of giving up their voting privilege.

And because they loved to exercise it, and the politicians had not yet abused it, it retained its prestige.

On conscription days, a din of drums and trumpets awakened the town. At an early hour, I would be in our small garden that faced the river and the open country, and, as a setting for my childhood games, combined the best features of the Far West, the Pampas, and the Sahara. Down the roads pounded today by the boots of the Wehrmacht, I could see the conscripts coming, their flags unfurled, their songs uninhibited.

In the afternoon, the authorities marched up the main street, which now bears our name: the Prefect in his uniform, the Mayor with his tricolored sash, and the Deputy. A deputy then, later a senator, then deputy again until his death in 1919, at which time I became his successor; from 1869, he ran the district with an authority that sometimes had rather displeasing aspects against which I stood up and protested. But he was our duly elected representative, and one usually yielded. Just as one bowed low to the prefect, who only appeared on occasions of the utmost solemnity. Since then, it has become the custom for the foremost ministers of the Republic to present themselves prodigally at ceremonies of vast insignificance which the sub-prefects of an earlier day would not have condescended to attend.

And the ritual began. Out of the little town-hall, scene of most of the stages of my public life, streamed the conscripts,

(ABOVE) DR. PAUL-BONCOUR LEAVING
FOR HIS ROUND OF CALLS

(BELOW) THE SAINT-AIGNAN
FAMILY RESIDENCE

A COURTYARD OF THE COLLEGE OF PONT-LEVOY

each with the number he had drawn pinned to his cap, amid a bright show of ribbons. Despite a slight tightening of the heart at the imminence of a military service which, in those days, was long and hard, they affected a noisy gaiety sustained by large libations at the inns. The fathers were less boisterous: a few of the lads sobbed intermittently, an indication that they had drawn a "bad number," sending them to Africa or into the Navy.

The Navy, in this case, meant the marines: for the maritime provinces continued to supply the men who worked the ships, drawn from a register of the nation's seafaring population, an admirable system instituted centuries before by Colbert, one of those great employes who made France. To our conscripts, service with the marine infantry meant duty in China or Tonkin, in colonial expeditions which, through parliamentary debate, were beginning to arouse public opinion. Even army service in Africa was causing considerable anxiety, at that time, among our home-loving peasantry. I have seen them lament being designated for it, whereas, in later years, their sons were eager to obtain an overseas assignment as a means of seeing the world. Without pretentious talk of empire, without the argument of primogeniture and other factors to which the expansion of Britain is attributed, young Frenchmen adapted themselves admirably to this colonial enterprise that was one of the triumphs of the Third Republic, and by no means the least.

Africa, where a portion of our conscripts was invariably despatched, hardly constituted a restful duty. Although Algeria had been pacified for the most part, there was frequent border agitation: columns were frequently on the march, and the Zouaves were as busy as in the years of the conquest. A war against pillaging tribes on the Algerian-Tunisian border was a prelude to the occupation of Tunisia, by which the Republic, even before Morocco, put its seal on the constitution of an African France, menaced today by our defeat in Europe.

On fair-days and holidays, in the waxworks or on violently-colored posters, reminiscent of early motion picture advertising, alongside the booths where the yokels' teeth were extracted amid a thunder of drums, one saw depicted the sailors of Courbet in combat with Chinese hordes, or a single small soldier, in the blood-red trousers of our infantry, about to be crushed to earth by a big blackamoor—although the Berbers, against whom our troops were fighting, were actually white.

Fathers and sons, at the close of conscription day, returned to their farms, often on foot—what marchers for our infantry!—revolving in their minds these new concepts of a France mutilated in Europe, but affirming her vitality in a conquest of territories overseas, where the Republic offered us revenge for our colonial losses at the end of the Eighteenth Century.

This, however, did not go without rather heavy parliamentary disturbances, which had their repercussions in local elections. The early days of the Third Republic were considerably agitated by this colonial question. I might observe that the monarchies of Charles X and Louis-Philippe had the same difficulties. Except for the Convention, dominated by the Committee of Public Safety, and carried forward by a magnificent and savage surge, our assemblies have a great deal of trouble foreseeing the future and the momentary sacrifices it requires.

The great Jules Ferry knew something of it. On the night of Lang-Son, when he was about to give Indo-China to France, after giving her Tunisia, he was overthrown by a speech of Clemenceau's, who thus added this splendid trophy to the bag of ministers felled by his caustic oratory. And in Ferry's pocket was a telegram that would have saved him, had he not promised Britain not to reveal its contents for a few days. Clemenceau was never gentle; that night, he was atrocious, and the commotion of that session, not particularly honorable for a parliamentary regime, still had an effect on the elections of 1885.

I can still see the poster on our wall, where the deputy, a member of the Opportunist party to which Ferry belonged, though I am not even sure that he voted for Ferry that night, was taken to task by the Right as well as by the Extreme Left.

These elections of 1885 would have brought the Republic

to disaster if, on a second vote, the Left had not come back into the fold. Fortunately, the republicans who, once in power, had hastened to quarrel among themselves, now showed equal haste in reuniting, as on the Sixteenth of May, introducing into our elections, this republican discipline of the "second vote" which has since played a useful part in preserving democracy.

But in this inexpiable war waged by Clemenceau and the radicals of the Extreme Left against Ferry and the Opportunists, the bitterness and the wounds of which I was to encounter again, twenty years later, in the entourage of Waldeck-Rousseau, if different conceptions of the nation's interest hurled them against each other with such violence, the idea of the Nation, the love of country remained intact.

Ferry, no more than Clemenceau, was not renouncing the cause of the lost provinces. He, with his great heart, cold expression, and sideburns of a legist, who said of himself, when his friends reproached him for not making more of an outward show of emotion, and thus renouncing more facile means of winning popularity, "My roses grow within!", was born in Lorraine and kept his roots there, even when his neighbors, momentarily misled, imitating the people of Paris who had shouted death threats, milled around his garden gate, screaming insults and imprecations. Deep inside, he cherished the hope of liberating the lost territory; but he did not believe that France would gain strength by falling back on this single objective. He remained faithful to the formula of Gambetta, toward whom Clemenceau had been equally unjust: "Let us think of it always, but speak of it never!"

I am not so sure that the formula is good: one is apt to stop thinking about something one has stopped talking about. Also, the formula of Gambetta had exceeded his intention. It was only against the vain blustering of a shallow chauvinism that Gambetta protested. In the background of his speeches, there is a vibrant sorrow over the fate of Alsace and Lorraine; if he spoke of it but little in public, it recurred incessantly in his private talk. How many times I heard the echo of it in my close association with Waldeck-Rousseau!

But Ferry thought—and rightly, I believe—as did Gambetta,

who supported him in the Tunisian affair and the Treaty of the Bardo, that a great conquered country like France, not only had many economic and political reasons for being present at any division of the world's territory, but it also had need of a field of activity that would sustain the nation's initiative, courage, and military spirit.

On this last point, the Clemenceau of 1918 had to concede that Ferry was right. In the great peril we had so narrowly escaped, military manpower had come to our aid from these colonial possessions—something Ferry himself had not thought of, as often the results of great works surpass the expectations of those who plan them.

But the Clemenceau of the 1880's, partisan, but always a patriot, saw things differently. Besides detesting the Opportunists for their timidity and their concessions to a social conservation which he was then fighting bitterly, his turn of mind, rectilinear, absolute, refused to consider the complexity of problems. He seized one, made his decision, followed through. In 1917, he said, "To the end!" And that became his sole destination. After 1870, he wanted revenge. He trampled pitilessly on anything he thought would turn our gaze away from the Vosges frontier which, by one of those coincidences that reunite beyond the grave those who have battled bitterly in life, was the place where Ferry wanted to be laid to rest.

Thus, Opportunists and Radicals, even at the peak of the struggle which was to carry the latter to power—where they hastened, as was generally and happily the case when the national interest was at stake, to carry on the very work they had so strenuously opposed—were animated by the same flame of patriotism. Better even; following the Jacobin tradition, the Radicals increased their patriotic fervor, and found the Opportunists too lukewarm. This was clearly demonstrated when, after the Radical ministry of M. Bourgeois, a more moderate ministry was formed by Meline, with M. Hanotaux as Minister of Foreign Affairs; and, hopefully embarking on a course of goodwill toward Germany, sent a warship to some ceremony at Kiel. The Radicals raged; and not just the Radicals. Jaures wrote in that great newspaper of our southwest, *La Depeche de Toulouse*, "We'll talk with Germany, when we're on the bridge at Kehl."

In those early days of the Republic, and for a long time after, until the years when the Dreyfus Affair was to change many things, French patriotism knew no atheists.

The Socialists were as ardent as anyone in this common religion which, underneath the bitterness of political combat inevitable in a free country, at least maintained our unity.

Who would have protested, among all those Socialist leaders released from prison or returned from exile, with an ever-increasing number of followers? The Old Man, Blanqui, of the innumerable imprisonments, the subject of an admirable book, *L'Enfermé*, written by a disciple of Clemenceau, Gustave Geoffroy? Every day, during the Siege of Paris, Blanqui penned those fiery pages of his newspaper, *La Patrie en Danger*, the first announcement of which I have carefully preserved.* The working classes, after petitioning for his release from prison, elected him to the Chamber of Deputies, acclaiming in him the intransigent patriot, quite as much as the indomitable revolutionist, who had roared at those who talked of capitulation, "Paris, for a drop of milk!"

Vaillant? Guesde? They had fortified their doctrine in exile; they came back more determinedly Marxist than when they left; but they had lost none of their French sense. This was evident when, toward the end of their lives, at the outbreak of war in 1914, they found again the patriotic ardor of their youth and urged the young not to give way to a pacifist deviation which, after their death, accentuated its ravages and divided French Socialism so profoundly when facing the growing menace of the totalitarian countries.

And the lesser elements, the rank-and-file of the Revolution, the amnestied supporters of the Commune, for whom the prison gates were opened when Gambetta bullied a timid Assembly into ordering their release "to do away with this last tattered vestige of civil war"? Not all of them had their railroad fare. I saw them plodding along the highways, ragged and dirty, glared at by the farmers, but taken into our hos-

* The unexpected gift of M. Doriot, at the time he gave an exposition of souvenirs of the Commune in his town-hall at Saint-Denis.

pital where, for a few days at least, they could rest their weakened bodies, undermined by the hardships of prison life. My father, who was in charge of the hospital, often permitted me to accompany him on his rounds, when he talked with them understandingly and sympathetically. From being present at these interviews, I obtained a markedly different impression than the one generally accepted in our circle.

Were these men guilty? They rebelled, with the enemy occupying the heights surrounding Paris, against a capitulation which aroused the violent protests of Gambetta and the deputies of Alsace-Lorraine also.

The proof is that, in a situation similar to ours today, these insurgents were joined by officers of the regular army, whose only reason for fighting in their ranks was a desire to continue the struggle wherever they could find anyone with the will to resist. I am thinking of De Gaulle and his companions. And of Major Rossel of 1871, his face profiled clearly against the dark background of the Commune, the memory of which, so recent, continued to haunt the bourgeoisie of the 1880's; and yet, it cannot be said that those Frenchmen who found the memory exalting, and feted the return of the outlaws of the Commune from their prisons, drew from it any lessons in defeatism.*

It was later, and under quite different influences, that an obvious and dangerous contradiction started and gradually widened a rift between Socialism and the Nation. There will be frequent mention of it in these recollections; and I am personally aware that, at certain periods, it alarmed Jaures.

The young Republic, ardently patriotic, though still proceeding with moderation, managed to keep social progress

* The memory of the Commune long remained vivid in socialist traditions. I am not sure of what happened, in 1939, to the customary commemoration of March 18th and the annual pilgrimage to the Wall of the Federated in the Pere-Lachaise cemetery on the anniversary of that blood-spattered week in May. I still recall seeing, in the years that followed the war of 1914, the socialists parading to the spot. And I have heard the miners of Carmaux singing the old song:

Vive la Commune, ma mere,
Vive la Commune, maman!

on an equal footing with the resurgence of France. Mostly of the middle class, her leaders, because they were republican, presented the working class with that most precious of boons: the freedom to form their own unions.

Under the influence of the liberal Emile Ollivier, the Second Empire, always inconsistent and incapable of completing any of its policies, foreign or domestic—as Jaures has pointed out in some pages of rare historical value—had given the workers the right to strike without giving them the right to organize, which was dangerous or ineffectual, or both. The Third Republic rectified this.

One evening in 1899, after dining with Waldeck-Rousseau, shortly after becoming associated with his law office, we were looking through his collection of souvenirs, when a photograph of him, taken in 1884, came to light. It accentuated his youth and good looks. He presented it to me, with these words inscribed thereon: "To my future friend. . . ."

Very future, indeed. The year I entered college, I had no idea that a law was being passed, the results of which were to have such a great influence on the orientation of my mind and my life, and that I would work with, and lose all too soon, as did the Republic, the man to whom, incontestably, the merit belonged.

It is necessary to think back to that period, to the atmosphere, to the strength of an opposition still all-powerful, especially in social matters, and particularly in the Senate, where the conservatives held solid positions, because of their number quite as much as by the quality of their leaders, to judge the accomplishment of the man Gambetta had chosen to be the youngest of the Republic's ministers, and who, in Ferry's cabinet, again occupied the post of Minister of the Interior. Re-reading the debates, as I did later, the better to know my superior, it is illuminating to note the singularly daring vision Waldeck-Rousseau had of things to come and of the way his law would develop. For it was really his. It was he who imposed it—the word is not too strong—on a rebellious Senate, by the power and conviction of his demonstration, granting to the workers not only the right to form their unions, but for the unions to unite among themselves, not pronouncing the name but drawing the curve that was to culminate in the famous *Confederation Generale du Travail.*

"If unions are legal," said Waldeck-Rousseau, "how can you protest that a union of many unions is illegal . . .?"

The ultimate development of the labor union movement did not emerge from a naive lack of foresight on the part of the legislator of 1884, as has often been said, in an effort to diminish the value of one of the essential achievements of the Third Republic. They weighed the risks, and chose liberty. Sixteen years later, looking back at his work, Waldeck-Rousseau wrote in the preface he did me the honor of supplying for my book on the labor movement*: "We have chosen liberty, let us have confidence in it." Which does not imply that order should not be maintained. For his part, Waldeck-Rousseau did not fail in this.

Obviously, all this took place at a considerable distance from my college preoccupations. The high walls that sheltered us kept away many outside rumors and discussions; if any reached us, through the comments of our teachers or from conversations heard during vacation, they were less concerned with the debates of the Republic than with its existence and its legitimacy.

It was a very old school, situated in the plain between the Loire and the Cher, and my brothers, my father, my great-grandfather had attended it. It dated, it was said, from 1034. A large feudal tower, flanking it, and which had served as a dungeon before being transformed into an armory, where I made my acting debut, gave evidence of its age. It was a protection to the establishment during a fire that broke out during my sojourn, preventing the flames from spreading. I have no idea why the Germans rebuilt it, and filmed it, after putting the torch to other noble edifices that had traversed the centuries.

For this college of Pontlevoy had been successively a Benedictine abbey and a military school. Richelieu stayed there, and the splendors of a church in the soaring style of

* *Le Federalisme Economique.* A study of the closed shop, by J. Paul-Boncour, Paris. Alcan, 1901.

Cluny adjoined a magnificent eighteenth century facade, adorned with warlike trophies.

Isolated in the countryside, its river, its riding-school, its terraces for games, its dimensions, its diversity of architecture, its customs, the portraits of earlier teachers and pupils, gave the place a rather uncommon air comparable only to the fine Lycee of Caen, lodged in William the Conqueror's abbey, where my Norman uncles were schooled. When I first visited Oxford and Cambridge, where England raised its young and assured its continuity, and again when I lectured there on the League of Nations, I had the impression of being on familiar ground.

As a member of the Ministry of Beaux Arts in 1912, my reports reflected these influences of my schooldays; and I was able to safeguard, by obtaining for them the classification of historic monuments, these places where a part of my youth was spent, without the occupants, or the parents of the pupils, many of them my political adversaries, knowing whence this protection came.

Very prosperous at the time when instruction was a monopoly, when only the colleges of Pont-Leroy, Soreze, and Juilly were privileged to teach freely, the families of the bourgeoisie and the nobility, unwilling to entrust their children to the state schools, sent them to these religious institutions which flourished under the charming motto: *Religioni et Patriae Floreant.* The Falloux law, encouraging the founding of ecclesiastical schools in the great cities, the Jesuits particularly, cut into the attendance at the rural colleges and reduced their area of recruiting to neighboring sections of Touraine, Berry, and the Nivernais, but without modifying any of their methods.

Which is to say that I encountered there a considerable amount of monarchist feeling, continuing all during the first days of the Republic, and making the task of its founders very difficult. Although he had been dead a year, the letters VHV *(Vive Henri V)* were repeatedly scrawled on the walls, and on the bucklers we used in our games of "*balle au roi*," M. de Charette, descendant of the counter-revolutionary leader in years gone by, and himself the commander of the Papal

Zouaves at Patay and Coulmiers in the war of 1870, came to preside at the distribution of prizes! In this rather closed circle, far from the big cities and their agitation, young men were being raised with practically no contact with the world outside.

However we were not so remote, and our walls were not so high, that the refrains of Boulangist songs failed to reach us. Especially since, in its second manner, Boulangism was awakening a good deal of hope in political circles such as those to which the families of my school companions belonged. And, on our return from vacation, we brought back some of the discussions we had listened to at home.

For not all were in complete accord as to how to use the General, who had begun as a member of the Radicals, but was hopefully regarded as a future General Monk by some of the Royalists. Controversies over this had replaced those concerning the older branch and the younger, a quarrel which had so long divided the conservatives and aided M. Thiers in founding the Republic.

Boulangism!

How faraway and small it seems, in the lights of the events we have just experienced! And how we are tempted to smile indulgently at the attempt to make a dictator of this amiable, attractive person! We have watched the unleashing of so many brutal dictators! It is necessary to view the episode from the standpoint of the facile and civilized period when it took place to evaluate some of the consequences it had on the evolution of the Republic.

As in other movements that I shall evoke here, I confine myself to history, if one can call history these minor episodes, compared to what we now face. I shall speak only of the memories it left me. But it is they, it seems, that fix concretely certain aspects necessary to their exact comprehension. To grasp them, there is nothing like the microcosm of our little towns, encircled by rural areas, penetrated by them, having their roots in the peasantry, whose adhesion or opposition ultimately makes or breaks political ventures in France. Paris, the great cities, the industrial centers start the movements: if the provinces do not follow along, and in the provinces, the rural areas, sooner or later the movement fails. This what Gambetta and his friends understood so well; thanks to them the Republic, which had failed twice, became firmly implanted when it won the country districts and the little towns where, on market-days, the farmers form their opinions, or have them formed for them.

And here is where the Boulangist movement failed to break through. One can even ask if, on that evening of January 27th, 1889, when the crowd in the Paris streets and on the boulevards acclaimed him, and the police refused to intervene, the General had marched upon the Elysee, instead of going to his mistress, Madame de Bonnemain, the *coup d'Etat* would have succeeded?

Who can tell? In a centralized country such as France, where the spirit is much more critical than revolutionary, he who controls the wheels of power can do a lot. What is happening today gives evidence of this.

But in the days of Boulangism, the Germans were not present and the Republic was young. The question did not arise.

Save in a few departments, where the Bonapartist tradition continued, the resistance of the rural areas saved the regime, as on the 16th of May, and more than on the 16th of May, because some of the cities had wavered. Freely anticlerical and passionately in favor of equality, our farmers were impressed with the General who, backed by Clemenceau, insisted that the priests perform their military service in regiments of the line, with knapsack on back and full marching equipment, and took away from the princes military commands that had become theirs by right of birth. And, moreover, as Minister of War, the General had thought of the soldier's well-being. He had improved the food. The workers had liked his declaration that, in case of a strike, the troops would share their rations with the strikers. But when the General turned "reactionary," the reaction to him was sudden and decisive.

Although the speech outlining his program was given at Tours, our provincial capital, it had little repercussion. He had tried to keep M. Naquet and Count Dillon, Rightist agent, on an equal footing. But there was considerable Rightist resistance, for many had refused to take part in the adventure.

Young as I was, I could judge this by what happened in a friendly house. It had belonged to Royer-Collard, deputy from the Marne district, but who spent the last years of his life at Chateauvieux, near Saint-Aignan. His grandson, Paul Andral, who had been vice-president of the Council of State, continued the conservative and liberal tradition of a statesman, liberal enough to have declared, during the Restoration, his opposition to a proposal of a law regarding sacrilege, which seemed to him an attack on freedom of conscience, in these revolutionary words: "If you pass this law, I swear to disobey it!"

For three generations, our two families had been closely united: my father, as a child, had sat on the knee of the great orator, whose relations with his neighbor, Talleyrand, were quite frigid. Talleyrand, on the contrary, had considerable esteem for M. Royer—as he was known in the neighborhood—and even entrusted him with his Memoirs, later. It was Talleyrand who decided to take the first step and pay M. Royer a visit. Having climbed, with some difficulty, the slippery slope that led to a charming eighteenth-century pavilion where his host awaited him, Talleyrand said, "You are, monsieur, hard to approach!"

My father had been an interne of Doctor Andral, Royer-Collard's son-in-law; he had attended his wife during her last illness and received, as a memento, a case of silver lancets—in those days, the practice of bleeding was extremely prevalent—which are now in the possession of my doctor-brother, who no longer "bleeds." When Doctor Andral's son Paul died, his widow presented me with his collection of law-books, which became the foundation of my library as a young lawyer. This, by way of explaining the freedom of conversation in our family circles.

How many times, in the great library of the Andral home, with its eighteenth century editions and the desk on which reposed the red morocco briefcase of Royer-Collard,* have I

* The manuscript of Talleyrand's Memoirs must have been there, in a first draft which has never been published integrally, I am told.

heard Paul Andral, through the smoke of his succession of cigars that continued uninterruptedly from morning to night, deplore the Boulangist adventure in which many of his conservative friends had plunged! With all the penetration of an extraordinarily fine judgment and the strong political tradition he had received from his grandfather, he considered it dangerous to call upon the demagogism of the Boulangist party to defend the conservatives. He had very little liking for generals in politics, and very little esteem for this particular one.

Quite understandably, though he paid little heed to politics, my father, as a liberal republican, shared completely the views of his old friend, who had been the comrade of his youth at a time when Paul Andral, a perfect Parisian, was well-acquainted with Hortense Schneider, and frequently gave my father tickets for the Varieties, where she was appearing.

But many visitors at Chateauvieux, the Andral home, who came to get political directives which they did not always follow, were disinclined to be guided by Paul's wisdom. They were in sympathy with the later phase of the Boulangist movement, and counted on using the General as "a battering-ram to break down the Republic," an expression used by one of them, an ex-major of artillery of the Imperial Guard, Bonapartist by conviction and temperament. His bristling hair, his mustache and goatee had whitened, but his ardor remained as it was in the days when he paraded his gold-braided uniform through the garrison-towns of the Second Empire. Of a remarkable turn of mind and a vast erudition, he spent a great deal of time, in a pretty dwelling with an Ionic portico, hidden deep in a large garden, now destroyed by the German occupation, reading more books than I have been able to, despite my reputation as a devourer of literature.

The peaceful, simple, relatively untroubled life of our little towns of that day, and the absence of ambition permitted a slow ripening of opinions. I have often heard—among these people, excluded from the nation's affairs because of political affiliations successively rejected by the electoral body—more profound conversation than that of some of our leaders, or those who consider themselves leaders. Another reason to regret that, moving against the great currents that are sweeping the nation, a whole section of the French middle class has been kept out—or keeps itself out of politics. The British Conservatives did not make this mistake. Having long collaborated at Geneva with some of their leaders, even a few die-hards, I had plenty of opportunities to note the difference and judge the errors of our own conservatives during the years when the Republic was setting a form and finding a rhythm.

To complete this miniature picture of Boulangism in our provinces, it is essential to underline the heteroclitical character of its composition. It disconcerted a public opinion accustomed to clear-cut classifications: conservatives and republicans, reds and whites. Thus, to the great surprise of the more advanced voters who had cast their ballots for him, Laisant, leader of the radical list, who, in the 1885 elections, had carried on a violent struggle against the outgoing deputy and the Opportunists, now turned up as one of Boulanger's lieutenants.

This confusion displeased our reasoning peasantry; and in our neighborhood, as elsewhere, it nullified the efforts of the Boulangist propaganda campaign, well-organized for an era preceding the existence of the motion picture and the radio and the loud-speaker, which have so profoundly modified political procedure in our time. And not to its advantage. The Boulangist publicity was louder and inferior to that of the Republicans of the Sixteenth of May; but always patriotic, super-patriotic, chauvinistic. Rest assured that, today, I use the word without disparagement; there are moments when any sort of patriotism is better than none. For all its clamor, the Boulangist propaganda had nothing in common with the theatricalities to which we have since been subjected by the dictators, red or white, and which would have shocked a people who retained any measure of moderation and good taste.

The Boulangists made considerable use of street-singers, bringing to us the refrains popularized in Paris by Paulus. Once again, the peddlers were offering for sale those simple, primary-colored patriotic prints, *images d'Epinal*, as they had on behalf of Napoleon during the Restoration and the

Monarchy of July, a permanent instrument of popular propaganda in a period that had no other. On their trays, the peddlers displayed snuff-boxes and pipes decorated with the gold-braided general's cap of Boulanger in place of the Zouave Jacob of earlier memory; and those huge cotton handkerchiefs such as the Republicans utilized on the Sixteenth of May.

But there was little heart in it; this time, the Republic was on the other side in the combat.

Even in the smallest localities, the Republic had its defenders. Immediately after some manifestations in Paris, Tassin, our deputy, came home very discouraged.

"The Republic is down the drain!" he sighed.

But our Mayor, a draper, whose business was prospering, and therefore remained a steadfast supporter of the regime, replied, "I just had a fellow thrown off the fair-ground for singing subversive songs. Do the same in Paris!"

We hear a lot today about the necessity for authority. It was not lacking in those days; and it was all the more freely accepted, because a long solidarity in the republican struggle had won for those who had to exercise it—mayors, deputies, senators, and other locally elected officials—the confidence of their constituents. Propelled by their voters into a show of energy, the parliamentarians rallied, and universal suffrage ended the adventure.

But precisely because it had been rather a heteroclitical movement—utilized, then monopolized by the Right, although it had originated with the Left, even the Extreme-Left—Boulangism had repercussions that survived its failure.

First, it united definitively the defense of the Republic with the defense of the parliamentary regime according to the Constitution of 1875. In the long run, this was not a happy thing. After the upheavals of the last war, the Republic had need of a strong executive branch capable of solving quickly and thoroughly, under the control of Parliament, new problems that presented themselves. The fact of having felt the nearness of danger, in the form of multiple candidatures, which the General presented, augmented the distrust—what am I saying?—the phobia inspired by the system of the plebiscite, already guilty of giving us Napoleon III. And yet, it is difficult to see how, in a Republic, there can be a strong and lasting executive branch if it does not draw its power from the same source as the legislative, that is to say, if it does not derive it from universal suffrage, either in one step, or preferably in two, as is the practice in the great American republic.

We shall again encounter this idea, and its systematic rejection. It has weighed heavily on the last years of the Third Republic. Perhaps, had it not been for this rejection, the Republic would have found the necessary strength to combat the enterprises of the totalitarian states, outside and inside France.

Then, because the Republic had momentarily found refuge in a return to the system of local balloting, the spirit of conservation, which works for parties as well as classes, aided in maintaining indefinitely an electoral pattern which, as Gambetta rightly observed, "was a broken mirror wherein France could not recognize herself."

Finally, Boulangism had succeeded in drawing off some of the republican strength, precisely where an exalted patriotism was the watchword. It removed, once and for all, from the republican ranks, the followers of Deroulede and the League of Patriots.

Deroulede had been a companion of Gambetta; he had been, and had remained, republican. One recalls his outburst, during a discussion among the Boulangist committee: "If the Pretender to the throne tries to return, I'll stop him with my own hand!" But the one thought in his mind was that of revenge against the Germans, and he spread the doctrine tirelessly in the cemeteries and on the battlefields hallowed by the war of 1870, draped in his long frock-coat which, on him, had the appearance of a flag upon its staff. He went to General Boulanger, who was doing a considerable amount of talking about revenge, and, at the time of the Schnoeble Affair, so nearly forced us into taking it that the name became a part of him. And Deroulede later followed "General Revenge" in his dubious political venture.

From an electoral and political point of view, this defection seemed unimportant. Cut off from the republicans, thrust necessarily toward the Right, the League of Patriots and its leader ceased to have any appppreciable influence on the course of events. But they also ceased to have any on the Republicans, as previously. And had this been entirely useless?

Since then, as I have observed so many rush headlong into servitude, I am inclined to believe it was not. It is never useless to keep recalling to a people a defeat which they are only too prompt to forget, so long as the reminder is not intended to invite them to submit to it. Up to the time of the Boulangist movement, Deroulede and his friends had been, from the patriotic standpoint, despite some slightly ridiculous moments, the marching wing of the republican party.*

When this marching wing withdrew, then fired on the main body of troops it had just abandoned, the latter were quick to distrust the exaltation of a sentiment that was perfectly right, but which they resented being used as a weapon against them. This was even more accentuated among the Socialists, some of whom, supporters of the Commune, had left them to follow Rochefort, and fought them with the violence customary between rival sects of the extremist parties.

Thus, from the time of Boulangism, before the Dreyfus Affair, which amplified it to the extreme, the exploitation, for political purposes, of a patriotic communion in which all had participated until then, inflicted a wound that widened, as we were to ascertain later.

* It is curious to note that Jaures so disdainful of duels and calumny, made an exception when it was Deroulede who attacked his patriotism. He met with him in a pistol encounter where his awkwardness was more dangerous to himself than to his adversary.

Chapter Two

THE REPUBLIC OF MY YOUTH

Brittany—My spiritual friends.—The Latin Quarter in the 1890's.—Our pleasures and our reading.—How I became a Socialist.—My first law-cases.—The last barricades.—The great Affair.

As little as I desire to speak of myself, except to recall events about which I am testifying, when it comes to some of them, and not the minor ones, where I have been personally involved through the men I have served, or through my own participation, it is necessary to state precisely the state of mind in which I approached them, and of what evolution it was the consequence.

The ceremony of the centennial of 1789 was at hand. The Republic, victorious over Boulangism, prepared to celebrate the historic date as best it could. The result was far from extraordinary; the Republic never seemed to have the gift for organizing public ceremonies and popular spectacles. However, it outshone the mediocre hundred-and-fiftieth anniversary celebration, which took place just before the war of 1939, and gave the impression that the Republic was already somewhat ashamed, while the populace ignored the proceedings more or less completely.

In 1889, the man chosen for the presidency bore a name that, to my mind, was the greatest in our Revolution; for without the genius of General Lazare Carnot, and the armies he organized, it would have succumbed; revolutions, like democracies, that do not think first of being strong, soon become an easy prey.

But in the college in Brittany where I was finishing my

studies, a small group of young men were preoccupied with other things than the centennial exposition, President Sadi Carnot, even the great ancestor, Lazare. They had reached the age of that intellectual puberty, of literary and philosophical frenzies which often determined the course of a life, in those fortunate days when grim material necessities did not seize youth by the throat right after leaving school, and when the adjustment to these problems could be prolonged until the completion of higher studies.

I had left the old college in our neighborhood, of which I spoke earlier. The idea of becoming a sailor had moved into my mind and taken possession. Odd, for one whose roots were in the rich farming soil of Touraine and Berry: the theorists would say, perhaps, it was the soul of the Viking invaders of centuries ago reawakening in me; I am inclined to place the responsibility with Jules Verne and the *Journal des Voyages*.

To prepare for the Naval Academy, I went to a college at Saint-Brieuc, a branch of the College Stanislas in Paris, which offered a special course for this purpose. In those days, the preparation had to start early, for the maximum age limit at the Naval Academy was eighteen. And much was made of mathematics.

Much too much for me. I discovered I was quite incapable of coping with it; geometry in space, notably, remained invulnerable, as far as I was concerned; when I had drawn the earth's line, I could never make myself understand why certain objects, the shape, size, and color of which were clearly defined in my mind, could be reduced to these dry, geometrical lines on a sheet of paper. May the memory of my friend Painlevé pardon me! It was his constant contention that, if I failed to absorb any knowledge of mathematics, his cherished subject, it was the teacher's fault. He was wrong: the professor of mathematics was excellent, as many of my classmates—captains and admirals in later life—would now attest, if a number of them were not at the bottom of the sea, or otherwise unavailable.

As for me, I had to renounce a maritime career. This was painful; the Navy held me in its spell, and for quite a long time. When I began studying law, I entered the Navy by way of the Commissariat, a department which combines the functions of the Army's departments of recruiting, administration, and supplies; a fine corps, with silver stripes instead of gold, and long tours of sea-duty in the Pacific or the China Sea, waters which had haunted my early dreams of belonging to the fleet.

I resumed my study of literature, but I remained in Brittany, which had quite conquered me. I found there certain features of the rocky section of Normandy, which adjoins it, and where, for eighteen years, I had spent my vacations in an old property of my grandmother's, between Avranches and Mortain, hidden away among woods and sunken roads, not far from Mont Saint-Michel, rising out of the sands, at the uncertain and oft-disputed border line between the two provinces. But if I found certain resemblances to the Normandy landscape, there was an added note of poetry, mysticism, that accord of scene and soul which makes Brittany so homogeneous, and enabling one to understand why she is so determined to retain her individuality.

They were not talking then about that autonomy which has caused so much discussion in the last few years, to the extent that the Germans were fooled by it, and thought for a moment they could make use of it. They rued it; Brittany, in the matter of resistance to the invader, led all the rest. But a literary and regional renaissance, such as had not been seen since the days of the poet Brizeux, was in full swing in my youth. Louis Tiercelin had just founded *Le Parnasse Breton* and *L'Hermine*, gathering round him writers and poets of real worth, Edouard Beaufils, Charles Bernard, Le Goffic, and that Le Braz, who sang of Brittany like a lover:

"*La Bretagne, ma douce, etant à l'agonie. . .*"

A poet's imagination, because Brittany was not dying at all, and her state of health was exuberantly robust. All this prose and poetry reached us at the school and exalted the Breton soul of my comrades, and, on the rebound, mine. Added to our intensive study of the classics, it helped put us in a state of receptivity, which was heightened by the rather cloistered life we led, with little other distractions than our reading—that prescribed by our study program and others that were not.

We each had our spiritual friends, where we looked for the expression of sentiments welling within us.

Mine were, first of all, those whose books I had read in my father's library, slender but tenderly selected, where Balzac and Paul-Louis Courier were ranged alongside medical remedies and some archeological fragments found as he was making his daily rounds, for he was keenly interested in anything pertaining to our province's past. Reconciled, at least on our bookshelves, were the estranged lovers Musset and George Sand, our George Sand of the neighboring province of Berry, of which she sang as the poets of *L'Hermine* sang of Brittany.

Lamartine, I am not sure why, was not represented in the collection; I only knew the excerpts from his works published in our school anthologies. But one day, during vacation, I found in a cupboard, among a stack of old books such as usually turn up in old houses—a sampling of the divergent tastes of succeeding generation—alongside *Les Jacobins Polonais* and the apocryphal *Memoires de Robespierre*, one of the numbers, published serially, of that *Cours Familier de Litterature*, which the aging Lamartine had to grind out as a livelihood. In these pages, Musset protested that Lamartine treats him like a poor, abandoned child. The number in question was devoted to Musset and Goethe, and, to fill it out, Lamartine, a Belisarius of democracy holding out his helmet to the reader, had added *in extenso* a letter from Musset, which he never answered, and which starts with the sumptuous poetic line:

"*Lorsque le grand Byron allait quitter Ravenne . . .*"

In the room, its shutters closed, while the heat of summer crackled outside, Byron, Lamartine, Musset aroused in me an emotion, the memory of which remains with me today, so that when I close my eyes, I can see the dear old house—not as it is now, in the hands of the enemy—but as it was. . . .

"*Quand la maison vibrait, comme un grand coeur de pierre,*
De tous ces coeurs joyeux, qui battaient sous ses toits."

I have been faithful to this admiration of my adolescence. For a long time, I never travelled without a copy of *Les Meditations* in my valise, or during the war, in my pack.

Very quickly, Lamartine the poet led me to Lamartine the orator, every bit as great as the poet, and from Lamartine the author to Lamartine the politician. One can imagine, from what I have said about my family background, the attraction for me of this former officer of the Royal Bodyguard, liberated from his monarchist fidelity by the fall of the legitimate monarchy, and who gave himself all the more completely to the democratic ideal because, in his estimation, only a democracy could replace the principle of heredity that permits neither arrangement nor compromise.

Lamartine, a visionary? Yes, like Jaures, very far-sighted: at the time when the ashes of Napoleon were brought back to Paris, Lamartine foresaw the tidal wave of Bonapartism which was to sweep away the Republic on December 2, 1851; on the question of the railroads, he was right, and Thiers was wrong; in the matter of indirect taxes, he was right, and our relative, M. Duchatel,* seated on the government bench, was wrong; and on many other subjects. There are two volumes of his speeches which should be read by some of our self-styled wise men, who call anyone who can see farther than themselves—because he is higher than themselves—utopian. Utopia is often merely a premature truth.

Emerson said one should hitch one's wagon to a star. Mine, in truth, was not ill-chosen.

There was another influence that exerted itself on the little group of close friends we had formed, a group which had the approval of our teachers for its eagerness and its inquisitiveness, but at the same time worried them by its independence.

In Brittany, where our elders had reawakened the memories of the region and enriched its patrimony, there was a place which had been the scene of one of the most pathetic spiritual dramas of the nineteenth century. It was brought very near to us by the fact that many of our playmates and classmates bore the names of those who had walked in these woods before Rome condemned the master and dispersed the disciples: La Chenaie, Maurice de Guerin, Du Breil de Marzan, le Val de l'Arguenon, the beautiful and mysterious

* His father, who drew up the law on registration during the Revolution, was the maternal uncle of my grandmother.

love-story that unfolded around the death-bed of Marie de la Morvonnais, all of these fired our imagination. The noble experiment of Lacordaire, Montalembert, and the young men of L'Avenir fired our hearts.

As Catholics, we had not gone as far as Lamennais. Although I already suspected that the severities of our teachers toward him were a little unjust. When a man can arouse as much devotion and fervor as this outcast, and among a veritable elite of young students, it would have been surprising if something within him did not justify it. I had already read the *Paroles d'un Croyant* in a first edition, picked up by my father at a sale of the library of an old republican of Saint-Aignan who had recently died. The outcries of the great heart of Lamennais, so violent yet so tender, led me to think there must be more to his case than a cassock being ripped off noisily in a moment of rage.

I was even more convinced later, when Bouglé, who had not yet become director of the Ecole Normale, started his *Collection des Reformateurs Sociaux du Dix-Neuvieme Siecle* and asked me to take charge of one of the volumes. He thought I was going to choose Proud'hon, Saint-Simon, Blanqui . . . He was quite astonished when I chose Lamennais. I alone knew what memories Lamennais stirred in me. And I devoted a little book to him, which went practically unnoticed, I must admit, although it is the one into which I put my heart.*

At least, Lacordaire was left to us. Reading him was even recommended by our professor of rhetoric, Abbé Leber, an eminent man whose great heart equalled his intelligence, and to whom I owe so much. I continued to visit him in Paris when, after his elevation to the post of director of the College Stanislas, the shaping of my ideas had carried me far from him, but had not weakened my gratitude, which continues to this day.

Was it the result of reading Lacordaire that led one of us, a very dear friend, and who has remained so, to join the Order of St. Dominic, to which the great preacher of Notre-Dame belonged, and gain new laurels for the Dominicans by his

* Lammenais, by J. Paul-Boncour, Alcan, Paris, 1928.

remarkable treatises on evangelical interpretations? For myself, it made me eager to verify the exact motives of that attempt of *L'Avenir*, the dual combat for freedom and faith, for the Church and for democracy, which roused so much youthful enthusiasm in its time. The July Monarchy had been disturbed by it, and dragged on to the benches of its law-courts the cassock of Lamennais and the white robe of Lacordaire. The jury had acquitted them; but the Pope had also been disturbed, which was much more serious. On November 15th, 1831, Lamennais announced that publication of *L'Avenir* would be suspended pending the pontifical decision; in which connection, Lacordaire and Montalembert, "the two pilgrims of liberty," were leaving for Rome. But their pleadings were in vain; the Pope condemned the movement. Lacordaire and Montalembert accepted the verdict; Lamennais resisted, then revolted openly; the movement was re-condemned.

I have long regretted it. Its success would have given our political history a different orientation, and the progress of democracy a less spasmodic rhythm. I merely mention it here to evoke the influence it still had, after so many years, on a young man in search of his destiny.

It answered so many of my intimate aspirations; it reconciled so many seeming contradictions; it set for me, out of the shining talent and moving sincerity of its protagonists, an example of the spiritual power and social renovation that could evolve from the union they dreamed of. And I must confess that it has haunted me all through my public life.

Later, by chance, as Socialist Deputy of the Tarn, I again found Lacordaire at Sorreze and Maurice de Guerin at Cayla. Between political meetings, I often took the time to renew, after so many years, the ties of that spiritual family whose company had made such a strong impression on my youth.

One day, at the cemetery of Andillac, visiting the tombs of Maurice and Eugenie, I was preceded by a young American woman who had made a rather strange and touching voyage: she had sailed from New York to Havre, dashed through Paris without stopping, took the train to Gaillac, hired a carriage to Andillac, then walked to Le Cayla down the sunken road and under the great oaks where Maurice had heard the Centaur galloping; and she entered the old, tile-roofed house, sat in the kitchen beside the big rustic table where, in front of the hearth, Eugenie worked, or read, or wrote to Louise de Boigne those letters, the publication of which I was able to facilitate for Abbé Barthes, canon of Albi, who, together with M. Zyromski, father of my terrible comrade, is the most authoritative commentator on "the sweet hostess." The visiting American lady meditated awhile in the touchingly simple bedroom of this Child of Mary where on the plain wallpaper Eugenie had pinned a few holy cards and a drawing of the Chateau de Saint-Point by Lamartine. She walked as far as the Cross of Farewell on the road where Eugenie accompanied Maurice at the time of his departures, urging that the marks of the horseshoes be left until the wind and the rain effaced them. Then, after her stop at the cemetery, she climbed into her hired carriage, took the train at Gaillac, retraversed Paris non-stop, took ship at Havre, and returned to New York without ever deviating from her pilgrimage, without seeing anything but the dwelling where the brother and sister had lived their quiet life, so solitary and so rich.

The cult of the Guerins knows well these fervors. In the common burying-place at Pere-Lachaise, where he wanted to be laid to rest, poor Lamennais attracted no such attention. But peace has come to his memory; a short time before the war, the hour had sounded, this time in full conformity with pontifical directives, for the resurgence of some of the very ideas for which he had suffered.

May they survive the defeat: we will need them more than ever in the necessary reconstruction of French unity.

One can imagine the explosive enthusaism when, after seven or eight years of practically monastic school discipline, we left our provinces and were turned loose in Paris, quite on our own, in the Latin Quarter. For, in spite of the song, there still was a Latin Quarter. It was an old song that my father sometimes hummed, to the rhythm of the hoofbeats of his tired little horse, as we returned from his rounds where he dispensed not only his medical knowledge but the endless treasures of his kindliness.

"*Mais il n'est plus de vieux Quartier Latin . . .*"

However, in my father's time it still existed. And even in my time. And they would seem to have resembled each other.

The Boulevard Saint-Michel, the "Boul'Mich" as we called it, was still there. It is today. But when we travelled up and down it, debating incessantly, dressed to the limit of our sartorial resources, in frock-coats and crush-hats, or great flowing ties and immense soft hats, we must have looked more like Chaunard and Rudolph of *La Boheme* than like the bare-headed, sports-coated young men I see when I walk in that vicinity with my nostalgic memories. And our little sweet-hearts were like sisters of Musetta and Mimi or Jenny "with a contented heart, contented with little," the contemporaries of *Louise*, whose musical reincarnation we were to love so much.

In spite of the penury of our resources, life was relatively easy; all the easier because our tastes and necessities simplified it even more. I no longer recall which of our songwriting com-rades sang the praises of the restaurant where for twenty-three sous we endangered our twenty-year-old stomachs.

"*Quand on n'a pas le Vefour que l'on aime,*
Il faut aimer le vingt-trois sous qu'on a . . ."

But to quote from one of the books of Pierre Louys, whose fine head and flowing hair often attracted our glances at the Taverne du Pantheon in those days when he was deep in his study of the young glory of Aphrodite, "we had nights that consoled us for our days."

I spoke of songs. There was a great deal of singing in the Latin Quarter of my youth, a province within a city, possess-ing its own folklore. Its songwriters echoed those of Mont-martre and The Black Cat, then at the peak of its popularity, toward which emigrated those of us who had succeeded. Such as Xanrof, student, and, I believe, doctor of law, who became famous thanks to the extraordinary talent of the singer, Yvette Guilbert, but whose little verses were first tried out on us.

And our choral-groups! I must admit there was a touch of the guard-house about their repertoire: then I recall the gay rooms, deserted little by little, the community life, full of ardor and labor, lived by our comrades of the medical school, the long hours in the hospitals to be near the afflicted.

We sang our songs far into the night. In those days, athletics were not of sufficient importance to prevent us from being night-owls. Except for fencing and boating, we indulged very little in sports. The taverns of the Rue Soufflot and the Boulevard Saint-Michel attracted us more. As on the Right Bank, where the delicate white-and-gold decors of the Cafe Anglais and Tortoni were gradually disappearing, the style in favor was that of the German beerhouses with their oak-panelling and stained-glass windows. When the smoke of our pipes befogged the air, and the piles of little felt pads, indicating the number of tankards consumed, rose higher, the setting suggested a scene from *Faust*, with the students singing, and the old doctor hit hard by the somewhat brutal impact of youth.

In his early writings, Maurice Barres touched interestingly on this life we led, light of pocket, even lighter of heart, and with the appetites of young wolves. These pages appeared in a little review, *Les Pattes de Mouche*, short-lived like others of its type. They were subsequently published in book-form and became a collector's item after the author had become a celebrity, a member of the Academie Francaise, and a prominent parliamentarian representing the Right. I believe I detect a development of these student sketches in certain pages of *Les Deracinés*, the first of a trilogy, biased but admirable, continued in *L'Appel au Soldat* and *Leurs Figures*.

What ardor we put into everything: pleasure and work. I recall that nostalgic comment of Leon-Paul Fargue in *Refuges:* ". . . a time when poetry and literary art had the importance that electricity, sport, and politics have today . . . ." Such an intoxication of poetry and literature, philosophy and social science! Our comrades studying medicine were held down by the hospital, the practical application and responsibilities that came to them as internes, that rugged school of practitioners where our great doctors were formed, and where my brother followed in my father's footsteps. We students of Law worked hard on the eve of our examinations, much less rigorous than they are now, when it is necessary to sift the excessive affluence toward the liberal professions; but the rest of the time, what truants we were, amid all the things that kept popping up for our delighted investigation, in the official decor of a Republic that was beginning to fall asleep!

In the minds of most of us, the wind blew toward the Left. With no attempt to solicit texts, or draw toward the Republic writers who, in several instances, paid little heed to it, it seems to me, out of my memories and impressions, that the greatest of them had a human ideal very close to hers.

I am speaking not only of the revolutionists like Valles and Leon Cladel, nor the anarchists, like poor Tailhade, who, after singing its praises in the ballad of Solness:

"*Anarchie, o claire tour qui sur les flots domine. . . .*"

was wounded by a bomb tossed in a restaurant; nor controversialists like Octave Mirbeau. I am thinking of the great stars, as one would say today, the authors of the best-sellers whose successes are stacked high in the windows of bookshops: Zola, Maupassant, Daudet.

Even before the Dreyfus Affair and his trilogy, *Lourdes*, *Rome*, *Paris*, Zola's entire works, at once a truculent summation and a vast fresco, destined him for the front-line of the Dreyfus battle and a leading position in the Extreme Left, which he promptly assumed.

Although influenced by the pretended impassiveness of the great Flaubert, there are so many pages of Maupassant's from which rises a human cry of revolt against injustice, war, and suffering. And even when, unlike his master, a taste for the social world took hold of the rugged Norman lad—and which we cannot quite regret, since we owe to it *Notre Coeur*—there is hardly one of his books in which one does not find it echoed. I wonder if it is not due to this dominant note in Maupassant's work that he is treated with a sort of disdain which the conformist authors of today feel obliged to display toward him, at a time when, following the stars, the least of the scribblers tries to affirm his conservatism.

And the charming, sensitive, profound Daudet, so widely read by people of all classes in those days; and today, much less; which is a great pity, for he is our Dickens! How his keen sense of humanity, his pity for the little ones, for the humble, those crushed by life, recruited young readers for political ideas which were probably not his own! Although his *Numa Roumestan* is not at all tender toward the Right, any more than *L'Immortel* is for the Academic Francaise, that conservative citadel of the Republic of Letters, the attraction of which, for a writer with any pretensions of independence, I have never been able to understand, as he most certainly must suffer from the proximity of certain members elected without regard to literary talent or thought.

Many passages of the Goncourt Journal, which has caused so much ink to flow, testify that they were nothing less than favorable to the republican regime. Exclusively artists and disdainful of the rest; it is nevertheless true that *Germinie Lacerteux, La Fille Elisa, Soeur Philomene* were filled with a sensitiveness very near to that which guided us toward advanced ideas.

It matters little what the personal political opinions of an author are, always supposing he has any; it is the way he presents life, the pictures he suggests, that influence the reader, creating the atmosphere in which a generation grows.

Ours was very different from that in which our successors of recent years have lived. In the 1890's, at least among authors who, by the number of their readers, could have an effect upon public opinion, one would have looked in vain for that rigidly Rightist thinking which, through fashion or conviction, was the rage on the eve of the two wars.

In art, we loved Carriere and his Maternités, Rodin and his daring. Even in the field of caricature, which then played a large part in political controversies and brought on innumerable lawsuits, everything contributed to keep us in that atmosphere of the Left. Mornings, on our way to class, we handed around the drawings of Steinlen, which answered our anger of the moment. Forain, the deadly Forain, before becoming a member of the *Institut* and a staunch Rightist, but then, as always, with the Opposition, riddled with his pencil sketches —as biting as the etchings he turned to later, in the manner of the great Daumier—the Middle Class and the Opportunists.

And Willette, the exquisite, the Watteau of Montmartre,

before taking to religion and having masses said for his fellow-artists, liked to put a Phrygian cap on his little nudes.

But Barres?

His influence on us was incontestable. However, the Barres of the 90's was not exactly the Barres of the Dreyfus Affair. Neither *L'Ennemi des Lois*, nor *Sous l'Oeil des Barbares*, nor *Le Jardin de Berenice* indicated him as a conformist. His transitory connection with Boulangism, since the movement was of Leftist origin and pretty much of a political melange, also failed to presage his journey to the Right. This was even the time when he wrote a brochure, clearly of socialist inspiration, *De Hegel aux Cantines du Nord;* not too well-known, it is of interest to anyone desiring to follow closely the evolution of "*la pensee barresienne.*" It was then that he was on the point of being the socialist candidate in an election at Neuilly. One of our comrades of the Latin Quarter, Sautumier was selected instead, and won, only to die prematurely and tragically, before giving the full measure of his capabilities. "And now this boy departs from us before the night falls," said Jaures, over the grave.

In truth, Barres was at the cross-roads; it would have taken little to change his direction. I had always suspected this, and it was confirmed in an intimate conversation with him during the war. I was with the Staff of our 8th Army at Flavigny; he was resting at his country-place at Charmes-sur-Moselle, where he had taken root in the soil of Lorraine: called to the bedside of his son, wounded while serving in the same unit of *chasseurs-à-pied* where the son of Jaures had been killed, he rode to the railway station at Nancy in my car. The anguished father was in a talking mood; he knew of my friendly admiration for him. As he questioned me about my reasons for adhering to the Socialist party, I asked, "But you yourself, in the 90's, when I was a student, weren't you tempted to do the same?"

He nodded. However, in addition to certain contacts displeasing to this rather disdainful aristocrat, it was the aspect of internationalism, which already figured on the Socialist program, that turned him away. I explained how I saw it, and how Jaures saw it. "A little internationalism draws one away from one's country; a lot of internationalism brings one back." It was after this conversation that, when he sent me a copy of his *Colline Inspiree*—a hill I had often climbed, thinking of him, during that winter of 1917, when it loomed over our headquarters—he enclosed a letter in which, using an expression that translated my thought better than I had been able to do, he wrote, "I understand that, as you see it, internationalism is a sort of enlargement of France."

I am thinking of Barres now, on this 24th of November, 1940, the anniversary of his death, after just listening to the voice of that son for whom he trembled, broadcasting from London, where he went to join the forces of Free France.

One would have an incomplete view of the movement of minds and influences of those years, without taking into account the great inspiration that came to us from Russia. Not Official Russia, that of the Franco-Russian alliance. Admiral Avellan and his sailors from Cronstadt preoccupied us less than the Russian Novel, a literary revelation owed to a French gentleman, who doubtless never realized the contribution he was making toward the advancement of advanced ideas among the youth of France, when he wrote a book urging us to read Tolstoi, Dostoievski, and the others. Diplomat and man of letters, M. de Vogué had used his leisure hours, while secretary of our embassy at St. Petersburg, to guide us through the literature of the country to which he was accredited. These appreciative tastes were frequently encountered among our diplomatic representatives; it was a source of pride to me, when I had the honor of being their chief; I have never noted that it put them in a state of inferiority. Now that it has become the custom to charge our diplomacy with the mistakes of the military, the talk is that these "dilettantes" were the cause of our downfall. Even the shade of M. de Gobineau, who was one of them, and who really invented the racial theory and that of the tall blond aryan, has not sufficed to protect them.

Thanks to M. de Vogué's book, and the curiosity it aroused, the few editions of Russian novels available, rather incomplete, gave way to a steady stream where we drank long and deep, especially those of us from the provinces, who had not yet tasted a drop.

Bringing a new vision of the world, overflowing with an infinitely rich inner life, these Primitives of literature went beyond the somewhat systematic and brutal objectivity of our naturalism. A great feeling for humanity swept over us. As Maurice Colrat, one of my predecessors, mockingly remarked in a sparkling speech, as First Secretary of the Conference of Lawyers, "We loved our fellowmen to the point of madness."

The arcades of the Odeon and its book-stalls offered to our hunger for literature and our thin purses the gratuity of reading in the open. The deep silences of the Bibliotheque Sainte-Genevieve and the Faculty of Law likewise sheltered our curiosity. But, above all, it was the library of the Students' Association—the "A"—that lured us. Founded a few years before, the "A" was presided over by Henry Beranger, then in the midst of a splendid thirst for idealism, director and animator of *L'Art et La Vie*, a youthful review, white-covered, not to be confused with *La Revue Blanche*, another proving-ground for advanced ideas, where I believe Leon Blum made his debut as a writer. I was to meet Beranger again, when he had become a most circumspect senator and President of the Commission For Foreign Affairs, after having been strongly anticlerical when Emile Combes was head of the government.

Not as well-stocked as the great libraries of the State, it was more homelike, more intimate; and our dramatic discussions often interrupted the reading.

It was there that, for the first time, I came in contact with Socialism, which had immediately jarred my young bourgeois sensibilities by its tone and outward manifestations, its violent defense of violence following the labor troubles at Decazeville.

Let me confess to some excellent comrades of my old party: I was not converted by Karl Marx, but by the pages of Benoit Malon's *Revue Socialiste*. It was at the drab door of this publication that Jaures knocked one day, after climbing the slopes of Montmartre, a fugitive—as M. Ribot pointed out at the trial of the great Socialist leader's assassin—from the Left

MINISTER OF LABOR (1911)

GOUVERNEMENT MILITAIRE DE PARIS

Armée de Paris,
Habitants de Paris,

Les Membres du Gouvernement de la République ont quitté Paris pour donner une impulsion nouvelle à la défense nationale.

J'ai reçu le mandat de défendre Paris contre l'envahisseur.

Ce mandat, je le remplirai jusqu'au bout.

Paris, le 3 Septembre 1914.

Le Gouverneur Militaire de Paris,
Commandant l'Armée de Paris,

GALLIENI

Center group, where he had first sat, and where he could not "spread his huge wings." Neither Marx nor the historic materialism, which never occupied much of my time, influenced my formation. On the other hand, I was attracted, conquered by that idealistic and generous socialism—Malon termed it "integral"—which took root in the long tradition of French Socialists, themselves directly affiliated with the Revolution, that has never ceased to make my old heart beat faster. I have never admitted that it was a complete separation, a trench dug between the Old France and the New; it is at the very center of our history; it is as absurd to attempt to cut it away, as some are now trying to do, as it is petty to attempt to efface with a stroke of the pen the centuries of monarchial rule that had prepared it.

It seemed to me that there was a magnificent story there—for which I have often regretted that certain friends of mine displayed an unjust disdain—a living tradition where Socialism always appears as the culmination of democracy and which encountered in me the deep currents that have swept me along since my college days.

What attracted me in these French Socialists was the action they urged, much more than their economic theories, already left behind in the rush of events. But how many others, Marxism to begin with, which seemed more solid, have been left behind also! "All theory is but dust," Goethe said, "and it is the verdant tree that bears the fruits of life."

I have never read, nor had any desire to read, the several pages wherein Blanqui has set down the outlines of a rather poor social system. But the life of Blanqui, his trials, his role during the Siege of Paris, the copies of his newspaper, *La Patrie en Danger*, always awaken in me a renewed admiration. What a splendid story of revolutionary energy! One that is tied together by the unbroken thread of his conspiracies, sudden raids, battles, sufferings, imprisonments, as well as the fervor of his followers, which continued beyond his death, a half-century of French political history, heated by the concentrated flame of this fragile little man. I understood why old Ranc always kept over his desk that picture of Blanqui, which is now in my possession. He had placed beside it that of

Gambetta: death and history are accustomed to these conciliations; the one thrusting forward and sowing for the future, the other reassuring and laying a foundation.

And Proudhon, with his solid common-sense, the cares of his critical task warning him against utopia. More than his social constructions, his "mutualism," by-passed by economic evolution, we look to him for directives of action, forceful ideas, that remain fecund. We re-read *La Justice dans la Revolution et dans l'Eglise*, and *De la Capacité des Classes Ouvrieres*. We weigh the value of his "hierarchy of the workshop," so similar to that of Saint-Simon, another picturesque and dynamic figure, who opened the way to a spirit of enterprise which, since socialism was not yet sufficiently strong to do anything with it, was taken over by the great capitalism of the nineteenth century. We gather from the old individualist this truth, which it behooves Socialism to penetrate if it wants to organize, command, govern: that there is no production possible without the acceptance of discipline.

Along with these retrospective itineraries through the origins of French Socialism, where the commentators of the *Revue Socialiste* were my guides, I was stirred by the articles of socialist or socializing contemporaries in the daily press which, realizing what was in the wind, gave them considerable space in those days. It was, I believe, in *Le Matin* that, ascending the Rue Soufflot on my way to class, I avidly sought the articles of Severine, the daughter—in spirit—of Valles. Brought back from Boulangism—and from Belgium, where she had placed the last red carnation, the party's symbol, on the tomb of the General and his mistress—Severine was now nothing more than a great-hearted woman, suffering with all who suffered, and raging against those who caused the suffering. A chalk-drawing of her youth, which she later presented to me, bears testimony to the distant and anonymous friendship of a young student for her.

The day came when I felt the need of incorporating in a doctrine these scattered aspirations. I recall reading, re-reading, meditating, annotating a weighty volume with a red cover, Benoit Malon's *Le Socialisme Integral*, a sort of Summa of French Socialism. Ethics, art, philosophy, all the manifestations of human activity were interpreted, by means of the faith which had moved, if not his mountains of Forez, at least the little shepherd who guarded his flocks there.

I was aware that all this was necessarily summary, primary even. This self-taught man, a proof-reader after having been a sheep-herder, then a militant member of the Commune, for which he was exiled, had nothing of the savant about him, and still less of the pedant. Yet it was toward him, his review, and his disciples, that Jaures turned. Later, Jaures wrote, for another book of Benoit Malon's, *La Morale Sociale*—preceded by the story of Malon's heroic life, by Leon Cladel—an admirable preface that gives the best idea of the great task Jaures had set for himself, alongside his purely political work: an attempt at a synthesis of the economic materialism of Marx and the idealism of the French Socialists of the Nineteenth Century, which gave the Socialist Party in France a scope and a strength which had not diminished in forty years, until the day of the abdications of Bordeaux and Vichy.*

In that year of my youth, I had a long vacation period before me, between my Second Year examinations at Law School and my military service. In the interests of better work, I had moved out of my own room into a guest room; except for my older brother and his wife, guests were rare, for death and old age had struck heavily about us. It was a large room, with blue wallpaper and curtains and white percale. The window overlooked, beyond a vine-covered trellis, the stable-yard. Every morning, before making his medical rounds, my father came in and opened the shutters to let the clear light of a morning in Touraine greet my eyes, and to start his own day, which was invariably long and hard, with a few moments of welcome relaxation.

In this peaceful setting, without any determining influence from the outside, except books and the dead, I became a Socialist.

I have remained one, although it was much later when I officially joined the party. I am not systematically a non-conformist, an "out-of-liner," according to the picturesque

* Since then, the Socialist Party, purged and renovated, has played a magnificent role in the Resistance. (1944)

expression of De Monzie; I have never underestimated the necessity and the force of an organization. However, a discipline a little too strict, an excessive doctrinism in some of its most influential leaders, and—as will be readily understood, in view of certain family ties, a certain upbringing which I have never denied—the anti-religious attitude of the party, still strong at the time, these things prevented me from enrolling in any of its political formations.

Participating in the anti-clerical movement, common at that period to all republican factions and explained by the struggle conducted by the Church against the Republic, Socialism, which was the *avant-garde*, carried it to the extreme, particularly in the central regions, where it was more an expression of super-Republicanism than specifically in favor of the working class. It often went past the boundary between Anticlericalism, a political position, and Irreligion. It took considerable effort on the part of the leaders to cut out of the *Carmagnole*, which was gradually replaced by the *Internationale*, but then very much in vogue, the couplet concerning Christ and the Virgin, of which Vandervelde rightly remarked that it was enough to turn the stomach of anyone who retained a respect for Christianity. And among the proletariat, at the labor union meetings I frequently attended, I recall the stupefaction of the delegates returning from Trades Union banquets in England, which began with a prayer and ended with a toast to the Queen.

It required considerable time for French Socialism, which remained rigorously laic, to respect religious faith and to permit a devout Catholic to occupy a ministerial post in the Popular Front government of Leon Blum without violent objection on that score. In fact, without any mention of it whatsoever, which I find regrettable; for it would have shown the injustice of the charge of sectarianism against Blum, who should rather have been reproached for a turn of mind too full of nuances and a lack of that solid decision so vital to energetic political action.

Other factors that kept me apart from the party, a sympathizer but not a member, an independent socialist in the true sense of the word, were its antimilitarism—introduced after the Dreyfus Affair—and an attitude of negation toward all patriotism from some of its supporters, too easily tolerated by the others, in spite of the efforts of Guesde and Jaures; and the refusal to vote appropriations for national defense, practically a rule of the party before 1914, on the pretext that it was wrong to maintain the army of a Bourgeois state.

I shall set forth the circumstances and the reasons for my joining the party in 1916, and for my leaving it in 1931.

But in heart, mind, and action later on, I was a socialist. And from that moment, although I was given rather frequent opportunities to enter parliament, I never consented to run against a socialist, nor to combat one. After leaving the party, I followed the same rule. I stood aside, in order to safeguard points of view as dear to me as socialism itself. Never against it.

As a young lawyer, I soon had occasion, right in my profession, to serve the ideas which had established themselves within me.

It was not out of a special vocation that I had studied law, although the profession was greatly esteemed in my family. My mother's brother, Lenfranc de Panthou, president of the society of barristers, after having been attorney-general, was, for years, one of the most celebrated lawyers of that splendid bar of Caen, and had been schooled by Demolombe and other great legal luminaries. The family hoped for a similar career for me. But, still haunted by my dreams of seafaring, and unable to pursue it by way of the Ecole Navale on account of my incompetence in mathematics, I expected to realize my ambition through the Naval Commissariat, for which a degree in Law was required. Until I obtained the degree, such was my goal.

But immediately after I obtained it, a new doctorate of Public Law and Political Economy came into being. It encountered within me the evolution I have described, the political preoccupations, my leanings toward socialism. The legal profession, and its independence, appeared to me as the one way to reconcile these inclinations with the necessity of earning a living. Although one earned precious little in those first years at the Palace of Justice! But my living problem was simple; a modest allowance from my parents permitted me to wait and see; I pursued concurrently my trial period as a probationer and my studies for the new doctorate, the latter with considerable ardor.

At the same time, I began to engage in struggles in which I have continued to be involved until my present retirement, and hope to resume, the opportunity and my strength permitting.

This was a period when, after several remarkably unremarkable governments, the persuasive and conciliatory Leon Bourgeois had his hour of conflict and of popularity. A cabinet homogeneously leftist, the support of the socialists, M. Doumer's project for a tax on personal income, had stirred up great uneasiness on one side and great hopes on the other; and I am fairly certain that I shouted, "Down with the Senate!" in the demonstrations caused by the hostility of the Upper House toward a political program which it finally defeated.

The reaction which followed was, by today's standards, quite gentle. Meline, a moderate, and the farmer's friend, let the folds of his agricultural frock-coat cover a good deal of it. Barthou, who subsequently tried to make us forget it, directed the reaction from the Ministry of the Interior with habitual heartiness, removing a few prefects from their posts—oh, very few—and calling out the gendarmes against the striking workmen. Those of Carmaux still remembered in 1924, and said that an attempt had been made to arrest Jaures.

Along about this time, I joined some of my friends and confreres in founding a judicial council at the *Bourse du Travail* in Paris, an idea which has since had a large and useful development. In the beginning, it had no other resources than our legal knowledge, freshly acquired and somewhat summary, and our inexhaustible good will.

Thus, the first contact I had with the working class brought me in touch with its most vital element, the labor unions—to which, a few years later, I was to devote my thesis. Thirty-four years later, it shortened my presidential destinies.

We passed quickly from the role of counsellor to that of defense lawyer. The unions were only too happy to accept our gratuitous assistance, especially since the governments of the period were rather severe in their methods of repressing strikes. My friend Alphonse Richard and I were called upon to defend some poor devils on strike in the fur industry, Polish refugees, dragged into the lower court on a charge which escapes me at the moment. Their situation was complicated by the fact that, being Poles, a condemnation would result in their deportation, and the justice of the Czar or the Kaiser inspired in them less confidence than that of a bourgeois republic.

I kept more or less within the limits befitting a beginner. But my friend was more violent; he spoke of "the danger threatening a modern slave who dares to disturb the digestion of his masters." But, he added, "we are a force to be reckoned with!"

It was a noisy hearing! The Solicitor General, M. Blondel, was a magistrate of much merit, but staunchly conservative, as a goodly number of his colleagues were, and have remained. With the exception of the suspension of the law of irremovability, a reprisal for the Sixteenth of May incident, our genial Republic has not done in fifty years a hundredth part of what has been perpetrated in the last three months. Pounding his desk, Blondel roared:

"So you are a force to be reckoned with? Well, we are the Law, and as long as we are the Law, I promise you that your force can do nothing!"

Our clients got the maximum. . . .

My friend, who himself became a magistrate, and presided with great severity over one of the Paris police courts, found the lesson fruitful. Indeed, he made all who appeared before him feel the full force of the Law. True, they were mostly peddlers and petty thieves, not too interesting, and my friend was able to reconcile his new-found passion for authority with the effervescences of his youth. Later, he was promoted to Counsellor of the Appellate Court and, as I was reading yesterday, "after a career entirely devoted to the State, he had been allowed to assert his retirement rights."

I continud to plead for the strikers, but, preferably, alone.

The political reactions to the Dreyfus Affair were about to

remove me momentarily from the Palace of Justice, due largely to a most unexpected encounter, and I did not return there until 1902, where I remained from then on, with the exception of the war years and those when I was in the government.

The Dreyfus Affair!

That, too, how far away it is!

I have checked with my children and their friends, and discovered that it had become practically unintelligible to them.

Yet, what an influence it had on our generation; and what political consequences followed it!

It happened when we were still students, having performed our military service, and with a few years of Paris behind us, all ready to rush into political battles, provided there was one that aroused our interest.

Save for a short interruption occasioned by the Radical ministry of Leon Bourgeois, and the wrath it stirred up, we watched, with varying degrees of disinterest, a passing parade of rather dim and equivocal governments. Already, with the founders gone from the scene, Waldeck-Rousseau out of the running and occupied with carving for himself a royal and unequalled place in the palace, quite a few profiteers started to push their way into power, alongside authentic republicans of the early battles, a preview of what happened, on a greater scale, in the years preceding the present war.

The Extreme-Left of the Radical party had lost its leader, more feared than loved, but who had given it the impression of strength by the succession of governments it had overthrown, thanks to him. Clemenceau had been beaten in the 1893 elections, after a jungle-like campaign where all those who, as Deroulede expressed it, had trembled before his pitilessness, his pistol, and his pen, had taken revenge for the fear they had felt.

This had given him the opportunity to unleash all the resources of his energy. A speech he made at Salernes, principal town in the Canton du Var—his words were collected, printed in a brochure, and, fortunately, reprinted after his death, thanks to the initiative of Jeanneney and the Friends of

Clemenceau—would rival a page of *Conciones*, or, to be exact, one would have to go as far back as Demosthenes, to whom Clemenceau devoted a book, toward the end of his life.

It was a masterpiece of conciseness, vehemence, and pathos, direct in its eloquence, which was always Clemenceau's style; but this time, thrown to the beasts, lacerated, along with his cries of pain, he lashed back in a fury of invective he never surpassed.

Jaures, converted to Socialism, had been returned to the Chamber of Deputies, and his booming voice was again heard. But the votes at his disposal were not sufficient to seriously alarm or activate these "dead-center" governments.

Like France at the close of Louis-Philippe's reign, the Latin Quarter was bored. Catholics and students of the Left and Extreme-Left, we all joined in hooting M. Hanotaux, the Minister of Foreign Affairs, for his complacency toward the Sultan of Turkey and the massacre of the Armenians. Happy era, when the young were indignant over distant massacres!

A few years previous, the Quarter had even attempted a small insurrection. A young man, Nuger by name, had been killed on the terrace of the D'Harcourt during a slight riot that began at one of those Quat'z-Arts balls, where young women displayed their anatomies without a single veil, to the great indignation of M. Beranger, the "*Pere la Pudeur*" of Willette's drawings. The Quarter was studded with barricades fashioned of overturned omnibuses, and some quite lively melees had taken place. A committee was in session at the Cafe de la Source where, in those easy years, a number of lawyers and doctors had done their studying. Zevaes was there, an Extreme-Leftist who became one of Jules Guesde's lieutenants, and later, for reasons that escape me, the lawyer for the assassin of Jaures, before returning to his political origins, vigorously defending, at many a court-martial or penal tribunal, militants who often had less to answer for than those who sent them. There was Jean Carrere, who turned to literature and sounded his *Buccins d'Or* in the bosom of Italy, which had adopted him. There were others present, and I shall not play them the nasty trick of citing their names; too many grave magistrates, members of the Council of Order, men of the government, or who believed they were, would be surprised to learn that they had been, for one day at least, insurgents.

A good-humored insurrection, which would have passed with little damage, had it not been for the corpse that caused it; an old-fashioned insurrection, such as Victor Hugo pictured in his immortal Gavroche:

"Je suis tombé par terre,
C'est la faute à Voltaire,
Le nez dans le ruisseau,
C'est la faute à Rousseau."

Its protagonists formed a rather picturesque assemblage, where all the parties rubbed elbows, somewhat similar to that Youth Congress in 1900, where I sat between Jacques Bainville, the royalist historian, and an anarchist poet from Provence, who began his speech by saying—and with what an accent—"Laws, like young girls, are made to be violated!"

The insurrection ended with a question in the Chamber of Deputies, where M. Charles Dupuy triumphed a bit heavily as the savior of Law and Order, less well-inspired than on that other occasion when, presiding at the session at which the anarchist Vaillant tossed a bomb, he said simply, "The session continues!"

The insurrection marked the last time that student solidarity manifested itself. I mean politically. It had, alas, other modes and other reasons for self-expression, amid the economic and scholastic difficulties created for young people by the last war, and still further aggravated by the present one.

To a young generation, frequently frustrated and kept apart from political action, if not from political principles, the Dreyfus Affair, involving questions of law, conscience, and politics, was about to bring unexpected developments. But at the same time, it was about to divide deeply the Latin Quarter and its extensions: the law probationers in residence, the internes at the hospitals, and the Great Schools. It was divided just as deeply on the eve of this present war. I am told that now, it has been unified against the invader by a vibrant patriotism.

Zola's *J'Accuse* was, for many of us, the live coal of Isaiah.

We plunged into the fight, all the more ardently because the old politicians, who were probably not so old, but seemed ancient to us, just as we do to the youth of today, began by misunderstanding it.

The Dreyfus Affair became political, and it had profound and lasting repercussions on our politics, because those in power failed to decide, authoritatively and immediately, a legal problem which could not be evaded, once it had been placed before them. Some, who were certainly far from being revolutionists, were not deceived. I distinctly recall attending a dinner at the home of M. Ployer, President of the Bar Association, in the early days of the Affair. The Keeper of the Seals, M. Milliard, who had been invited, was late. There was a discussion in the Senate over an interpellation by M. Scheurer-Kestner, the first of many which the Affair was to bring forth. M. Milliard finally arrived, sprightly, a smile in his eyes, becomingly white-bearded, and said, as he took his seat at the table, speaking of the interpellation, which had been announced as promising sensational revelations, "Nothing in the hands! Nothing in the pockets!"

I was seated beside M. Devin, a typical member of the old Palace of Justice group, where one encountered so much culture, good sense, and shrewdness. He leaned toward me and said quietly, "The Keeper of the Seals speaks frivolously of an affair that could become serious."

It became so serious, it cut France in two.

Oh, the vertical slash was not perfect, with the right on one side and the left on the other. More than one radical, who was among the noisy laborers of the twelfth hour, remained quiet at first, yielding to demagogism and fear, unwilling to defend an officer and a Jew against the rising wrath of the moment. The Socialists were far from being unanimous. A debate in the Chamber of Deputies brought a serious clash between Millerand and Reinach, who, a short time later, were to fight on the same side. Millerand said to Reinach, "You should, first of all, do a little house-cleaning in your own family." Guesde, after praising Zola's letter as a revolutionary act, and reproaching the moderates of the party for not having the courage to seize upon it, retreated from his position of doctrinal intransigent, unwilling for socialist action to be absorbed in a matter where classes and parties were intermingled.

On the other hand, among the liberal-minded moderates, who inevitably turn up on the good side, in the Boulangist question, the Dreyfus Affair, or Vichy, some were not deceived from the very start: Waldeck-Rousseau, Scheurer-Kestner, Trarieux, De Pressensé. Certain devout Catholic consciences were troubled. And the army was by no means united behind the General Staff. A little courage in defying the Staff's leadership, which thought it was defending the army, by defending something which was, to say the least, a monstrous judicial error, would have sufficed to rectify the error without too much damage to anyone.

This was only accomplished some years later, when the affair had become political, and the Rightists, determined to use it to the full against the Republicans, forced the latter to seek out Waldeck-Rousseau, who had gone into retirement ten years ago.

Chapter Three

THE LAST OF THE THREE

Waldeck-Rousseau.—How I became his collaborator.—The secrets of mastery.—The great ministry.—Millerand and Galliffet.—The papers of the High Court.—After Fachoda.—Waldeck and our alliances.—The Law of Associations.—Election night.

Waldeck-Rousseau was sought because, at that time, in spite of a few relinquishments, the republican feeling was sufficiently alive, and in days of danger, one remembered and one chose well. He was "the last of the Three," to whom one turned, in memory of better times, when the Republic was young and vigorous. Gambetta, Ferry, Waldeck-Rousseau, of different age and even more different temperament, formed one of those triptychs, chromo-colored, such as the peasants keep over their hearths. These men were the incarnation of a Republic which was neither the conservative Republic of Thiers, nor the Extreme-Left Republic of Clemenceau, nor the one that socialism extolled, but a republican Republic, without complacencies or excesses, a response to the middle-of-the-road sentiment of a nation which remained deeply attached, not only to the form of its institutions, but to their spirit. Ready to move forward, but not too fast.

Gambetta had died young, inaugurating a series of premature passings, wherein Waldeck-Rousseau was to follow him, before Berteaux and Jaures; deaths that weighed heavily on the destiny of the Republic. Ferry, too, was dead, much older, his death hastened by the bitter attacks upon him.

Waldeck-Rousseau remained. Minister in the Cabinet of Ferry and of Gambetta, who had noted him particularly and made him the youngest minister of the Republic, his return to the practice of law had spared him the competition and the rivalries, less hectic than those we knew, but which already existed, and above which he moved majestically, in the midst of his memories, preparing himself by his very withdrawal from the political scene to be its arbiter, the man designated to head the union of republicans when the day should come.

It came with danger.

Absent five years from Parliament, five more years of what amounted to silence in the Senate, he had only reoccupied the center of the stage quite recently, in the matter of the Dreyfus Affair, with an admirable speech on the law of dispossession. I listened from a seat deep in the gallery, trembling with emotion and proud of having been invited to work with him, as he told the assembly, "You have tarnished the conscience of France, that clear mirror where so many generous ideas had been reflected. . . . So, then, there are memories that no longer grip the hearts of the sons of those exiles of 1852. . . ." Ah, how many of those memories should assail us today! And what sins have been charged to the conscience of our beloved country!

Thus, after the fall of the equivocal cabinet of Charles Dupuy, and the failure of attempts by Raymond Poincaré, Casimir Perier, and Leon Bourgeois, there was no other recourse than to call upon Waldeck-Rousseau at his law office in the Rue de l'Université, and ask him to form a government. His position was strengthened because everyone knew he had no desire to take such a step, and that it would demand certain sacrifices on his part.

He took command at a time when, according to his own ironic observation, "the avenues of approach to the position of leader were unusually uncrowded"; the clever and the wary not caring to come to grips with a situation which, if not desperate, had been made difficult by the compromises and weaknesses of preceding governments.

Because he had fought and won—a bit more than he wished—by his long ministry of three years, longest on record in the republic, he proved—as Clemenceau did later, by other methods— that ministerial stability was not incompatible with Republican institutions, *provided they have a chief*. When he had gone, the political formation over which he had presided determined, in the ensuing years, an orientation for the regime which, after his crushing victory in the 1902 elections, he believed he should relinquish to others.

I would like to try, by personal and direct recollections, to shed new light upon this fine figure of a statesman, reticent and enigmatic, whose career has been over-simplified, in my opinion, in premature biographies published just after he died, too early to take the exact measure of the man. I shall ignore the detractors, who have failed to hit the mark, even though the talented Jacques Bainville tried.*

As a contribution to the portrait of the man, here is how I became his collaborator, and what he said to me.

Admitted to the Bar two years previously, doing an honest day's work pleading cases of divorce-by-default and other legal minutiae, interspersed with really ardent efforts on behalf of the labor unions, the idea had not occurred to me to brave the Conference of Lawyers, the secretariat of which is the Staff College of our peaceful battles, a training-ground for future Field-Marshals of Forensics, even preparing for other brilliant careers, commencing with that of President of the Council.

Nor did I attend its preliminary lectures at the Demolombe, the Harlay, and other private courses, all bearing the names of past jurisconsults, and held evenings at the Palace of Justice. There, my young confreres exercised their talents on a given legal problem or imaginary criminal case, free to choose the side of the prosecution or the defense.

Contrary to legend, I never frequented—except to hear my friends, later—the Conference Molé, where our junior barristers played at being parliamentarians. A young provincial, I had few acquaintances to lure me out of the Latin Quarter. In addition, a highly-developed shyness held me more or less

* Since writing these lines, the first volume of the *Memoires* of Joseph Caillaux has appeared. I have read with emotion the pages he has devoted to my master, whom he salutes as his, in his impressions as a young cabinet-member. Inevitable repetitions will be found in our two books, since, at different degrees, we both have served him and loved him.

aloof. The slightest speech before a magistrate was a victory over myself; to hear my voice rise alone in an assembly froze me with terror. Shall I confess? Long after my efforts were sufficiently successful to warrant a feeling of assurance, this apprehension persisted.

"Who is the . . . who pretends he's never been afraid?" said an old soldier.

It took all the insistence of my friends, who had more confidence in my oratorical possibilities than I, to persuade me to address the redoubtable Conference. As an added inducement, one of the subjects listed for the competitors was near to my heart, for it concerned labor unions and the rights ofworkers.

Believe it or not, I succeeded so well that I failed to get any pleasure from it. I was convinced that it was due to sheer luck, or to the choice of subject, and that I could never live up to the reputation so suddenly acquired, already pointing to me as the future first secretary. Veterans of the Palace know what that means. I was sure that the second test, following this trial gallop, would go all the harder for me because my confreres and the judges had shown such enthusiasm the first time.

Such was not the opinion of the President of the Corporation of Barristers, M. Ployer. And here I would like to bring to him the grateful homage of a young lawyer, quite without influential friends, unsure of himself, to whom the benevolence of his superior opened a career, with its satisfactions and its bitterness, but who, without this encouragement, would never have known the best of it.

An affable and astute man, of old Parisian bourgeois stock, a clever lawyer, possessing a comfortable income which permitted him, like other eminent confreres of the 1890's, to avoid the ravages of the occupational disease known as "brief-case fever"—the unseemly chase for clients—and allowed him the leisure for long conversations in the great waiting-hall of the Palace, where he dispensed a good deal of wit and learning. Conservative by inclination, he was the attorney for the General Staff of the Army, therefore anti-Dreyfus, as much as his kindliness and indulgence, a bit ironic and undeceived, permitted him to be "anti" anything. It seemed unlikely that he would be disposed to give to me so spontaneously, when I had done nothing to hide my sentiments and tendencies which differed considerably from his, the unexpected boon of his support. Unlikely, were it not for the habit, which I hope has not been completely lost, of certain veterans of the profession to aid the young barrister to climb in a career where they had succeeded, and to serve the Order to which they were attached.

I can see myself, on the afternoon of the day I competed, still trembling from my effort of the morning, and perplexed by my unanticipated success, entering his office with its portraits of past presidents, outside which the famous Leon, beadle of the Order, sternly maintained the dignified silence suited to such a spot, where the young lawyers of that time waited respectfully. Let our bolder young confreres of today hide their mocking smiles; tradition has its uses.

After trying to make me understand that I seemed not to realize the importance this day could have for my chosen career, he questioned me about my origins, my family. He remarked:

"I hear you're a socialist?"

"That is correct, *monsieur le batonnier*."

"Odd choice," he said, in that gentle voice of his. "Have you a patron?"

"No, *monsieur le batonnier*."

"You must get one. A great lawyer, who'll be happy to put you to work."

"I don't know anyone."

"What would you say to going into Waldeck-Rousseau's office? I'll ask him to put you on."

It is important to realize Waldeck-Rousseau's prestige around the Palace of Justice at that time, even greater with probationers like us, who watched him pass by, the eternal cigarette dangling from his lips, without a toque, which was then an eccentricity, almost a demonstration of independence. Not one of us would have ever dared to address him.

He was hardly talkative with his peers. A late arrival at the Paris Bar, after a long period of preparation at Nantes and Rennes, to which he often told me he attributed his thorough formation, and his two interludes of power as a young cabinet minister, he had quickly conquered one of the first places in the legal profession, if not *the* first. He encountered a certain amount of jealousy, and made few friends. His extraordinary —for a lawyer—gift of silence, his taste for solitude, kept him away from those charming conversations indulged in by even the busiest, at an epoch when one was not too hurried to give some time to an exchange of ideas and anecdotes. He appeared at the Palace, accompanied by the faithful Ulrich, sailed into court, generally delivered a masterpiece, then went back to work at his office with its mountains of dossiers, or relaxed with chosen friends at his apartment, among his books, paintings, and objects of art, on the Rue de l'Université. For he stressed the importance of these things: he knew the value attached to the *decor* of our labors and anxieties, what one's mental equilibrium owes to the size of a piece of furniture, the harmony of a lamp, the view from a window. His speeches were quoted, his fees cited.

The Council of the Order had received him without any campaigning on his part, unhurriedly, but proud just the same to have him in their midst, and realizing how ridiculous it would be if he were not. Those with a certain independence of mind, the President Ployer leading them, designated him for leadership.

Imagine, then, what his unexpected, unhoped-for offer meant to me; the chance to work with Waldeck-Rousseau.

Nevertheless, I raised an objection: it concerned that brief period when the former member of the cabinets of Gambetta and Ferry, and who was soon to be the chief of the republican Ministry of Defense, rather far away from the radicals, unable to forget their attacks upon his masters, had moved close to the moderates, already allied with the conservatives. He had not been favorable toward the government of Leon Bourgeois, for whom—I do not know why, but I observed it several times, and observed also that Bourgeois was affected by it—he had little liking. He supported Meline's ministry. All this in the distant, reserved manner that went with his temperament, and explained the persistency with which, concentrating on his legal career, he had remained aloof for years from active politics. At the *Grand Cercle Republicain* and elsewhere, he had made speeches fairly hostile to socialism, which caused me, in all honesty, to reply to M. Ployer:

"First, Monsieur Waldeck-Rousseau should be told that I'm a socialist."

M. Ployer smiled. He pointed out that I was not going to work for the politician, but the lawyer; and, as a lawyer, the man deserved my admiration, which was strictly true.

M. Ployer went to see Waldeck-Rousseau, spoke of me in terms which I can well imagine, after his benevolent treatment of me, and asked him to employ me as secretary, after mentioning the reservation I had made about the political point of view.

Waldeck-Rousseau, interested, and perhaps amused at this youthful intransigent, replied:

"This young man pleases me, with his reservations. Send him to me."

An appointment was made for the following week. I waited a few moments in the secretaries' office, which faced his, close to, but apart from, his private house, so as to keep separate his work and his repose, his business appointments and his social gatherings, according to the rigorous routine he applied to everything, from the preparation of his speeches to the management of his life. Thereafter, I was to return often to this secretarial office, and to ask people to wait—not clients particularly, for Waldeck-Rousseau saw them but little, claiming that the dossier taught him more about them than their explanations—but politicians, ambassadors, sovereigns, who, immediately after his departure from the government, following his great triumph, called upon him, quite sure he would return to power.

Then, came my direct contact with the man who was to be my mentor.

A certain coldness, from which I have never seen him deviate—no matter what those who claim to have had this privilege may say—did not prevent a kindly reception, which he made even kindlier the more timid the visitor appeared to be. Such was my case. He assured me that everything M. Ployer had told him about me disposed him to number me among his collaborators. He spoke of my thesis, on which I was then working, and said that the subject was still dear to his heart: he was interested to note, in the mind of a young man whose tendencies he knew, the progression of ideas, and perhaps the unexpected consequences of this labor union movement which he had been the first to pass into law.

Finally, he indicated to me his method of work and collaboration. As I had confessed my lack of experience, adding that I counted on his advice to learn my *metier* and aid him in his, he made this suggestion, rather an unusual one for a jurist:

"The best advice I can give you, is to read a great deal of Balzac."

It was not exactly needed; for my father had long initiated me in the cult, and I had remained faithful. It still exists, and, in my present exile, very much alone, Balzac is one of my refuges. But, at first, I was somewhat uncertain of what it signified.

Since then, being in a position to study my mentor's speeches, not only in their stenographic and printed versions, but right from his notes themselves—and I shall speak of their marvelous order, and the way they reproduce the movement of his thought—I understood.

This brief, almost enigmatic, remark, which could have seemed nothing more than a pleasantry, gave me the key to what was, not the only, nor the most apparent, but certainly one of the reasons for his mastery at the Bar, which assured him, with his success before the judges, the eminent and almost unique place he held. For, from him dates a type and style of plea quite unequalled, and after him, other styles that had gained fame, appeared so outmoded, they were discarded.

For if one studies, enlightened by this strange advice he gave me at our first interview, the speeches of Waldeck-Rousseau, one notices that a number of them—the one in the case of the Recipon will, the Lebaudy affair, the will of the Marquise de Plessis-Belliere, the Eiffel case, that of Burdeau, the forgotten affair of Madame Achet (one of the very rare occasions when he pleaded in a criminal case)—are constructed like a novel of Balzac. It does not consist of an exposé of the facts, on the one hand, and on the other, a demonstration; the story he relates covers so well the legal argument, so solid, incidentally, constituting an unassailable basis, that the listener—in this instance, the judge—while he thinks he is merely following the story and its incidents, is led to accept, as a natural conclusion, the very one where the lawyer guided him.

"Read a great deal of Balzac. . . ." Yes, it had a lot to do with his courtroom successes.

But there was more that bore his stamp, at the Bar as well as on the parliamentary scene: for he was equally effective in both, which is rare: a liking for simplicity, the exact adaptation of phrase and thought, the purity of style, which made him an adherent of classicism; certain pages of his speeches have the rhythm of Racine, and Viviani made the remark that he had, like Racine, a limited vocabulary, all the effect resulting from the arrangement of words, not their number and their richness. I can still hear the start of his speech on behalf of the actor Coquelin. I quote from memory:

"It is not without regret that one pleads against the House of Moliere. We are all under some obligation to it. Through it, authors who had been merely the property of our young memories, have become the joy of our imaginations. It is like another Louvre, where the masterpieces of the past are preserved, but find each night the spark of life that sets them palpitating before our eyes. . . ."

Contrary to what one might suppose, so perfect it was, and unlike Poincaré who wrote everything out, Waldeck-Rousseau meditated a great deal, constructing his speech in his mind, putting down only a few notes on great sheets of white paper. But the choice of the essential words that marked his thoughts, underscored with pencils of different colors, was so judicious, the words so well arranged, reproducing as if linearly the construction of the phrase he had in mind, that after hearing the speech, with the aid of one's memory, one could repeat it almost integrally by reading his notes. Many times, I have experienced this with his political addresses, which were prepared by the same method as his legal pleas. For he was so sure of his thought and his language, that he hardly ever looked at the stenography; he left that to me, at the same time that he turned over to me his dossiers, as carefully classified and arranged as his legal ones.

How I would have liked to see his legal pleas placed in the archives of our Order, the political speeches in the library of the Chamber of Deputies and the Senate! What models!

We have at least a slight sampling, thanks to Peguy. Madame Waldeck-Rousseau, who kept alive his memory, after having been an incomparable companion, but who, with his dislike of outside manifestations in his working hours, had never been allowed to hear him speak in public, had placed in Peguy's hands, for publication in the *Cahiers de la Quinzaine*, the speech he had been about to make in the Senate against the separation of Church and State, when sickness struck him down. With his characteristic typographical care, Peguy reproduced the exact disposition of these notes, replacing by one, two, or three underscoring lines the black, blue, or red notations Waldeck-Rousseau had made for his own guidance. A precious document for anyone seeking the secret of a great master.

There should be added the long and solitary preparation on which his mastery is based, that constant effort of the will that set the course of Waldeck's life, surmounting a shyness coming through in his letters to his mother and others near him, at the beginning of his career, during the studious years at Nantes and Rennes, tied down to the most routine tasks of legal procedure, bridling an imagination which led him to write—and destroy—as he confided to me one day, several adventure stories. He had retained a taste for this type of fiction, not with the idea of creating, but of reading for relaxation, never going to sleep without trying it.

It was this same will-power, tenacious but not brutal, which explains the summary and contradictory opinions I read, right after his death, in newspaper articles appearing about him; some denying his heart, others believing themselves obliged to bring him back to the common level of facile sensibilities. Statesmen, party chiefs, leaders of peoples, those who are qualified to carry on their shoulders the weight of collective responsibilties, have not this amount of leisure. Clemenceau was ferocious. Of the good Jaures, Anatole France said that he loved others "as the Christian loves his neighbor." Waldeck's sentimental side existed, certainly, and I have experienced it. But he hid it well.

It had taken long and considerable effort on his part to acquire that impassibility which rendered him, at least in appearance, invulnerable to attacks and capable of coldly carrying out his resolutions, calculatedly hiding under a mask of impassiveness the beating of a heart that, like all hearts, sometimes pounded passionately.

I have known silent men. They were babblers compared to Waldeck. His powers of silence and isolation were unprecedented. I have always thought that it was during these long meditations, a cigarette in his lips each time his obligations or his courtesy allowed him the leisure—for he had no peer in the fine art of stopping a bore—that he worked at his political constructions and the unwritten preparation of his speeches, the form of which was too perfect not to have been carried long in his head.

An example among many: after the fashion of the English political leaders, and having much of their demeanor, he adopted their tradition of the week-end, in an era when this usage was far less frequent. Except in the gravest of circumstances, each Sunday would find him in the country. Until he bought a house at Corbeil, overlooking the Seine—the house where he died, and which he loved because the river view reminded him of Nantes—his customary week-end retreat was the property of his friends, the Dreyfus-Gonzales, the lovely chateau of Pontchartrain, once a possession of the favorite of Louis XIV, Louise de la Valliere, and later that of La Paiva, celebrated courtesan of the Second Empire. Under the autumn-reddened vines, a bust with its heart pierced by an arrow perpetuated the memory of the tenderest of royal mistresses, who became a Carmelite nun, Sister Louise of the Misericordia. The chateau, pleasantly filled with these souvenirs of profane love, was somewhat sanctified in a more contemporary style by the sojourns of an eminent Jesuit, whose name often arose in controversies of the period. Pere Dulac was the director of that school in the Rue des Postes, where so many military and naval leaders were educated, and were still strongly influenced by him. He was said to play an important, but discreet, political role. Along with Waldeck, he shared the sympathy and the confidence of Madame Dreyfus-Gonzales, a Spanish catholic, widow of Waldeck's first client in Paris, following his ministry of 1884. Waldeck appeared on behalf of the husband in the Chilean Guanos case. The hostess took great care to see that Jesuit and the chief of the government of Republican Defense, the author of the Law of Associations, did not meet. But in those days, it was the custom to be as courteous in social relations as one was rigid in politics; and whenever they discussed each other with their hostess, the tone was gracious.

It was I who usually accompanied Waldeck on these week-ends; I believe he chose me because he had verified my capacity for respecting his silence. Pontchartrain was situated just a few kilometers from Trappes. No automobiles, or practically none, at that time; we left the Place Beauvau in a horse-drawn coupé, took the train at the Gare Montparnasse, passed through Versailles and St. Cyr; at the Trappes station, a carriage was waiting to take us to Pontchartrain. A matter of two good hours in all. Frequently, from the moment I greeted him in the courtyard of the Place Beauvau until our arrival at the steps of the chateau, Waldeck had not opened his mouth. Nor had I, of course.

One Sunday evening, returning to Paris in a train packed with excursionists, as we stopped at a suburban station, a man tried to get into the compartment reserved for us; the employee held him back, saying, "It's the President of the Council." This happened at a time when a violent nationalist struggle was in progress; royalists and nationalists had been arrested and accused of treason before the High Court; the trial continued; passions were aroused; and the excursionist, holding the compartment door open, glared at Waldeck and gave his personal opinion of the President of the Council in a few ill-chosen words. I was sitting across from Waldeck. He did not flinch. Neither did I. A good five minutes later, removing his cigarette from his lips, he expressed his opinion of the man. "Imbecile!" he said. And that was all.

I had, that evening, a good lesson in composure.

Obviously, these long silences were only possible with his intimates; elsewhere, he had his professional, political, or social obligations. For he loved to go out of an evening, to relax at the theatre or with friends. But even then, he was not particularly prodigal with his words; just what was necessary to examine a question, if it was a business matter, or to preserve an attitude of politeness toward his hosts and guests. He loved to laugh, and to be made to laugh, discreetly, as always. The younger Coquelin, a very good friend, excelled at this. The older Coquelin, who had been an admirer of Gambetta, was a bit too inclined to talk politics; but he amused Waldeck by his perpetual enthusiasm, which the audiences did not always ratify, for the roles tailored for him at the Theatre de la Porte-Saint-Martin, after his departure from the Comedie-Francaise. With the exception of Cyrano, they were not as good as those of the old house he had left, but they gave him the pleasure of incarnating successively some of the great figures of History, Napoleon, Jean Bart, and the like.

When Waldeck was looking for relaxation, he had no desire to hear about business. I have heard him reply to a politician, invited to dinner at the Place Beauvau, who ventured to remind his host of a political favor he had requested, just as the coffee was being passed, "My dear fellow, I have set aside Wednesday mornings for members of parliament who wish to speak with me."

Luncheon, however, was a part of his working day, and it was used to continue his political task, between the morning interviews and the afternoon schedule. Every day, for two years, I attended these luncheons, where I saw a passing parade of committee presidents, group leaders, influential members of the majority, to whom he talked attentively about their reports or their action, exercising at every instant a control over the parliamentary machine.

"Well, *mon cher ami*, how is your report coming along?"

"*Monsieur le president*, it advances."

"When do you believe you can submit it to the committee?"

"in a few weeks."

"Rather long. Make an extra effort, will you? I should like to have it up for discussion at one of our next sessions. . . ."

Presidents, leaders, and those preparing the reports, felt flattered, encouraged, listened to reason, or were animated by a desire to please; the parliamentary machinery rolled on; it had something it could not function without: a motor, a government.

With the press, he was courteous, but distant. And the press was deferential; I speak of those who supported his policy; he ignored the others. He personally saw, though infrequently, several of the great newspaper editors, and quite often Pognon, an important personage of the *Agence Havas*, keeping close watch on their news-gathering. More frequent contacts were left to his secretary-general Demagny, who handled this sort of thing marvelously, knowing just when to be inflexible and when to be obliging. I have seen potentates, at a call from whom some of our recent cabinet ministers would have rushed around submissively, enter Demagny's office sheepishly and receive a tongue-lashing for insufficient zeal.

Except in matters of foreign policy, where he was disturbed about possible repercussions outside the country and interpretations unfavorable to us, he never attached the importance to press campaigns that, in our day, cause so much fear and trembling. He valued opinion and took it into account before making a decision, but when he had settled upon a line of procedure, the press and its editorials left him indifferent; he knew the majority of them were on his side. Although the press bureau of the Ministry of the Interior, a ministry closely attached to the presidency of the Council and deriving considerable importance from it, was efficient and well-equipped, we ourselves were on the alert, like any self-respecting cabinet, in going over the analyses of the newspaper reports before placing them on his desk each morning. I generally found them untouched.

Writing this, and comparing it with what I saw, heard, and experienced during my years in power, I seem to be dealing with ancient history. Poor Elie Blois, who went to his death in London, reproached me for trying to keep alive this tradition and for bringing to a thieves' market the manners of another age.

I entered the law office of Waldeck in 1898. By June, 1899, the political situation had drawn Waldeck away again; and I went with him. And not in the direction M. Ployer had imagined, when he confided my new-born socialism to this great moderate.

This moderate, according to an expression he often used, and which will flow often from my pen, was not moderately republican; he was even more ardently liberal and attached to the right by temperament and profession, as much as by family tradition.

His father had been one of those exiles of 1852, whose memory he reproached the Republican Senate for forgetting, at the moment of his return to politics, on the occasion of the dispute about the law of dispossession. From that day in February, 1899, his political ideas had taken a new orientation, or rather, returned to their point of departure, renewing, over the heads of the moderates who had lost it, the living tradition of Gambetta and Ferry.

However, when called upon to form a cabinet, he still wanted to trust his companions of old, and urged them to join him in defending the Republic. Encountering a certain indifference, which said a lot for the devolution that had led them to this condition, and wanting above all to save this Republic which, without the slightest romanticism, he judged to be in peril, a judicial affair having been turned into a conspiracy against her, he audaciously sought the elements of his majority even in the bosom of the socialist party.

He chose Millerand. Considered a member of the right wing of the extreme left, he had nevertheless made a speech at Saint-Mande, in 1895, in which he preached the doctrine of collective ownership, praised a policy of daring reforms, tracing a program of governmental socialism approved by almost all the members of a party which was never more united than in the days before it was unified.

There was a beautiful uproar! All that I have heard said about the Cartel in 1924, the Popular Front in 1936, I heard in 1899 at Millerand's entrance into the ministry of Waldeck. I had heard it originally, in my childhood, about the Republic itself; for that reason, it has never moved me much.

Millerand proceeded to give the lie to the current opinion, which covers a multitude of backslidings, that a jacobin who becomes a minister is not always a jacobin minister. He remained a socialist in the government, a socialist of the government, as he had always been. And when I fought, later on, within the party for participation in a non-Socialist cabinet, persuaded that one gets nothing achieved without being in power, I had a time of it trying to remind my friends that, during his first months in the government—in that Ministry of Commerce, where social legislation was then centered, before the creation of a Ministry of Labor—Millerand had, in a series of decrees, made more progress in this field than years of parliamentary discussion would have accomplished. At the same time, in his ministerial practice, he had called for the collaboration of the labor unions, long before me, although I have been widely blamed for it.

He fearlessly wore his revolutionary cockade even in the ministerial drawing-rooms. To someone who slandered the Revolution, the Bonapartist Princesse Mathilde replied, "You forget that, without it, I'd be selling oranges in the square at Ajaccio." One evening, at dinner at Waldeck's, a guest spoke scathingly of the Commune, and Millerand replied, with one of his rare smiles, "Excuse me for not going along with you. I can't forget that, if it hadn't been for the Commune, I wouldn't be here!"

Nor can I forget what he said about Jaures, and his admiration for him, to Waldeck, who had never met Jaures. It was only later on, during the duration of the ministry, that the two came in contact. Jaures, wanting the meeting to be handled with discretion, as a sop to the susceptibilities of the party's purists, would not go directly to Waldeck's office. Instead, he came to mine, accompanied by Gerault-Richard, who directed *La Petite Republique*, organ of the independent socialists prior to unification and the founding of L'Humanité. It had been arranged that after a few minutes conversation with me, Waldeck was to express a desire to see them. Which was done. As they were about to go in, Gerault-Richard, a former upholsterer with a newly acquired taste for elegance, noticed that Jaures' trousers were torn: "And I dressed so carefully," sighed Jaures. But the interview went off well. Waldeck was grateful to Jaures, who was leading a courageous fight for the new government; and Leon Blum has told me the very considerable effect Waldeck's term at the head of the government had upon the thinking of Jaures, and what esteem he had for Waldeck's character and talent.

When the Exposition of 1900 opened, it was the function of Millerand to inaugurate it as Minister of Commerce, with Waldeck at his side. Waldeck had a horror of this sort of thing, and hated making a speech when there was nothing to explain. He asked me to furnish him a few notes, which we worked on with De Jouvenel, who often visited me at my office in the Rue des Saussaies, where I was a neighbor of André Tardieu. Waldeck promptly discarded most of the notes, finding them too lyrical. Millerand, however, was as lyrical as he was socialist and thundered an invocation to Labor that had a certain swing, and ended:

"O Labor, it is thou that liberates. . . thou that consoles. . . ."

It was all somewhat of an anticipation of 1936, a symbol that socialism could have used to its advantage had not the uncompromising attitude of some of its best minds, including poor Renaudel, started by attacking Millerand, destroying the fruits of this policy of participation in the government, a policy set aside thereafter.

Was it this injustice? Undeniably. Was it because of these attacks, in spite of his hippopotamus hide, that Millerand, whose entire career had been made as a socialist, decided not only to abandon it, but to take a stand against it? Or did Millerand submit to the envelopment of large enterprises, for which his capacity for hard work and his solidity made him the ideal lawyer, after the death of Waldeck-Rousseau, who greatly appreciated his talents, gave him a good part of Waldeck's clientele? I suffered the consequences too much, not to have often asked myself this question. Millerand's term of office as head of the government, and the use he made of it, were often subjects of controversy in our debates on participation. The objection was made to those of us who defended the participation policy, "See what it has led to!" This was objectively false: during its entire duration, as I could testify as an observer and a participant, socialism—socialism in government, the only kind that matters, unless one is conducting a revolution—drew nothing that was not advantageous.

Another audacious stroke, in an opposite direction, was no less disconcerting to those who failed to grasp the masterly idea behind Waldeck's formation of his cabinet. It was his purpose to group together all those he judged capable of bringing order to the endangered Republic. With that in mind, he chose the socialist Millerand. And for that reason, he selected as his Finance Minister Joseph Caillaux, son of one of the ministers in the government of Moral Order, but whose courageous vote against his colleague of the Sarthe, M. Cavaignac, now on the side of the nationalists, and what had been reported to him about the keen intelligence and competence of Caillaux, made him decide to include him in his team.

He did even more. Until the final hours of the combination, one place remained vacant; under the circumstances, the most important of all. For Waldeck-Rousseau, the essential thing was, not so much the rehabilitation of Dreyfus—except for a few fanatics, no one doubted now that Dreyfus had been unjustly and illegally condemned—but to silence the fomenters of coups d'etat, and to put back in line certain military leaders, who, if not directly implicated, were at least in favor of the political action which the battle against a review of the trial had become. It was urgent to get the army back to work at its proper function, preparation for war; an energetic call for discipline and silence was necessary; rigorous measures were required.

Like a wise statesman, Waldeck-Rousseau, who had first thought of taking over the Ministry of War himself, realized that such a task, to be accepted by the army, could only be undertaken by a soldier of undisputed merit. I can recall the evening when, dining quietly—for even during this cabinet crisis, Waldeck, at the close of his day, shut his door to all but his most intimate friends, relaxing with them and gathering strength against tomorrow—told us how he had made a trip to the environs of Paris where, in retirement at the home of an elderly belle, the General Marquis de Galliffet, the hero of Sedan, passed the time agreeably massacring magpies. The General had been on the retired list since 1895.

Waldeck was aware that, like others, Galliffet was the victim of a legend that made of him a dashing, swashbuckling cavalryman, and nothing more. Counsellor of Gambetta, reorganizer of the cavalry in the 1880's, inspector-general of the army and director of the maneuvers of Bléré, Burgundy, and Beauce, much given to pitiless and brilliant criticism,* it was the intention of M. de Freycinet, then a member of the government of National Defense, to appoint him generalissimo. Still energetic and full of go, in spite of his seventy years, he was the right man for the place Waldeck had picked for him.

The humiliation of the defeat, the collapse of an army he had believed in, the bitter reflections of captivity, had marked rather deeply the temperament of Galliffet and oriented his destiny. Without losing any of his impetuosity, nor depriving himself of any of his pleasures and his witticisms, the somewhat hare-brained officer of the Second Empire—festive companion of Grammnot-Caderousse, acting in the plays put on by the Empress Eugenie and her court at Compiegne, magnificent soldier in Italy, Crimea, Mexico, Algeria, and the War of 1870, a general at forty—was to become a leader eager to learn, to renew, to prepare our revenge. I am thinking of

* It was at one of these criticisms that an aged general, interrupting him, said bleatingly, "But, General, it seems to me that before 1870 . . ." Galliffet cut in, "Before 1870, we were all asses!" (He used a more brutal expression which I cannot reproduce here.)

Captain Gilbert, unforgettably described by Jaures in *L'Armee Nouvelle;* from his hospital bed, immobilized by wounds, he continued to write in burning words the lessons learned, for the benefit of officialdom. It is to men like this, Galliffet included, that we owed, in the years that followed 1870, a spirit of research, an effort of the imagination, in a word, a military renaissance such as only the German General Staff seemed to have a taste for, after our victory of 1919.

Waldeck's choice was therefore not merely a piece of clever politics, an audacious move to counter-balance his selection of Millerand; it was based on a knowledge of the man, whom he had met with Gambetta, and retained as a friend.

The plan came near upsetting everything; for one evening, the unexpected choice threatened to sabotage the formation of the cabinet. It must be confessed that, after the doubly daring experiment of using Millerand and Galliffet in the same government, the idea of teaming them together seemed entirely too much. That page written by Galliffet in the repression of the Commune was a bloody one: civil war is a nasty business. . . . Jaures bounded to his feet; the socialists opposed to participation found in it a serious argument to reinforce their position. But Waldeck-Rousseau held firm. He wrote to Joseph Reinach, who played a rather important role during the crisis, "Tonight, at nine o'clock, it will be all put together, or all smashed. . . ."

Millerand's mind was easily made up. Jaures made no effort to hide the fact that it was a difficult decision for him, but finally accepted and declared it was necessary to go ahead.

The complete cabinet presented itself to the Chamber of Deputies and the Senate on June 26, 1899. This was the first time I entered these premises, where I was to spend so much time, without ever having much affection for them.

Politics, a field so fertile in irony, had saved somethnig special for this occasion: after a somewhat more than tumultuous reception for this disconcerting governmental picture, "Waldeck's last water-color," said a deputy from the Aveyron by no means lacking in wit, and a mere majority of several votes having been laboriously obtained, the ministry lasted three long years!

WALDECK-ROUSSEAU IN 1884

THE INTERVIEW WITH JOFFRE AT SAINT-NICHOLAS-DU-PORT (1915)

At the opening of the session, the unleashed socialists and a goodly number of hostile radicals greeted the new Minister of War with repeated shouts of "Assassin! Assassin!" Moving to his seat with the short, abrupt step of a horseman walking, he answered calmly and banteringly, "The Assassin? Here I am!"

Three months later, from the same side of the house, came endless applause when, taking his place on the rostrum for the first time, he made the famous speech in which, with a cutting gesture to indicate the falling blade of a guillotine, he enumerated the measures taken against some undisciplined generals: "General So-and-So? Talked well. Talked too much. Out!"

That is history.

What is also history, but less well-known, is the sort of liking Galliffet began to feel toward the socialists. Was it their ardor, their discipline, not yet dulled by a taste of power and the arrival of new generations less solidly constituted?

Did Millerand, who represented them in the government, win him over with his precise mind and sturdy obstinacy? I am not sure, but in the many times we gathered at Waldeck's table—and once in even friendlier fashion—this tendency was demonstrated.

He had taken a liking for the young man I was then, who, with the impetuosity of youth, did not fear to affirm his socialism in official circles, or to talk freely. Waldeck-Rousseau, who knew this, had entrusted me with the liaison between the Ministry of the Interior and the Ministry of War. One summer day in 1899, while the trial of Dreyfus was under way at Rennes, I had to hand a secret message to Galliffet. He gave his reply, and as a trusted secretary was copying it—they took precautions in the ministries in those days—Galliffet paced the office, which I had no idea I would occupy some day, stopped beside me, tapped me on the shoulder, and said, "My boy, you are right. If I were starting my career all over again, I'd become a socialist." Then, in a tone where authority once more took command, he added, "But never forget, there are some people born to command, and idiots born to obey them!" (Only, as during his criticism at maneuvers, he used a much stronger word.)

The speech of a condottiere, when one recalls Galliffet's past. Where did this devil of a man, perpetually active despite his seventy years, find again some of the reactions that caused him to write a surprising letter to his sister, out of the depths of his captivity in Germany? He seemed to be so vividly impressed with the all-out resistance organized by the Republic, that one could readily see where his sympathies were. From the pen of this favorite of the Empire, whose services were sought by some who were plotting enterprises of restoration instead of working to halt the invader, it is heartening to read, in contrast to other capitulations:

"*. . . I laugh just as much at the anger of some as at the advances of others. Even the little that a citizen army, energetically led, has been able to do, has doubled the disgrace of the capitulations at Sedan and Metz. I am doing my utmost to obtain an exchange which would permit me to wash away, in combat, the sin of which I am not guilty, but freely accept the responsibility. . . .*

. . . Certainly, I have less deserved this fate than . . . (here follow the names of generals) . . . who, without orders, fled the battlefield at Sedan at eight in the morning. Instead of a court-martial, which they only avoided on account of the surrender, they received a promotion. . . .

*. . . Gambetta and Trochu have all my esteem; their energy doubles my shame. . . .**

Evidently, there is where one should look for the beginning of his friendship for Gambetta. Old Gambettists, who were in Waldeck-Rousseau's circle, affirmed that Galliffet played an important part in their leader's entourage, advising him, guiding his choices and enlightening him about a military personnel which the few months' duration of his government of National Defense had not permitted Gambetta to know sufficiently.

A real friendship, which touched the heart of a hard man. I have heard it said to Etienne, another frequent visitor at Jardies, that when the body of Gambetta was placed on the bier, Galliffet, who had rushed over from Tours where he commanded an army corps, took one of the bouquets brought

* Louis Thomas, *Le General de Galliffet*, page 93.

by the delegations of Alsace and Lorraine, and placed it over the heart that had beaten so constantly for them. Later, at Paris, in the room at the Palais Bourbon where the body lay in state, Galliffet, in dress uniform, was there with the guard of honor. Forty-nine years later, not a general was present when we conducted the body of the assassinated Jaures to the Pantheon.

There was a lot of talk, some of it supremely silly, in Galliffet's world and among his clubmates, about his reasons for accepting a post in the 1899 cabinet. As a matter of fact, I believe Galliffet cared as little about the Republic as he did about Dreyfus.* From his German prison, he wrote, "Whether it be the Emperor, the Republic, or the Orleanists in power, I want to go on fighting and wash away the shame with which the surrender at Sedan has covered us." What would he have said about Bordeaux, today?

But, patriot and warrior that he was, I imagine him a little like those Czarist officers, in Poland and elsewhere, who were willing to fight alongside the Bolshevists, so long as it was Russia's war. His heart was with the army; and the army that was being fashioned stubbornly and pitiably by the bureaucrats of the General Staff—he referred to them irreverently as the "senators of the army," for which I can only apologize to the senators of the Senate—did not please him. He went back into the service solely to keep them in line.

Thus, with Millerand, he was at once a star and a target; and shortly after the tumultuous session at the Chamber of Deputies, the famous military review of the Fourteenth of July was a difficult situation for him and for the ministry. There were fears of incidents—perhaps at Longchamp, where the reviews were then held, affording a little more space and attraction than those much curtailed ones in the Champs-Elysees from 1914 to 1939.

There had been discussions about Galliffet taking the salute on horseback. For reasons not at all equestrian, M. Brisson, deputy of the Tenth Arrondissement of Paris, one of the still

* Although, according to Caillanx, Galliffet was the first Minister of War who bothered to read the dossier. The others had merely affirmed, by hearsay, that Dreyfus was guilty.

venerated leaders of the Leftists, asked me to inform Waldeck that it was desirable; this having been the procedure at the review where General Ferron, who replaced Boulanger, had bravely faced considerable booing as he rode from the Ministry of War in the Rue Saint-Dominique to Longchamp. One had to swagger a little in front of the Paris population. Of course, certain precautions would have to be taken . . . and M. Brisson slipped into my hand, for transmission to my chief, the name of a trustworthy general to whom could be confided the command of the Paris garrison. These men, who had known the Empire, were haunted by fears of conspiracies and sudden outbreaks of violence. Their successors of recent years laughed at them; but since Bordeaux and Vichy, it does not seem quite so ridiculous. . . .

However, nothing serious occurred. Waldeck was a man of foresight; like all those of the republican generation wherein he had been raised, he was careful about persons and places, and put in command people in whom he had confidence. He had taken control with this proviso—which he had made clear to the President—that he had the right to change, even before appearing in front of the National Assembly, the prefect of police, the attorney-general, the public prosecutor, and to replace them with men he might consider more reliable and energetic. Nothing better for his own peace of mind.

General de Galliffet was little disposed to get on a horse again. He had said farewell to his handsome animals the day when, placed on the retired list, he no longer had the money to maintain such a stable; and he did not care to hire one. The most he would do was to go to his tailor and order a new uniform; since his retirement, he had not worn military attire. It was on the cushions of a landau, seated beside Waldeck-Rousseau, that he endured the hooting of the nationalists—which Waldeck-Rousseau insisted on sharing—grouped around the Municipal Council of Paris, and the acclamations of the populace among which he must have seen a number of faces similar to those he had glimpsed through the smoke of the barricades of the Commune and the powder of platoon fire.

The picture is clearly fixed in my memory: Waldeck-Rousseau in full dress and white tie—there was a respect for sartorial convention in 1900, sloppiness was not de rigeur, one did the people the courtesy of dressing up for them—impassive as usual, his head erect on the guillotine of his high collar. Galliffet, slim and svelte in his brand-new uniform, turning toward the crowd a face as indifferent to the booing as to the cheering, his mouth hard and mocking, and beneath his heavy black eyebrows, an eye without benevolence for the "patriots" so ready to subject the leader of the army to these street demonstrations.

Because, in his War Ministry, like Waldeck at the Ministry of the Interior, the General was cracking down: General Hartsschmitt who, in an order of the day addressed to the troops of the garrison at Angers, permitted himself to criticize the retrial of Dreyfus, was removed and placed in command of the infantry division of Rheims. General Roger, the one who talked well but talked too much, was sent to Belfort to command an infantry brigade. Along with these demotions, Colonel de Saxcé, of Rennes, who, by means of an order, had informed his troops of his controversy with a newspaper, was shifted to Poitiers. Displaced also was Lieutenant-Colonel de Coubertin, of the Second Cuirassiers, who advised his men "to remonstrate with violence when they heard anyone speak ill of the army, and even to use their weapons. . . ." General Jamont, inspector-general, and eventually generalissimo, exited noisily.

The much-disparaged Popular Front, which left almost all its adversaries in their places, never had such a record.

And, in addition to these individual executions, there was a permanent and organic measure: the suppression of the committees on classification, in effect from the month of September, marked the passage of Galliffet through the Ministry of War.

Long deliberated between Waldeck-Rousseau and himself, the terms of the report which preceded the decree clearly indicated its goal: "The lists established by the Commissions impose, in practice, upon the Government of the Republic, certain nominations without benefit of choice. This constitutes an abandonment of its powers; it becomes merely the compulsory executor for a commission composed of a few officers and generals in no way responsible to the Parliament. In the eyes of officers, who rightly have a hope of reaching high positions in the army, the Government and the Minister of War have no power, the Higher Commissions on Classification have it all. . . . *Any Minister of War, who knows exactly his duties and his responsibility, will refuse to exercise his functions in such a state of powerlessness.*"

When I took my seat in this same office of the Minister of War, I was unfavorably impressed to ascertain that, if the Commissions on Classification had not been revived, the Inspector General of the Army had become, even more authoritatively than the Commissions, the one in complete charge of all promotions in the higher ranks. I did not have behind me, unfortunately, the prestige of that heroic charge at Sedan, as had Galliffet, to quiet the murmurings; the least that I can say is that, despite the undeniable proofs of my devotion to the army, for which I was heavily attacked by the Communists and the extremists of my own party, life was made pretty disagreeable for me, simply because I sought to reestablish those rights without which, as the reports signed by Galliffet in 1899 correctly pointed out, *there is no longer a Minister of War or a Government.*

The misfortune was that Galliffet left too early.

I recall how bitter Waldeck-Rousseau felt about it. The rather cutting manner in which the general treated him was not the sole cause. The first requisite in this rebuilding of an army, sorely troubled and divided by the Dreyfus Affair and its political exploitation, was about to be lost. And, for that reason, the departure of Galliffet was more than an anecdote.

A police matter, rather obscure, was the apparent motive; more accurately, one of those police rivalries which are not least in the mishandling of certain affairs relative to the security of the State. That of the Prefecture of Police and the Sureté is a classic example. Since the Dreyfus Case, a Service of Information had been added—the *Service des Renseignments,* or S.R., an essential part of the Second Bureau and the Sureté. Never, rumor notwithstanding, did Galliffet or

Waldeck-Rousseau suppress the *Service des Renseignments;* they merely wanted to confine it to its original function, the gathering of information about the enemy, leaving to the Police the task of discovering enemy agents within our territory. After all the fantasies emanating from the *Service des Renseignments* during the Dreyfus Affair, public opinion would not have wanted it otherwise. This division of the work appeared logical.

I am not sure that it was a happy one; however ill-suited the military are to police work, for which they often have more taste than competency, it is quite difficult to separate the spies from the counter-spies, to call things by their name. Close collaboration between the *Service des Renseignments* and the Police is essential. As a matter of fact, it was generally and satisfactorily accomplished. It is not there that one has to look for the cause of the deficiencies in our Secret Service during the present war.

But, after the Dreyfus Affair, there was considerable friction. The *Service des Renseignments,* out of a sincere realization of its necessities—there are people in it whose merit I was able to appreciate during the last war—and because any department, military or civilian, hates to be dispossessed, was irked by the accomplished reformation. It made free use of the various procedures the police have at their disposal to harass those who disturb them. An over-zealous officer had handed to a journalist and to some politicians of the opposition documents intended to prove that the Sureté was not doing its job; that, in addition, there was an attempt to reopen the Dreyfus Case.

Passions were still easily roused; the incident took on proportions disproportionate with its real interest; questions on the floor of the Assembly came next. In the course of one debate, Waldeck-Rousseau termed the act of this officer a "felony." Was he wrong? Tumult, protests.

Suddenly, we saw General de Galliffet, his portfolio under his arm, storm out of the session. He was resigning.

No one could get him to change his decision. Ill, not in the mood to be disturbed, he went straight back to the home of the elderly belle—where Waldeck-Rousseau found him at the time he wanted him to join his cabinet—and popped into bed. However, one of his oldest friends, a Gambettist also, and opposed to the cabinet, Adrien de Montebello, "Big Adrien" he was called, and he was, indeed, a large man, had been able to see him. It is he who supplied me with an anecdote where, for once, the man of such acidulated witticisms—of which I know so many that have not been printed—was outdone by a woman, his own wife. She had not been near him for so many years, he no longer remembered exactly the length of time, as he told the King of Greece one day, when that monarch thought he should inquire.

While Adrien de Montebello was with the General, a letter was brought in. Galliffet opened it, read it, then passed it to Montebello. The letter was from Madame de Galliffet and read something like this:

"*Monsieur, I know the difficult moments you are traversing. I know that you don't want to see anyone. I pray that you will not forget that I am still your wife, and that here is the only place where no one would come looking for you.*"

Montebello added that the letter went unanswered. Just as, when he first entered Waldeck's ministry, mutual friends had sought to effect a somewhat tardy reunion of the husband and wife, he replied, "Since both of us are good Christians, we have all eternity in which to see each other again."

The stubborn general could no more be persuaded to take back a resignation, the causes and determining influences of which, have remained quite unsolved.

To replace him, some leading radicals indicated to Waldeck-Rousseau an artilleryman,* General André, who commanded the army corps at Le Mans. He was hastily summoned. His republicanism was well-known, his service record honorable, and behind the lenses of his glasses, his near-sighted eyes saw clearly enough the difficulties of a task he had not asked for, and which he assumed with a somewhat dull tenacity, but without weakness.

* At the time of Agadir, when he brought the High Council of War face to face with its responsibilities regarding heavy artillery, Messimy informed me that it was to this much abused artilleryman that we owed the first production of the Rimailho 155.

It was evident that he was not sufficiently imposing a military figure to override the hostility of that part of the army that resented the Republic's attempt to reorganize it. Having suffered from this mental attitude in the course of his career, as had so many republican officers, he attempted to break down this resistance by less brutal means than those of his predecessor, but more distasteful. A bitter struggle began, fed by controversies in the press and in parliament. Waldeck-Rousseau kept close watch to see that his minister, unjustly attacked, was not goaded into reactions that might turn him away from the objectivity necessary in his function. He had a courteous but firm way with his ministers, as I had occasion to observe during the three years he was in power: he was the "Premier" in the fullest meaning of the word. The day he was no longer there, the entourage of General André moved into that affair of the "files" that hindered, more than it helped, a necessary enterprise. More than any other government, that of the Republic had to see to it that the leaders of its army were not overly hostile toward the government; it turned out to be a costly oversight, when it forgot this. But there was a way of doing it.

The gallop of General the Marquis de Galliffet through the politics of the Republic has caused me to lose track of chronology. The man was so picturesque! And I found again, thirty years later, some of the problems he had cut with his saber, and which I tried to solve by milder means—for which I received no thanks.

But while he was putting the general in line and the army in order, other events, of no less importance, were taking place: at Rennes, the Dreyfus trial; in Paris, the treason case before the High Court. In the latter, with my colleague Tardieu—both secretaries to the President of the Council—we collaborated a bit, if he will forgive my mentioning it today.

With wordless energy, the moderate republican Waldeck-Rousseau had accomplished more than all the upraised fists of the Popular Front under which—in spite of the efforts of poor Dormoy, who paid for it with his life—the conspiracy of the Sixth of February, 1934, prepared a revenge.

Having persuaded himself, politically and judicially, that a plot existed, one fine morning, bounding out of bed, he had the plotters arrested. They, as in the days of Boulangism, were not in accord on anything, except that the government should be overthrown. I have already mentioned that Deroulede declared he would stop with his own hands any pretender who tried to usurp the power; and I quite believe he would have done so. I have since had occasion to discuss it with Marcel Habert, who was faithful to him and thought like him—and, toward the end of his life, thought more as I did. But a sort of exasperated nationalism led them astray in this affair.

Supporters of the plebiscite, Royalists, Bonapartists, and some agitators without any well-defined doctrine were arrested, intermingled in a measured repression which Waldeck insisted should conform strictly to the exigencies of the penal code. He opened this procedure of the High Court, which I regret was not used to advantage at certain recent instances, where the quotation from *Athalie* fitted the case perfectly:

"*De ligues, de complots, pernicieux auteur. . . .*"

This stipulation was the reason that Tardieu and I, for several weeks in the summer of 1899, had to handle the heavy dossier from which the Attorney General had to take his requisitions before the Senate, and the Keeper of the Seals, M. Monis, who was to become my President of the Council in 1911, had transmitted to his dossier.

Not completely satisfied with the way the things had been presented, he wanted the judicial link between the scattered actions of the plotters, yet all converging toward one goal, should be solidly established. Trusting only himself and his mastery of the Law, he had confided to his two young secretaries the task of preparing the elements on which he was to work.

As in all police reports, there was a little of everything in this dossier: a little discrimination was needed. We were much amused one day when, among the organizations judged to be subversive by one of the police, just as zealous as he was ill-informed about the pleasures of Paris, Tardieu, who was *well*-informed on that subject, noticed the name, "Royal Sapphire."

The Royal Sapphire in question was not a royalist group, but an establishment where young men in quest of adventure could dance with unquestioning young women. The name of the place all but resulted in deep difficulty for those who frequented it, and who were certainly not there with political intent.

But there were more serious implications: nothing as bad as we have seen recently, and which have gone unpunished. If Waldeck-Rousseau had less of a sense of proportion, the arrests would have been more widespread. As often happens, when a regime is supposed to be toppling, a good many people began making premature replacements. The night before the incident at Reuilly, where Deroulede, as in the Boulangist period and in his habitual manner, was at once audacious and faint-hearted, there had been a meeting in the home of a former magistrate, who had become an ardent nationalist.* Parliamentarians and generals had started distributing places to each other, in case of success. Nothing was seen of them afterward. Because, in spite of themselves, they had not resorted to action in the matter, Waldeck thought it unnecessary to inculpate them.

In the matter of sanctions taken, they were not gentle; exile is painful to patriots, such as Deroulede and his companions incontestably were. But it was done without too much personal injury, without the prolonged and illegal detentions, since they are not even sustained by trials carried through to completion, with which the regime of today strikes at its adversaries; they were, in fact, equivalent to the act; whoever attempts, by means which the Law condemns, to change the government which the nation has freely chosen, he is ordered to go and live elsewhere. This will be worth remembering when, with the Republic restored and renovated, the time comes to put those who killed it, under the protection of the enemy, where they can no longer be harmful.

The Law, which is not the same thing as the "fooorm" of Judge Bridoison in *The Marriage of Figaro*, but which main-

* I have found in the *Memoires* of Caillaux, confirmation of what I saw in the dossier; since he has written it, I can say that the magistrate was M. Grosjean, deputy of Paris.

tains in politics, and even in the necessary acts of authority, a minimum guaranty of liberty for the citizens.

The Law! It keeps returning in every line of this brief outline of events which, at the time, so strongly affected public opinion, and which now appears to us, in this age we live in, as very distant and less tragic. It is none the less true that, if calm was reestablished in the streets, if not in the minds, if the opposition was made to understand that only legal ways were open to it—and it used them widely—if, to sum up, the Republic and its institutions came out of it strengthened, it is because the statesman was also one of those legists who, in various epochs, Monarchy, Revolution, Republic, have made France and served the State.

This purely political passage, necessarily repressive owing to the circumstances under which he took over the government, was not the one closest to his heart. He had to accomplish it. He accomplished it right to the end. Nothing stopped him; certainly not the attacks. He neither sought them nor feared them. Nor did he yield to any considerations of a social nature—to which he might have been susceptible, belonging to polite society, and having established, during his years of high repute as a lawyer, interspersed with travel and fashionable leisure, very varied relationships—when he set out to defend the Republic by any appropriate means.

But, as soon as order was restored, he lost no time in moving on to the constructive part of his program. Abroad, our alliances; at home, the Law of Associations.

Our alliances! It is false that our foreign policy had been weakened by our internal struggles. The dates are there. It was at the time of the Government of Republican Defense and the Leftist Group that two of the three treaties which sustained us in 1914 were drawn up and signed.

And certainly they showed the imprint and signature of Delcassé; the advantages derived from his long stay at the Quai d'Orsay can hardly be over-estimated. But I was in a position to know how much of the credit belonged to Waldeck-Rousseau; the initiative and the guidance date from his arrival in power.

He had assumed the leadership following the Fachoda incident, which had resulted in a great deal of tension between the English and ourselves. Without a day's delay, he set about easing it, then arranging the Entente, persuaded, as anyone worthy of the name of statesman of France would be, that for our country, adjoining Germany and always more or less menaced by her, there was no other policy. He felt that any attempt at an entente with Germany, which he was far from excluding—for it was only after him that a treaty with the one could appear to be directed against the other—would be a deception and a danger, if France did not seem to be in accord with England. Waldeck-Rousseau really worked at a European treaty organization; in short, he worked for peace.

And peace with England had just been seriously threatened. Capitulation was all that saved it. But the wound bled. It was kept open, poisoned by the angry reactions unleashed by the nationalist crisis that stemmed from the Dreyfus Affair.

Nothing is negligible in preparing such reconciliations. Waldeck-Rousseau neglected nothing. So disdainful of personal attacks on him by the press, he was extremely concerned about those directed, from a certain quarter, at "perfidious Albion." Even caricatures were by no means indifferently regarded; I remember the trouble he went to, in an effort to attenuate the effect produced in England by a page in *Le Rire*, where the good Leandre, a talented cartoonist I knew in Montmartre in my younger days, had allowed himself to depict Queen Victoria in an outrageous manner, insulting the triple majesty of the woman, her age, and the Crown.

For the good of his enterprise, he made an even greater sacrifice: one day, from the window of the office I occupied, before installing myself with Tardieu on the ground-floor of the Rue des Saussaies, and which gave on to the inner courtyard of the Ministry, I saw an elderly man with a square-cut beard, a long frock-coat of almost ecclesiastical appearance, and the top-hat in which he was popularly caricatured, get out of his carriage and enter the wing which housed Waldeck's office. He reappeared in a few moments, a bit more careworn, a bit sadder, and resumed his difficult pilgrimage, which recalled that of Thiers in 1871. At lunch, Waldeck-Rousseau told us how much he regretted having to refuse to receive the Boer leader, President Kruger, so as not to awaken English susceptibilities and give rise to a misunderstanding that might hinder the great work he had begun.

He was conducting it concurrently with our ambassador Cambon in London and the British ambassador in Paris. The latter highly appreciated the many evidences of a liking for things English in Waldeck's habits and tastes, particularly his love of good dogs—he was one of the first Frenchmen to own a Chow—and an exchange of views on the care of them sometimes interrupted the gravest conversations.

I am not aware what subjects were under discussion, not yet having entered the arena of international negotiations. I can only attest the earnest desire of my master to see them successfully concluded, and his perseverance on behalf of the plan he had conceived in the first days of his arrival in power, when public opinion decried its very possibility. He knew that time would prove him right. Happily, time was granted him.

Which did not prevent him from taking every precaution. Watching everything himself and supervising his ministers, at the moment of this touchy reconciliation, in July 1899, I recall seeing a voluminous dossier on his neatly-arranged desk; mobilization plans and those of our defenses against England. He had been painfully surprised to note its omissions and deficiencies, notably in our coastal defense and the organization of their forts and redoubts, at a time when we had been drawn into a policy that might oblige us to use them. He went on negotiating, but wanted to be ready for any eventuality.

I mentioned this unabashedly to my English colleagues at the League of Nations in Geneva. It did not displease them. They had just such an example from higher up. Shortly after the end of his ministry, when Waldeck had returned to Law and was handling a hunting dispute for an ex-deputy, the Marquis de Breteuil, who was not only a friend of Waldeck's but also of King Edward VII, the Marquis told me that, at a dinner-party, he had expressed his delight at the treaty about to be concluded, to which His Majesty, puffing a cigar, said smilingly, "Good, but just the same, keep up a strong fleet!"

This is what Waldeck-Rousseau tried to do, agreeing with King Edward that foreign policy is not based on sentimental effusions, as we are only too inclined to wish for in France, but on common interests and goals, and that treaties are best arranged between peoples capable of bringing an equal contribution to the task they are to undertake together. In place of our vanished army, may we at least have, on the day of peace deliberations, the fleet that has been left us!*

To carry to a successful culmination this enterprise—which was completed after his departure, but which he had guided well on its way—Waldeck-Rousseau had found a man, small in size, so small that, rumor has it, he had to have the legs of Vergennes' table** lowered so he could work more comfortably, but a great Foreign Minister, quiet, laborious, tenacious. Delcassé was as useful to Waldeck-Rousseau, as Waldeck was necessary to him. At first, the new Foreign Minister was somewhat less "English" than the anglophobes of those days—less boisterous than those of today, but still heard from—accused him of being. Waldeck showed him the way. As the work progressed, Waldeck warned him of his rather too frequent tendency, from which Delcassé did not always free himself, to want an alliance to counter-balance an enmity. Waldeck-Rousseau and Briand, both from Nantes, favored what one must call a European Entente, whatever repugnance one feels toward a term so detestable in its current usage.***

That was precisely the plan Waldeck-Rousseau pursued, long before Briand, in accord with Jaures.

To the preparation of the Franco-British Entente, so clairvoyant and audacious at the difficult time it was conceived, he added another project which he pushed even further, and which was not of lesser importance. It was not without reason

* November, 1942. Alas, why didn't it put to sea?

** Vergennes, the famous Foreign Minister of Louis XVI. The mutilated table in question is said to be only a copy. The inkwell alone authentically belonged to Vergennes.

*** Written in 1941, when the "necessity of forming a united Europe" served as an excuse for collaborating with the enemy.

that I often saw M. Barrere waiting for an appointment with Waldeck, sometimes in the company of Adrien de Montebello, both having just left their mutual friend, Galliffet.

Cambon, Barrere. Republican names. They themselves had, at least in their youth, belonged to the party. In their case, as elsewhere, the young Republic had no reason to regret renewing its personnel.

Not with any idea of enticement, for that outmoded game of philandering in the diplomatic field was not in Waldeck's manner, but to draw it into his peace plan, he had turned to Italy, which was then enmeshed in the Triple Alliance. He sought to clear up the almost uninterrupted series of misunderstandings that had marked our relations with that country, even though we played such an important role in its foundation, a fact one must be wary of recalling to them.

Waldeck-Rousseau's efforts were successful.

In 1902, an agreement was signed whereby Italy would remain neutral in the event France should be *attacked*. The vast benefit to us seemed to escape notice until 1914, at which time all the credit was given to Delcassé. Admittedly, in this negotiation, as in the one with England, Delcassé had a major part; in both, his perseverance was of value; he helped enormously by organizing President Loubet's visit to the Vatican, which had the additional result of causing a break in our relations with the Holy See. It is, however, a fact that not only the original idea, but also the whole plan of campaign was the work of Waldeck. With the aid of his ambassador Barrere, and the loyal accord of his Minister of Foreign Affairs, he even had direct relations with the Italian premier, Zanardelli, whose officious intermediary I saw several times at the Place Beauvau. I remembered this, thirty years after, when I attempted, in March 1938, to renew with Italy the tie that had been broken since the departure of M. de Chambrun.

The alliance with Russia had already been accomplished, and had started to break down the isolation in which our defeat had left us. But Waldeck-Rousseau watched it carefully, bringing to it his prudence, calming some of Delcassé's excessive confidence. Waldeck had been influenced by an incident that happened at a cabinet-meeting just prior to the arrival of Czar Nicholas on a state visit to France in 1901. The incident arose from the great liberties Galliffet was accustomed to take in governmental deliberations. As Delcassé was speaking enthusiastically of the Czar's visit—an enthusiasm he reserved for all things Russian—Galliffet roamed around the room, hands in the pockets of his pants, which were set well forward, cavalry style, and finally stopped to say curtly, "I know every army in Europe. The Russians are not as solid as you think. A lot of facade!" The reviews of Tsarskoie-Selo impressed him little. Actually, the general went too far. The Russian army rendered us a rugged service at the time of the Marne, forcing Germany to weaken its marching wing by despatching an army corps to East Prussia.

However, Galliffet's observation sounded a warning to Waldeck, who was at that moment giving a good deal of attention to the Far Eastern situation, in which he foresaw that our ally was about to become involved. Reserved as he was in his conversations on the affairs of State, I have been told that —while members of his cabinet, and especially their ladies, were overcome with delight at the festivities at Compiegne and the military review at Betheny, Waldeck spent some time in a serious talk with the Czar and President Loubet, a particularly practical president.

The Czar did not give the impression of being very consistent, or determined in his resolutions, but kindly, gentle, seeking to counteract by his amiability the worried rigidity of the Czarina, who seemed to be convinced that she was among savages.

Waldeck received a rather different, but equally unfavorable impression during a picturesque interview with Emperor Wilhelm II. As to the reason for the meeting, it is necessary to realize the immense prestige enjoyed by Waldeck-Rousseau in the final days of his ministry, not only in France, but abroad; in fact, it was even greater abroad, where they were all too aware of the important place he had won for France in the affairs of Europe.

As soon as he stepped down from his post as Premier, before returning to the practice of Law, he took a long vacation. In June, he visited the Norwegian fjords as a guest of Gaston Menier, the Chocolate King, aboard his yacht. I had certain family ties with Menier, and it is from him I obtained the details of the interview. The Kaiser was cruising in these same waters, a favorite recreation of his; it was here that he sailed in 1914, right after Serajevo, while war preparations were in progress. He had a keen desire to meet Waldeck-Rousseau, who was expected, after a slight rest, to return to the position of power he had voluntarily abandoned. Waldeck, much more ceremonious than His Imperial Majesty, was reluctant to chat with the Kaiser without proper diplomatic overtures. Furthermore, he had not cared for several anti-British suggestions advanced by the Kaiser at the time the British were having trouble in Transvaal, suggestions which His Imperial Majesty later sought to attribute to France.

But Wilhelm II was strong-willed; so, when he wanted this meeting with the great French Premier, he simply arranged things so that it was inescapable. One evening, apparently quite by chance, the same fjord sheltered the imperial yacht and Gaston Menier's *Ariane*. Etiquette demanded an exchange of greetings. The Kaiser issued an invitation; then was invited. He displayed considerable charm, a Parisian turn of mind, talked fashion with the ladies, and spoke of graver things with Waldeck-Rousseau, including some incautious observations which, if repeated, might have embroiled a good many European chiefs-of-state. But with the taciturn Waldeck, there was no risk. When I went to see Waldeck on his return, and questioned him about this sensational interview, which had aroused considerable speculation in the press, and asked him about his impressions of the Kaiser, he merely said, "An X with a crown." Only, instead of X, he actually cited the name of a French politician he considered pretty much of a lightweight; I shall not mention the name here; his sad end and the death of his son in the last war demand a certain amount of respect for a man of honor whom, in my opinion, Waldeck-Rousseau judged too severely.

Gone are the days when the leaders of Germany pursued French statesmen for the purpose of chatting with them.

Thanks to the relentlessly methodical organization of his work and his life, and the authority which permitted him to impose it on others, the Parliament included, for three years, Waldeck-Rousseau was able to handle simultaneously this careful diplomacy, the heavy burden of internal politics, and a great constructive plan. He wanted, and secured the Law of Associations.

An organic law wrongly transformed, after his departure, into a law of combat. In his mind, it was in line with the one regulating trade groups, which he had succeeded in putting through during his ministry of 1884, and solved liberally a delicate and oft-debated question. It gave a legal existence, as an integral part of the Republican state, to those groups functioning for the good of the people, and covered all sorts of activities, including the spiritual.

But, by a strange misunderstanding of its real objective, in the eyes of those often misinformed by a partisan press, it seemed to be directed solely at the religious orders, control of which was only *one* of its goals. It was much more far-reaching and comprehensive. As in the law of the trade groups, this one had results that surpassed the reasons that had caused some to vote in favor of it, or to fight it; but not more than its far-seeing author had anticipated.

Neither Tardieu nor I were directly involved. Waldeck had chosen for his closest collaborator in this affair his chief-deputy, our colleague Marcel Peschaud, member of that Council of State which he held in such high esteem, like Caillaux, and others with a sense of manipulation of affairs of State, and which the Republic would have done well to call upon more often in its legislative work. As I did not fail to do, when I had to apply the Pension Law.

Peschaud, an excellent comrade, and who has remained one, even when our paths were quite different, was of moderate tendencies; he soon turned his talents to private industry, and became a high executive of the Paris-Orleans railway company. I am grateful to him for a number of transportation conveniences in this region, which I represented in Parliament, and where the German troop trains now roll. But, when he aided in the preparation of a law, the conception of which was as carefully devoted to liberty as to the rights of the State, he was in no way called upon to sacrifice his liberal ideas. He was loyal; and the work advanced as harmoniously and methodically as Waldeck could wish. M. Dumay, practically permanent director of Cults, added a certain amount of unction derived from his constant meetings with bishops. The contrast was great between the peaceful atmosphere in which the law was constructed and the lively, even violent, debates to which it was soon to be subjected.

For, parliamentarily speaking, the battle was furious. It is a mistake to believe that the last sessions of the Assembly outdid all others in ferocity; enough sins have been charged to them, without adding this; and it is not for this reason that manners had worsened, and the regime become weakened. I can distinctly remember discussions in the 1900's, as violent, if not more so, than those I took part in recently. When one spoke regretfully to Waldeck of this bitter opposition to his project, he was as unperturbed as on the rostrum and at the bar, and merely remarked that things had been worse at the beginning of the regime. Only, at that time, politicians' manners had been better. And their convictions stronger. It was that which made the struggles more intense, while the merit of the champions kept matters on a higher plane.

To mention only the Chamber of Deputies, the exchanges of dialogue between Waldeck-Rousseau, De Mun, Ribot, Pelletan, long-haired and lettered, Viviani, and Sembat—Jaures was no longer present, and Briand had not yet appeared—regardless of the *fortissimo* from the accompanying chorus of partisans, made these debates on the Law of Associations one of the most brilliant pages of our parliamentary history. I lived it day by day, accompanying my superior to the two Assemblies, for it was my duty to check the stenographic report of his replies to the objections of the opposition, replies which he never bothered to re-read, certain of what he wanted to say and how he said it.

And God knows there were plenty of replies required, and great discourses, including that regarding the rival youth groups which began the battle and went far toward giving a foretaste of the divided France of the future. This speech was made outside of Parliament, at Toulouse, under the auspices of the newspaper, *La Depeche*. I believe it was the one that gave him the most trouble. Yielding to the suggestions of the press, which had assembled, along with a swarm of prefects and sub-prefects from Languedoc and all the rest of France, impatiently demanding a first look at the important pages, he was compelled to write out the speech in advance. That evening, at the Prefecture, where my room was near his suite, while he tried to relax after a devastating day in which everyone of importance, bishops and generals included, had come to pay him homage, he said, "I shall never go through it again. It was too much." He was the only one to feel this way about the speech. This page, worthy of an anthology, opened in that ardently democratic region the great debate which was to absorb the attention of Parliament for months.

It took all Waldeck's admirable talent, his mastery as a debater, his legal and political science, to dominate, convince, or silence his eloquent contradictors, springing up on all sides, some reproaching him for his sectarianism, others denouncing his timidity.

For he had to bear all the weight of the struggle. At once, Premier and Minister of the Interior, none of his ministers was in a position to help him. However, he trusted no one but himself to carry to victory this law of his own authorship, as that of the trade groups had been. Unfortunately, this new one did not remain his to the end; and he was not around to apply it.

Yet his triumph had been complete. The 27th of April, 1902, right from the first ballot, universal suffrage carried and added to the majority which, for three years, had been faithful to him, providing a second, a countrywide victory to supplement that which his talent, his prestige, and his tenacity had won in the Chamber of Deputies and the Senate.

Two weeks later, the night of the 11th of May accentuated the success of the first ballot. Republican discipline then functioned at full strength, giving even less opportunity for dissidents and traitors to conduct their operations, because it overwhelmed them with a convergence of voters, rather than the less well-organized maneuverings of parties. Politicians, journalists, and the usual officious personages who swarm about at these times, all-too-recent friends rallying round the victor, jammed the corridors of the ministry, the waiting-rooms, my office, that of Tardieu, those of Waldeck and Ulrich; the faithful followers of the master, even those who had no part in the conflict, noisily acclaimed the victory.

Alone in his study, before the portrait of Philippe de Champaigne, which he had brought over from the Rue de l'Université, so as to have, in this official decor, something lovely on which to rest his gaze, Waldeck meditated, calm as ever, the eternal cigarette at his lips. When I entered to hand him the latest results, I heard him say to himself, "Too much!"

That was all.

Next day, at lunch, he tried to quiet my juvenile enthusiasm with the comment that he feared the effect of this overwhelming victory; in crushing the opposition so completely, it could lead the victors to run riot and commit mistakes.

He was right. The three days of all-out celebration to which any conquering army would be entitled lasted a little too long.

But that is another story.

Before relating it, I should like to dwell upon some recollections that are without a cloud: those brought to me by the great popular and social current which, in those years, journeyed through literature and art.

Chapter Four

REPUBLICAN MYSTICISM IN THE 1900'S

The Intellectuals and the Dreyfus Affair.—Painlevé, Basch, Pressensé, Bouglé, Seailles, Anatole France.—Les Cahiers de la Quinzaine.—*University socialism.—Jaures.—The People's Universities.—Our battles of* Hernani. *—Civic festivals.—The Muse of the People.*

The electoral victory of 1902 was accompanied by a movement of the minds; the strengthening of our institutions was followed by a renewal of a republican mysticism. The political development of the Dreyfus Affair had drawn toward the more advanced republican ideas and toward socialism a large proportion of an intellectual elite that otherwise might have stayed in their libraries and laboratories. Many left their ivory towers, never to return, bringing to the Republic new strength it sorely needed.

It was a master-stroke of Clemenceau, returning to the front line of politics with the Affair, and, with Zola and Jaures, a champion of the cause, to call the protest which followed Zola's *J'Accuse* a "Manifesto of the intellectuals." One is always flattered to be in such good company. It was, as a matter of fact, exact; a good part of French intellectuality was represented. Not at all astonishing, when one recalls the atmosphere in which we had been raised, the literary and artistic tendencies of the 1890's, the books we were reading, the ideas that exalted us, which I evoked earlier in my recollections of the Latin Quarter. It was a favorable field for the words of Zola, Clemenceau, and Jaures, calling for a rehearing of an unjust trial, the liberation of the Prisoner of Devil's Island.

But, thus accelerated by a prior orientation of the mind,

the rush toward the Dreyfus Affair, and the political repercussions it engendered gave much more amplitude to this movement of the intellectuals toward the left, and forced them to take a more definite stand. At the same time, it gave rise to a more determined opposition, and new political groupings among those who chose the other side, the most characteristic and the most durable being *L'Action Francaise.*

One of the first, Painlevé, aglow with his young scientific glory, already a rival of Poincaré in the field of mathematics, rushed into the fray with all the fury of his liberal temperament. And from that moment, he was one of those who never left the political scene, carving a new career, Minister of War, Minister of Public Instruction, President of the Council, but always himself, a tireless fighter for whatever he thought was just. Heading the Air Ministry in 1932, he became embroiled in a rather obscure affair, in which the Second Bureau of the General Staff had intervened. Without consulting me, although I was his superior, he re-exhibited his ardor of the Dreyfus days, using up the last energy of a worn-out heart in defending one of his subordinates, the son of a former minister, Chaumié, judging him to be innocent of the accusations brought against him, and in fact he was.

He had also remained faithful to mathematics, and had kept his chair at the Ecole Polytechnique. They were his relaxation, his repose, and his last consolation. When I became Premier, desirous of retaining him in my cabinet, still hoping he would regain his health, I had provided him with a subsecretary of State in whom I had great confidence, my friend Bernier, who filled in for him during his illness. Whenever I went to confer with Painlevé, who continued to follow the affairs of his ministry, I noticed he always had a book of transcendental mathematics at hand, to keep him company. He even insisted on reading some of it aloud to me, unwilling to admit that those he loved would not love mathematics. I understood none of it, just as I understood none of the descriptive geometry when I was trying to prepare for the Ecole Navale; but I never told him.

I had known Victor Basch for quite some time. It was he

who gave me my bachelor's degree, when he was a professor at Rennes. I reminded him of this, when he kindly consented to speak at a banquet offered me at the time of my departure as Minister of Foreign Affairs in April 1938. I even recalled to him the text he had given me to explain. Among the optional authors, I had chosen the *Sermons* of Bossuet and commented with commendable fire the one that begins. "How beautiful thy banners, O Israel; how shining thy tents, O Jacob!" A supporter of Dreyfus from the beginning, he had stood fast at Rennes with a courage that never left him, a courage that continues at this very hour when, a refugee, ill, mourning his son who committed suicide—as did Doctor Thierry de Martel—when the Germans marched into Paris, he can see the collapse of everything he loved, and can watch the persecution of his race.

Member and leader of that League of the Rights of Man, which played a decisive role in the Affair and ever since—and which has been called, I know not why, a branch of Free-Masonry, when so many who have no connection whatsoever with Free-Masonry, myself for instance, were on its executive committee—Basch became its president, after Ferdinand Buisson, who followed Pressensé.

Pressensé! Another conservative drawn into socialism by the Dreyfus Affair, and from that moment, a front-line combatant. Son of a Protestant minister, he wrote in *Le Temps* serious and luminous chronicles of foreign politics, and articles in such right-thinking magazines as the *Revue des Deux Mondes*. Having retained from his protestant education an uncompromising conscience, he simply would not forgive repentant partisans of Dreyfus, or those who did not seem to him to have remained faithful to the just cause for which they had fought. On this subject, I heard him deliver one of the most moving speeches in all my parliamentary memories.

To enumerate the strength of the Dreyfus camp, one would have had to check an entire section of the University in those days. I speak only of those I knew personally, and fought alongside, during and after the Affair.

There was Bouglé. In my public talks, I had often quoted from a little book of his, which I would like to see re-read, or read—for I cannot believe its pages have received the slightest attention from those who now speak so lightly of the lack of patriotism, the base materialism of the educators of our youth under the old regime. No one could have written more comprehensively and with more respect for all the spiritual values. In this book, there is a phrase—and I ask his forgiveness for having sometimes forgotten to credit him with the quotation, which had become the expression of my own thought: "France, great by turns, because she was the oldest daughter of the Church and the mother of the Revolution."

After the Dreyfus Affair, he remained faithful to the University, and to his task as educator, sub-director, then director of the Ecole Normale. Called upon by him to speak to his young people on the subject of the League of Nations and collective security, I shall not forget the atmosphere of free research and a mutual respect for each other's convictions which he had been able to maintain among his students, despite their divided opinions. He died in time to avoid the spectacle of his colleagues summarily dismissed, and his democratic faith—as patriotic as it was democratic—scoffed at and trampled upon by those who claimed to be reorganizing the unity of France.

I was also well acquainted with Seailles, professor of moral philosophy at the Sorbonne, working beside him, in Paris and Vendome, in those people's universities which were an outgrowth of the Dreyfus Affair. Seailles had a candid mind, well-expressed in a reply which Anatole France related to me. During the Zola trial, France and Seailles were lunching at the Restaurant Laperouse, near the Palace of Justice. Seailles, preoccupied with the testimony he was to give at the afternoon session, said: "And if the presiding judge asks me, 'How do you explain, Professor, that with those opinions, you teach the *Phedon* to your students?' I shall answer . . ."

France interrupted him. "Yes, but he won't ask you."

Anatole France had granted the use of his name to the partisans of a retrial for Dreyfus, and, after the victory, was among those who continued the combat. France, the sceptic, the pure stylist, who appeared merely destined to polish his phrases and air his irony, was touched by grace and became, as much as his indolent nature and love of comfort permitted, a militant socialist, devoted, attentive not only to the movement of ideas, but to the inner life of the socialist party, to which he brought the inestimable advantage of a talent that the Royalist, Charles Maurras, with his respect for classic style, bowed before.

The duties of a socialist militant made him uncomfortable, at times. Happy to have him, the organizers often dragged him away from his library and his desk where his dear friend, Madame de Caillavet, watched over him—and made him preside at their meetings. At one of the "pro and con" assemblies we were holding at the Porte-Saint-Martin, a contradictor, in the act of contradicting, came perilously close to being shoved over the balcony railing. In the midst of the scuffle, Anatole France rose and in a trembling voice made this slightly incongruous observation:

"Citizens, let us show by our calm that we are right. . . ."

He acquitted himself of these painful duties with perfect good grace. It was easy to see that he was happier in the mornings, when he received his admirers in his own villa, while sensuously caressing his statuettes, or in the salon of Madame de Caillavet, which was for many years, along with that of Madame Menard-Dorian, a rallying-place for Dreyfusards and Republicans, while the enemy assembled in the salon of Madame de Loynes, where Jules Lemaitre reigned.

A short time before the present debacle, I saw again many souvenirs of our intimate friendship at the country-seat of Anatole France, La Bechellerie, where he died in our lovely province of Touraine which he had adopted, on a beautiful day in October, where the soft sunlight he loved bathed the purple vines. What has become of all that?

Many intellectuals who turned to the Left at the time of the Affair, did as the old Master did; they passed by the old parties, already half-emptied of their substance, and headed straight for socialism, the doctrinal and moral aspects of which were better suited to their work and former tastes. All did not stay, and some even turned against it. "Fashion had given them to us," said Jaures, "and fashion took them away."

But there were many who came. Peguy, to begin with. One

is too inclined to forget that before finding a hero's death in a wheatfield at the Battle of the Marne and becoming the great Catholic and Nationalist poet piously exhumed by a battered France in search of her sources, Peguy began as a socialist. Not in a sense of blind obedience, but sincerely, ardently, a member of a party not yet unified, hence even more alive. His *Cahiers de la Quinzaine* were wide open to its varying aspects, at the same time that he wrote certain pages that equal *Les Provinciales*, and where his non-conformism mocks committees, bureaucrats, and high priests, He jeered at the meetings in the Rue Portefoin, where first the scattered factions reassembled; he claimed that Vaillant repeated sixty-three times the words, "a war of the classes." But what verve and drive in a faith which he later directed toward other objectives, without, to my knowledge, ever denying its initial manifestation; socialism being in perfect accord with his cult of Joan of Arc.

I was one of the first subscribers to the *Cahiers de la Quinzaine*, of happy typographical memory, and my collection, I hope, awaits me in Paris, so that I may find again the traces of those felicitous days and of so many ideas to which I remain attached.

Without quite such brilliance, due to the ardent mind of its founder, there were other publications dealing with what M. Bourguin, who was a supporter of the movement, but has lately denied it, called in a recent diatribe, "University socialism" of the 1900's. Unlike the *Cahiers*, some of these periodicals were rather obtuse and pedantic. I have in mind *Le Mouvement socialiste*, which I also collected assiduously. I shall be amused to reread the articles wherein M. Lagardelle,—who had a name suited to a musketeer, but not the soul of one, a future minister of the Vichy government, after officiating at the Palazzo Farnese as an envoy to Signor Mussolini, his comrade of revolutionary days—continued a purely Marxist indoctrination.

There was another review installed right in the library of the Ecole Normale, in which Lucien Herr exerted his influence. I only knew him through a rather disagreeable article about my book; but I knew a few people, among them Leon

Blum, who acknowledged the effect he had on their formation, and their esteem for him, which was shared by Jaures.

One of the most notable representatives of this "university socialism" was Andler, a professor at the Sorbonne, who was an authority on Germany and had written an excellent book on Bismarck. A few years later, in 1914, he warned his friends about their pacifist illusions. Jaures was annoyed at this; I do not know why, since it could only assist him in his fight against the antimilitarism which had attracted some of the party, and justified his book, *L'Armee nouvelle.*

Jaures! His name crops up incessantly in my story. He was the great persuader, the one responsible for this rush of the intellectuals to socialist ideas.

Having quickly obtained preeminence in the party by his prodigious eloquence, the Dreyfus Affair provided for him the opportunity to enlarge his sphere of action and to strengthen his position as the uncontested chief of the democratic forces, until an assassin's bullet finished him at the very hour when Socialism and France had the greatest need of him.

He had been beaten in the 1898 elections, after a savage campaign that lived on in people's memory when I was conducting my own fight in 1924, in the very same electoral district. He had been beaten, in spite of all the affection surrounding him in that territory of the Tarn where his ancestors, who then called themselves Juares, had settled, after journeying from Spain, in the 18th Century. The defeat at the polls brought tears to his eyes, as he stood in the midst of his old comrades at the City Hall of Carmaux.

Yet his defeat may have been a blessing, freeing him from the debilitating influences of Parliament, which affect even the hardiest, and from those eternal little deals that are concluded in the corridors, less harmful then than now, but already a part of party politics.

I have mentioned that most of the Leftist politicians began by being uncertain what position to take in regard to the Dreyfus Affair, and that it was only when the Right started to exploit it that they felt themselves menaced and struck back.

Jaures was not one of those who waited. Now that he was free of electoral and parliamentary restraint, he led the fight for truth and justice against falsehood and iniquity, one of the finest actions in our political history.

Often, in my pilgrimages to Bessoulet, sometimes called his "chateau," an old family property, part manor-house, part town-house, and altogether charming, I have walked under the elms where he loved to dream, with the roofs of Albi and its cathedral-fortress silhouetted in the sunset. And I recall the contrast between this peaceful setting and those pages, hot as flowing lava, he wrote under these trees, forming the series known as *Les Preuves*.

Politically unfettered, he could be unrestrainedly jubilant when the re-trial of Dreyfus was ordered. I can see him now, his face shining with light and joy, standing near one of the windows in the great hall of the High Court of Appeal, while Ballot-Beaupré read his report.

Jaures saw clearly, at the time Millerand was invited to join the government, all that socialism would gain from this coalition cabinet, and fought for it, as I did myself. The Socialists, allied with the Republicans, triumphed in the 1902 elections, after having opposed for some time this very alliance that brought them victory.

Let the influence of men upon events be denied! Without them, who would draw the rank-and-file of the parties? One saw this only too well when Jaures, Guesde, Vaillant, and others of the veteran leaders the party trusted were no longer there.

His vision verified, and victory achieved under his banner, Jaures led the unification of the socialist party. I am not sure that it was an unqualified boon. But because of his leadership, and because it maintained the solidarity of the Ecole Normale and the Sorbonne, many intellectuals, who would have deserted rapidly, stood fast, and the party benefited by the presence of so many of the high-minded in its assemblage.

Many others, without having crossed the threshold, joined the procession, and in their books, newspaper articles, or stage plays republicanized, socialized, democratized to a degree that suggested they were trying to outdo each other.

People's universities were set up in all the likelier locations; professors, literary men, artists stepped forward to share the fruits of their science or their art with the populace. "Go to the people!" I pity those who make fun of the phrase. Despite a certain disorder in the programming, these people's universities had their day and their usefulness. Not only for the listeners, but for those who taught; they learned to know and satisfy that touching desire for knowledge which I found intact, but lacking in opportunity, when, after the war of 1914, as a deputy for the second sector of the Seine, I was in contact with the Parisian audiences.

The Theatre, too, was visited by this mysticism. I have no idea what the political opinions of Antoine were, and care less, although at least once he made the annual pilgrimage to the Wall of the Federated, where the firing-squads were busy back in the days of the Commune. But at Antoine's *Theatre Libre*, and in the establishment on the Boulevard de Strasbourg, where his disciple Gemier continued the work of the master, how many of the plays presented were socialistic in their atmosphere, if not always in their conclusion! In any case, they echoed in our hearts and answered our aspirations; *Les Fossiles*, *Le Repas du Lion*, *Les Tisserands*, and others.

And when Lugné-Poe introduced us to the works of Ibsen and Bjoernson, *Les Soutiens de la Societe*, *Au dela des forces humaines*, we were not worried whether the old individualist, the bourgeois who drank his grog every day at the hotel in Christiania, would not have rejected our enthusiasms; we only retained that which animated them: a protest against the errors of society, against injustice, against stupidity.

Thus the battles over the Affair had unexpected repercussions in the new Theatre. I remember a performance of *L'Ennemi du peuple*, for which the souvenir program was the work of Steinlen, whose great talent had served our cause incessantly: each speech of the play was greeted with our wildest acclaim. And another drama in which the actors interpreting the script of Saint-Georges de Bouhelier had difficulty in making themselves heard, because Henri de Bruchard, an extremely accomplished agitator, standing in the front row of the orchestra seats, his back to the stage, was heckling the hecklers. Ah, youth!

The Civic Theatre of Louis Lumet, forerunner of the people's theatre which I commended in my 1910 report to the Ministry of Beaux-Arts, and which Gemier brought to reality, moved through the faubourgs of Paris with its social dramas. The repertory was composed of the somewhat cold, but noble works of Romain Rolland on various episodes of the Revolution.

For that period in our history had returned to occupy a place of honor. Its uniforms, scarves, plumes reappeared officially at one of our national theatres, in the presence of the President of the Republic, the day of that immense banquet in honor of the mayors of France, a banquet where the cuisine was mediocre but the cheering tremendous, recalling in a certain measure the old revolutionary Festival of the Federation.

In those 1900's, which were not really so ridiculous after all, our Republic had regained her youth, and overcome the assaults that threatened her. She had everything, including the settings and the showy ceremonies in the arrangement of which she had usually been so inept.

The Muse of Music also participated in this rush toward a human, popular, social ideal. The street-cries of a morning in Montmartre, the fanfares of the Coronation of the Muse rang out during the sessions of the Ministry of Republican Defense. And I can well believe that Gustave Charpentier, little versed in things political, perhaps vaguely anarchistic, when attending the Institute, cared not whether his harmonies were in tune with the policy of government pursued by the serious-minded but very artistic Waldeck-Rousseau. But it all went well together, and Charpentier's dangerous venture—in daring to put on the stage of the Opera or the Opera-Comique a story about the working-classes and the romance of a little seamstress—was carried to success on the flood-tide of a rejuvenated Republic. Ah, that *Louise*, how we loved

WALDECK-ROUSSEAU SEVERAL MONTHS BEFORE HIS DEATH

BATTALION-COMMANDER PAUL-BONCOUR ON THE LORRAINE FRONT (1917)

her—we who were young, too—when she sang of her happiness from the topmost rise of that sacred hill!

The success of the opera was prodigious; perhaps more than those who still applaud it can realize, for it has remained in the repertory now for over forty years.

It gave new confidence to our friend the composer, who was inclined to be distrustful of the spotlight and liked to lurk in the shadows. With Charpentier and Saint-Georges de Bouhelier, we brought to the workers' centers at Lens, Saint-Etienne, and elsewhere, *Le Couronnement de la Muse,* which had preceded *Louise,* and included some of its themes. This earlier work did not concern itself with the "pretty sister" of the artists of Montmartre; we were introduced to the Muse of the masses, the miners, the weavers, and the like. The wind blew to the Left and in spite of my official duties, neither prefects, nor high functionaries saw anything astonishing in the close association of an assistant to the President of the Council and a long-haired musician and the ballerinas of the Opera-Comique in the presentation of an opera where the rhythm of the Carmagnole could be heard in the distance.

It was, incidentally, a very beautiful and novel entertainment in which, along with the music and the ballet, the public itself participated. Wherever we played, the local workers acted as extras; at Lens, the miners; elsewhere, the metal-workers, the weavers, the peasants.

Obviously, this lacked the amplitude, the aggressiveness, the robot-like precision of those massive displays put on by the totalitarian countries, of which we had a surfeit in the cinema newsreels in the days of the Fifth Column. What we were doing had more of a feeling of good fellowship flowing from the sort of entertainment that belonged to our country and our people. I have known returning travelers of the present day whose eyes were dazzled by the great parades in the Red Square at Moscow. On my way to defend, before the Bolshevik tribunals, socialist revolutionaries, friends of Kerensky, I met in Berlin poor, dear Isadora Duncan, who had gone to Russia in quest of new inspiration and a government that protects the Arts. She claimed she had found all she looked for. If our government had gone to the trouble to encourage such initiatives as those of our younger days, our old, very old—too old—democracy would not have needed to look for lessons elsewhere.

This was one of the aspirations of my old friend Gemier, who always found himself too constrained on our stages, even when he tried to enlarge them and permit more effective groupings by adding a stairway, the great idea of a great director, already adopted by Reinhardt before he became an exile. Gemier, who has done so many splendid things in the theatre, never gave his full measure, and never found a government in France that understood these problems. Twice he went to Switzerland in search of masses to move, and a democracy which had the good sense to confide them to an artist. Like Isadora, he wanted to go to Russia. He was feted there; the Bolsheviks knew how to treat their guests, perhaps mindful of Potemkin, who could conjure up imaginary villages to impress the great Catherine. Gemier praised the theatrical production of the new Russia, and the marvelous artistic sense of its people, which seems to survive all regimes.

But much of what he encountered in that country shocked this liberty-loving visitor from France with the all-seeing eyes. Megard told me that, on one occasion, Gemier, returning to his hotel room, opened the door, put his hand to his mouth, and said, "*Vive la France!*"

Unfortunately, in the domain of art, popular art particularly, France and its governments grew increasingly indifferent. One might even say, ungrateful! When one saw a man like Antoine, who had renovated the drama and struggled with endless financial problems in trying to run a theatre which merited the name of "The Second Theatre of France," obliged to scrounge and scrape at his age for his very existence, one might well say that Louis XIV would have arranged this much better. For a long time, the Republic had replaced the pension system adopted by our kings, and handed out positions as directors of museums and curators of historic chateaux whereby writers and artists could shelter their improvident old age. Then, young men attached to the cabinet began usurping these posts little by little, until the day when, as a reaction, the introduction of a system of examinations was tried.

As writers and artists are not all inured to this sort of hardship, how many walked out, never to be seen again, after being the staunchest of socialists at the time of the Leftist Block!

The salons, the Academy, the influential magazines, the big newspapers attracted some of them, not to mention that law of succession which habitually makes the new generation rise up against the one that preceded it. "Each generation begins with an assassination," someone said.

The intellectual afflux which the Dreyfus Affair and its repercussions brought to the parties of the Left, no longer existed on the eve of 1914. And certainly not at the beginning of the present war.

Outside of these motives, mediocre but natural, and outside of the attraction of the salons, the Academy, the magazines, and the newspapers, there was an incentive of an ideological order, rising out of the Affair, but on the other side. Thanks to the bitter campaign waged by Maurras and *L'Action Francaise* against any retrial for Dreyfus, terming it a blow against the State, this group constituted a center of attraction which drew a number of conversions, and orientations in the opposite direction to that which I have summarily traced.

Just as, on the one side, there were many who aided in the spreading of socialist doctrine without adhering to the socialist party, there were many on the other side who, without being monarchists, yielded to the lure of a coherent program which looked to the glorious past of France in a search for the road to future grandeur. Each day, with the strength that comes from repetition and an incontestable talent, Maurras set forth this doctrine in his newspaper, the editorial policy of which satisfied a certain taste for violence and defamation often displayed by Rightists toward their adversaries. "The reactionaries are malicious," said Anatole France.

If one takes the trouble, it is not difficult to observe the very considerable influence of Maurras and the monarchists in much of the writing that appeared in the years preceding the 1914 war, and the present one. The logic of the authors errs in that they accept the premise and not the conclusion, the construction and not the culmination.

Except for the Socialists, the parties of the Left, too busy with their electioneering, did nothing to oppose the monarchist doctrine with one capable of keeping young hearts faithful to the Republic.

It was this mistake that led to a reduction of the Republican majority which the triumphs of Waldeck-Rousseau had established.

Chapter Five

"YOU KNOW HOW TO CONQUER, HANNIBAL . . ."

The grievous evening of Waldeck-Rousseau's life.—M. Combes, Albigensian.—The anticlerical struggle.—Controversy on Regionalism.—Trade Unions and the State.—The Congress of Amsterdam.—The Affair of the Files.—The Army of the Republic.

In his solidly constructed, but very biased *La Troisieme Republique*, Jacques Bainville, the noted Royalist writer, notes with injurious intent that a President of the Council enjoying considerable prestige, a veritable Premier, Waldeck-Rousseau, was so much the master of all he surveyed that he even designated his successor.

In conceding Waldeck's prestige, Bainville is correct, but to infer that he used it dictatorially is wrong. It was the custom for Presidents of the Republic to ask advice from a resigning Premier about a suitable successor; advice which they were perfectly free to disregard.

What made Waldeck's departure unique in the annals of the Third Republic, to my way of thinking, is that he resigned not because of a hostile intervention, but at a moment when he was at the peak of his popularity, following triumphal elections, with all the republicans of the Leftist Block eager to keep the man who had led them to victory. He had been in power for three years; he could double it, if he desired. It was of his own volition, firmly expressed, in spite of many entreaties, that he stepped down. I might have joined those who reproached him for it, had not his premature death made it apparent that he had already felt the first pangs of the implacable malady that was to carry him off.

Despite his disregard for power—one of his originalities—

and despite his eagerness to get back to his books, his paintings, his travels, and his preeminence in the legal profession, I do not think, if he felt he had the strength, that he would have left to others the application of a law which had been his own project, as that of 1884 had been, and which he had conceived along with a delicate judicial mechanism he certainly would have wanted to set in motion himself.

Combes, who had made the report on the law to the Senate, where Waldeck found useful support against certain impulsive movements in the Chamber of Deputies, was the man he designated to succeed him. "He adopted him," writes Jacques Bainville, "and the adoption led to one of those unexpected results that sometimes surprised the Caesars." Since Vichy, things have been better.

In truth, aside from a republican sincerity and integrity, no one was more different from Waldeck-Rousseau than Combes. Even in their conception of the ultimate development of this law, they had nothing in common. For Waldeck, it was a concordat; for Combes, an execution. One was a Gallican, the other, an Albigensian. . . .

I believed I had found the key to the rather special psychology of M. Combes—who was at once a spiritualist and a violent anticlerical, and was hooted at by anticlerical extremists one day, for speaking of God—when I discovered, in that department of the Tarn which I represented in Parliament, the real origins of this doctor from the Charente. He was born, raised, educated in the seminary here in this rugged country, where the religious wars have left lasting memories. Did I not hear, one day when we were inaugurating a bust of Jaures at Montpellier, the representative of a neighboring socialist federation refer to him as "the last victim of Simon de Montfort!" And, during the electoral campaign of 1924, holding a meeting in an isolated corner of the Black Mountain, I was reliably informed that a young protestant lad, engaged to a catholic girl, was unable to obtain the grandmother's consent to the marriage until she assured herself that the young man had no cloven foot!

M. Combes did not go quite so far. But I am inclined to agree with one of his biographers that, unlike many politicians, anticlericalism was not so much a political position with him, as the result of a certain philosophical conception, and even, paradoxical as it may appear, a religious conception, the revenge of an Albigensian against the Roman Church.

But this theology mattered little to his majority which, as Waldeck predicted, roared out of the bitter struggle it had been obliged to fight, and thought only of striking hard and often. After the Dreyfus Affair, as after the Sixteenth of May, the Church—certain of its organizations especially, who had thrust their way into the conflict much deeper than their spiritual leaders would have wished—had to pay for the defeat. It is always dangerous to bless the enterprises of reaction. Which is what many eminent members of the clergy, secular as well as regular, appear to have remembered in the present crisis; their attitude of reserve in respect to the new government of today and its policy, corrects certain imprudences at the beginning, and a few berets of the Legion on the heads of young curates. The highly patriotic attitude of bishops, priests, and monks safeguards the future and is, I hope, a guarantee against a reaction which would have brought us back to those struggles of the past, and which it is neither to the interest of the Church, nor the Republic, nor that of France to see reborn.

In the debates before the Chamber of 1902, they were in full swing; a massive blow against religious congregations, without discernment, preceded the separation of Church and State, which was precisely what Waldeck-Rousseau did not want.

I was in a position to study closely the anxiety he felt. Many of his old collaborators, who had looked upon his resignation less lightly, urged him to intervene. Unwilling to create difficulties for his successor, he confined himself to words of advice; and only decided to climb back on to the rostrum of the Senate, when he became convinced that the words of advice were going unheeded. It was a great blow when his speech was equally ineffectual. The majority, the one he had built, was being swept headlong toward solutions of great brutality. In the Senate, which was his house, and which he has sustained in all his work, he received a miserably small number of approving votes now. Only a few more than the three which, during the war, supported Clemenceau's cry of alarm; the same Clemenceau who stood up and reproached Waldeck for trying to halt the forces Waldeck's own law had set in motion against the Church.

It was his last speech. He was already hard hit. We who loved him were well aware of his condition, and were saddened to see this moral suffering added to the ravages of his physical ailment. He had no illusions about the latter, and chided his doctors—who, in view of the patient's importance, were disturbed over the possibility of an error becoming public—about their excessive caution.

"I told them," he confided to me, "to treat me as they would my gardener."

But when President Loubet's visit to Rome brought a violent Vatican reaction, which in turn prompted the anticlericals in our Assembly to denounce the Concordat, Waldeck determined to dominate his malady and ascend the rostrum for a final appeal. It was then that he prepared the speech I mentioned earlier, the one that appeared posthumously in Peguy's *Cahiers de la Quinzaine*, affording such precious information about his working methods.

He never gave the speech. After Gambetta and Ferry—and before Jaures—death struck him down at the age of fifty-eight, when he could have normally expected long years of action ahead of him. And with him died his law, or at least his conception of it, which differed so widely from the version substituted.

As we followed his casket out of the house at Corbeil that had sheltered the melancholy evening of his life, his Minister of Marine, M. de Lanessan, said to me, "I'm quite sure we'll be the last to have governed."

Which is often the opinion of those who step down from positions of power. Combes was governing . . . in his own manner. Clemenceau had a markedly different method which the war of 1914 permitted him to develop to the fullest extent, fortunately for France. But Waldeck's term of office was indeed the last time that, under peaceful conditions and strictly parliamentary procedure, a man's prestige, will-power, and a courteous but resolute desire to defend the Republic enabled him to retain, all through the legislature as well as throughout the country, the majority that had put their trust in him.

With Waldeck gone, this majority, deprived of their leader, failed to grasp the opportunity offered them to fortify, by founding appropriate institutions and accomplishing basic reforms, the regime they had saved. Largely by the fault of her adversaries, slightly by her own errors, the Republic was once again thrust into anticlerical struggles which drew her away from the constructive task that could have been undertaken right after her parliamentary victory. Old memories of schoolboy studies rise to mind, and out of my Latin textbooks, the words: "You know how to conquer, Hannibal, but you do not know how to profit from your victory. . . ."

For problems were already arising, and some of them would not wait.

Obviously, such was not the case with a question that seemed rather academic in the eyes of our Parliamentarians, accustomed to the smoke and tumult of legislative warfare, but to which a few of us—a slender squad scattered among various Leftist groups—had become attached. And yet, were we wrong in trying to persuade the conquering legislators that one of the constructive labors facing them was very closely tied to an ancient claim of our democracy?

It was the problem of decentralization which, under the Empire, had figured prominently on the programs of their predecessors, and, in the form of municipal autonomy, on those of the Radicals after the Commune. It still received an occasional salute, but was generally relegated to an exercise of style in speechmaking, getting little serious attention from the elector or the elected.

Furthermore, the formula had been surpassed; a concrete reality had replaced an administrative concept: "regionalism" was the order of the day for several young groups and their publications, as young as their publishers and just as unsound financially, therefore unable to reach a great number of readers. They sought to find again the life of the old provinces, mostly in their folklore, their literary and artistic manifestations, their customs, and the diversity of their intellectual and moral tendencies, rather than in any political expression.

Maurras had not been mistaken; blending conceptions familiar to the Comte de Chambord and the Comte de Paris, he had added to the monarchist doctrine—which he was enlivening and renewing—and transposed into political terms that attempt at a renaissance which some of us belonging to the Left also felt would serve to solidify and enrich our national life.

I had just published my *Federalisme Economique*. The research, the reflections induced, had established ineradicably in my mind the conviction that a government, whether Republican or Monarchist, can only be solid if it rises on a foundation of social groups equally solid. Which they cannot be unless they are largely autonomous. The State will be all the stronger in the prerogatives that properly belong to it and can only be exercised by it, when it has marked more clearly the limits of its domain. A conglomeration of individuals is not a society; it is as a group that they are important; and along with the voluntary assemblages given statutory liberty by Waldeck-Rousseau's law of association, there are natural and obligatory ones determined by the family to which one belongs, the place where one lives, or the profession one has chosen. I had set down my argument in favor of compulsory association, and was quite prepared to understand the necessity for widening the field of regionalism to include the old, almost-forgotten demands of the Early Republicans for decentralization. Here again, I was mindful of my days in Brittany.

A strong Republic, it seemed to me, could and should give back to the old provinces the sort of life that had proved so profitable to an earlier France. A well-ordered democracy must not neglect what a young socialistic writer, Paul-Louis Garnier, called "the superb determinism of the native soil." A phrase not unworthy of Barres.

Out of these pronouncements of mine came a controversy with Maurras, which aroused some interest in that happy era when people's minds were sufficiently free to think about this sort of thing, and adversaries were sufficiently courteous not to go after one another with a kitchen knife. So much so that one of the younger periodicals engaged in developing the regionalist movement, and, happily, having its own book-publishing house, asked Maurras and me for permission to compile a book from our articles, the volume to bear our names, a juxtaposition that caused considerable eyebrow-lifting at the time, and infinitely more with the passing years.*

Decentralization, thus revived, aroused additional articles and arguments. Clemenceau himself, ever youthful, ever attentive to the reactions of the young, and jealously guarding for the Republic the benefits of such a movement, rushed into print with a reply to an editorial in *Le Temps*. The author was, I believe, Andre Tardieu, and the editorial reproached Clemenceau for his silence on the subject of decentralization. Clemenceau, who was at the moment taking a cure at Carlsbad, answered by accusing the Moderates and the Opportunists of picking up the decentralization idea when the Radicals were in power, and of neglecting it completely when they controlled the government.

His article was violent and vivid. The old Jacobin harked back to Federalism, judging, like myself, that if the Jacobins were right in centralizing the government to save the endangered Republic, it was now time to decentralize to keep it alive. "The institutions of 1793," he said, "were notably liberal compared to those of the Year VIII." This was peremptory but exact. And he concluded, "Along with M. Paul-Boncour, I contend that we must put an end to the centralization of Napoleon's time, which has fallen into the hands of an anonymous State controlled by bureaucrats lounging on their leather cushions, running the government by a routine that kills all initiative, all responsibility. But let *Le Temps* take care. What it recommends is nothing less than a political and social revolution."

* *Un debat nouveau sur la Republique et la decentralisation*, by J. Paul-Boncour and Charles Maurras, societé provinciale d'edition, Toulouse, 1907.

Which did not happen. My friend Varenne replied, "First, The Church. Let us not run the risk, in decentralizing, of disarming the Republic before the battle with the Church is at an end."

Though not everyone had the frankness of this man from Auvergne, many agreed with him. As Waldeck-Rousseau had feared on election eve, the anticlerical struggle became the all-but-exclusive preoccupation of the elected, too concerned about the battle they had been through to give attention to new conflicts.

However, the more I think about it in relation to what has happened since, the more I am persuaded that in this debate—an episode soon forgotten by a legislature assailed by a profusion of other problems—the question we raised was not untimely. In the end, despite the disdainful reception from political veterans, our young ideas, expressed in our youthful publications, proved to be right.

A few days ago, I was reading in the *Journal de Geneve*—which affords a measure of escape from the present servitude of the French press under the Occupation—that it is a wise thing for a democratic regime not to remove any decision from its effects. "When the governing power lies far away, the sovereign expresses his opinion without first-hand knowledge of the problems he is asked to solve. He is under certain illusions as to the real possibilities of the State. Inclined to stress his rights, he neglects his duties." How true! Political life, at the level of the hamlet or the district, has this very considerable advantage; it gives the citizens a daily bath of reality, and, when it asks them to make their own decisions on local matters, it forces them to measure the consequences, the entire weight of which will be on their shoulders.

Switzerland is an example of this. Even with us, is it by mere chance that the same elected representative is more cautious in approving the expenditure of local funds called for in the budget of his community than in voting appropriations which will be paid for by the State?

But the problem was much more extensive, and indissolubly a part of what had become, in the second of the between-war periods, the growing weakness of the regime: governmental instability, lack of authority vested in the executive branch, and *an unwillingness to confer such authority because of a fear, not entirely unwarranted, of executive misuse of this power in a centralized administration.*

If there is one country where individualism could be expected to run riot, unshackled as it is by any historic tradition, that country is the United States. Yet, Federalism has succeeded in maintaining order and welding a strong nation which has twice come to our rescue. Within these federated states, one encounters precepts and laws, unprotestingly accepted by the citizens, which our centralized authority would have had enormous difficulty in imposing on us. Even the most tyrannical exigencies of collectivity—such as the problem of race—have received an obligatory protection which would have caused our liberals to stand aghast, and which the totalitarians have merely imitated, with somewhat more contempt for the human being.

As for the Federal government, and the discipline which the various states accept in the common interest, everyone knows that President Franklin D. Roosevelt, in internal as well as external affairs, exercises prerogatives that the parliaments of Europe have refused to grant to the proudest dynasties.

Why do the free citizens of Free America permit the placing of so much authority in the hands of one man? Because the federal government itself sets a limit to his powers. In their own sphere, these powers are strong, but only there; the president cannot arbitrarily extend them in accordance with his own interests or those of his party. Constitutionally and practically, in law as in fact, the president has only such powers as the states have entrusted to him for the good of all. Whereas, in a centralized government, the central authority, whether an individual or an assembly, in law as in fact, possesses all the power and only doles out to the various groups composing the nation whatever portion seems desirable.

Hence, one's fears of it. Hence, the paralyzing terror, blended with memories of actual or attempted *coups d'etat* made easier by a centralized regime, that arises to confront those who talk of reforming the State, even when such reform appears necessary. Reforming the State meant strengthening the Chief Executive, and that was the chief obstacle. Would not this repugnance have been more easily surmounted if the Republic, in happier days, when the post-war problems were not at its throat, had taken the time to establish, through a professional and regional federalism, groups strong enough to protect it from sudden blows, and not have resorted to a system of defense based upon the continuance of a feeble executive branch?

The federalizing of professions was progressing without official permission. Though regionalism allowed itself to be forgotten, following that unfruitful awakening occasioned by our juvenile audacity, Trade Unionism was somewhat rudely determined to make a place for itself, upsetting political formations and disconcerting the established parties.

Millerand, tired of unjustified attacks—for he had rendered incontestable services during his participation in the government—had left the Socialist party, starting an evolution which was to lead him quite far from his point of departure. But his work remained. Through him, but in an orderly and methodical fashion, Trades Unionism had come into the government and its surrouundings. And what is more significant, the head of the government, Waldeck-Rousseau, was the one who, in 1884, had given Trades Unionism its charter. The forward step had been taken with his approbation. The preface he wrote for the second edition of my book on Trades Unionism marked the orientation of his mind. "We have chosen liberty; let us have confidence in it." And this formula pleased him so well that, having entrusted me with the selection of a motto to be engraved on the commemorative medal struck in his honor by the Mint, he gave his approval when I chose the words mentioned above.

But Trades Unionism was no longer concerning itself with liberty, it wanted power; and the kind it outlined in its own domain verified what I have said about the possible reconciliation of social autonomy with a strong authority.

A labor union puts upon its members a heavier constraint than that of the State. Nevertheless, the most violently freedom-loving member will submit readily, though he will resist the slightest show of authority by the State. The unions, in turn, willingly yield some of their powers to a central group such as the *Confederation Generale du Travail.* Union functionaries possess, in fact, powers more real, efficacious, and lasting than that of cabinet ministers. "I thought I was listening to Louis XIV," says a character in the play, *Les Nouveaux Messieurs*, to the actor Victor Boucher, portraying the chief of the Confederation, who has just finished giving a few orders.

Why are the union leaders so secure in power? Because, however strong the authority to which one submits, however hard the rules which one accepts, these are disciplinary measures strictly limited to the needs they are concerned with, not imposed from above, but freely granted by the agreement of the interested parties and placed under direct control. This would have been all very well, if the unions had stayed within the boundaries of their competency. But there began to be some question about where this competency ended. It became necessary to rule on the relations between the unions and the Republic.

All the more so, inasmuch as the cabinet had substituted its own improvisations in place of a general formula. Pelletan, the rather bohemian Minister of Marine, generous, ardently patriotic—as he had demonstrated in certain critical hours before the Budget Commission—had settled in his own way, which was not that of his admirals, his business relations with the workers in the navy-yards. A settlement which was vigorously attacked. These personal onslaughts were as excessive as the accusation that he had ruined the navy, simply because his opinion in regard to big ships—not nearly as big as those so easily sent to the bottom by submarines and planes—did not conform to that of the experts.

Uncertainty reigned; the unions, received in some quarters, were disregarded in others. Since the decrees of Millerand, when he was Minister of Commerce, no one seemed to know exactly what new concessions should be made.

It was something else again when trade unionism moved from the workshop to the company offices. The white-collar worker now demanded his turn at achieving the benefits of union organization to improve his financial situation, which was far from brilliant, and to safeguard his dignity, which was generally disrespected. An immediate result was the disturbance in the Chamber of Deputies on November 7th, 1905, when an insidious question by Lasies, the Bonapartist *enfant terrible* who had defied old Cassagnac to his face, demanded an answer.

I was present at the beginning of this session. Gazing down on the eddying currents that all but swept away the Rouvier cabinet and left the various existing political groups and subgroups disordered and divided, I was able to discern the great conflicting streams which the social politics of tomorrow would let loose in Parliament. The wave of tolerance which, for several years, had covered the successive usurpations attempted by the professional group of those employed by the State, broke against their firm determination to enlarge the social, economic, and political consequences of their action.

It was then that I wrote a little book on this question and its increasing urgency, *Les Syndicats de Fonctionnaires**, in which I tried to set down a few rules that would permit some other treatment than brutality or complacency for a condition it was now impossible to stop. What I suggested would not only block all political meddling in purely administrative matters and office routine, it would also aid in the reformation and smoother functioning of the modern State, in some measure "substituting order for anarchy," as Henri de Jouvenel had urged, in an article defying the clamor of the conservatives, the very morning of the day this disturbing debate began in the Chamber of Deputies.

It was now impossible to destroy, or even repress, a movement that had been forming for years, often with the aid of the government.

Not only had unions been permitted to organize in government-owned enterprises such as tobacco factories, matchworks, powder and saltpeter works, arsenals and warehouses, offices of the army engineer corps, the construction and maintenance departments of the telephone and telegraph lines,

* *Les Syndicats de Fonctionnaires,* by J. Paul-Boncour. Preface by Anatole France. Cornely, Paris.

road-builders, sewer-workers, street-sweepers, and gardeners, but, during Millerand's term as Minister of Commerce and Postal Service, he had aided and applauded various professional associations of office-workers and laborers who were not at all under his jurisdiction.

Doubtless, these groups did not, at first, come under the heading of unions, but it was quite clear that their founders had that in mind. Not merely mutual aid societies, but truly protective, it was their express intention to push through, by constant pressure on public officials, economic and social laws that concerned their particular profession, as well as to keep their demands constantly before their hierarchical chiefs.

In the Department of Public Works, the toll-keepers, road-workers, and canal lock-keepers, utilizing to the fullest extent the law of 1901, had formed professional associations and merged them into federations which negotiated openly with municipalities and other public powers.

An even more significant movement, because of the category of state employes involved, was that of the teachers in public schools, grouped under cover of the name of "friendly societies." From the start, they affirmed, sometimes boisterously, their determination not to be bound by the anodyne appellation of their group and "to defend energetically against officialdom the material interests and the dignity of their members."

Not only cabinet ministers, but the heads of government, in the years of confidence, had lavished approbation and benevolence on them. It was a bit late now to step back when confronted with the unionization problem and to begin, over a question of nomenclature, a battle for which the Rouvier ministry was preparing, but which no government was able to carry through to the end.

The important thing was to determine exactly which government employes, because of the authority vested in them, or because they directly represented the State, were not entitled to benefit by the 1884 law of association. But if the idea was simple and sensible, its formula of application was complicated.

One proposal would have barred state employes in posts of authority and administration from joining a union. This was a bit curt. Because a postman or a local customs collector has the right to make certain demands upon a citizen, is he a wielder of political power? Judicial hair-splitting in an attempt to prevent the organizing of these employes. It would not work.

Another suggestion: state employes having the right to give orders and make decisions by virtue of authority delegated to them, and employes engaged in purely executorial and technical work, would be excluded. This was better, but the formula was still too generalized, and would be a jurist's delight.

For my part, I proposed a realistic approach often used in English law: to grant, in principle, to *all* functionaries the right to associate within the framework and limitations of the law of 1884, except for categories *expressly designated.* These were easily established, if one was willing to take a practical point of view. Obviously, certain functionaries exercise the right of constraint, of command, and make imperative decisions in the name of the State, while others, no matter what the moral and technical importance of their function, are merely managers of a public service, whether it be intellectual, economical, or commercial.

This precise designation of categories, not at all numerous, to which the right to associate would be denied, guaranteed the others against any ulterior alterations of policy and interpretation due to changing political majorities, and protected the State from the system of tolerance into which it slipped because of sheer indecision, thus paving the way for unionization and mutual defense, where the will and authority of its chiefs should have come into play.

For no decision was made.

Anatole France took it upon himself to present my little book to the public; in his ardor as a new convert, the grand old man spoke of this great movement of labor solidarity, "sweet as reason, terrible as love." It was a little optimistic. The government thought otherwise, though not at all sure what it wanted. The ministry of Rouvier, succeeding that of Combes, was headed by an able financier—at a time when it was rather easy to be one—but not well acquainted with social problems, and ill-prepared to cope with the one which now presented itself. It remained imminent and irritating; and what followed will show that it weighed heavily on French politics, adding to the causes of ministerial instability, and creating insurmountable difficulties for the best of them.

The political formation emerging from the elections of 1902, the Leftist Block, now knew the fall from favor that later befell the Cartel and the Popular Front, and which, from 1914 to 1939, gravely damaged the parliamentary regime, a legislature never ending as it had begun, that is to say, as the voters had wished.

Despite its anticlericalism, which appeared excessive to many staunch republicans, the Combes ministry played too strongly on the passions unleashed by the political exploitation of the Dreyfus Affair and the imprudent part taken by some of the religious orders not to be able to face the bitter struggle conducted by the opposition. The latter even sought to attack, through his son, the indisputable integrity of the Premier, one of the most refractory of men in matters of financial intrigue.

But two incidents proved disastrous for him.

The Leftist Block was sadly shattered at the International Socialist Congress at Amsterdam. Despite the efforts of Jaures, the Congress condemned, by the margin of a single vote, the systematic incorporation of the Socialists in the Leftist majority, and their permanent presence in Leftist delegations, notwithstanding the preponderant part they had already played, to the party's very considerable profit. The deciding vote was that of a Japanese socialist, Katamaya. This was not the least of the pleasantries which, during the post-war struggle to restore this participation, my friends and I tossed back at our anti-participationist comrades—who obstinately tried to keep untouchable a rule not only obsolete through circumstances born of war, but which, by its very origin, was marked as a strange paradox—the vote of a delegate from a remote country of the Far East, where his party played a very obscure role in the politics of his own nation, determining *our* political policy and the course to be taken by one of *our* great parties, just when it was about to take the place it merited by its manpower, organization, discipline, and ideals.

Jaures suffered, but submitted, sacrificing the Leftist Block on the altar of party unity.

Meeting Leon Blum, on the occasion of a theatrical opening, where he devoted the multiple resources of his mind to reviewing the new play, I voiced my regret over what had happened at Amsterdam, and we paced the corridors, outlining our future controversies on participation.

There was also a rather nasty business taking place in the Ministry of War. The Affair of the Files provided an honorable pretext for getting rid of a government which was governing much more to the Left than was pleasing to some who, while not daring to vote against it, would infinitely prefer not to have to vote *for* it any longer.

This Affair of the Files had worried Waldeck-Rousseau, warned of it by an officer in the ministerial cabinet. It contributed, together with his setback in the Senate, to the melancholy of the last months of his life, when, immobilized by his illness, he could only watch helplessly the unforeseen consequences of the policy of Republican Defense, and of national reconciliation, for which he had prepared the basis.

Strongly imbued with the theory of supremacy of the State, he had tried tenaciously to restore a spirit of obedience among the military leaders, and a respect for the laws of the nation among the religious orders. Galliffet, the hero of Sedan, his personal choice for the task, had hit hard, but aimed only at the head, convinced that the government had a right to demand from its chiefs, military or civilian, absolute loyalty, and absolute impartiality in the promotion of their subordinates. From the latter, all that is required is devotion to duty or, in the case of the civilian, doing his job to the best of his ability.

The error of General André, or of those he allowed to err for him, was that, not too sure of the republicanism of many of the high-ranking officers—and here he was *not* mistaken—he sought outside information, which soon led to individual denunciations, in making his selection.

Galliffet had put a stop to the uninterrupted abdication

of power by the Ministers of War in the matter of promotions by doing away with the army's classification committees. Once more the master of the High Command, it was the Minister's duty to staff it in such a way that the advancement of republican officers needed no other guarantee than the impartiality of their superiors.

The Affair of the Files impaired this necessary republicanization by unmasking the unpleasant processes used to accomplish it. Though far from equalling the unmitigated snooping that has thrived in our country since the present regime.

It had another disadvantage: it concealed the effectiveness of certain useful measures taken during the years when a new viewpoint was permitted in the offices of the Ministry of War. The deplorable Affair, noisily exploited, even to the slap in the face given General André by Syveton, made one forget the organic reforms. It was at the time when Galliffet, André, and Berteaux, were the successive Ministers of War, and Waldeck and Combes were Premiers, that the regulations were modernized to conform to the new army, with its reduced term of service, which did not turn out too badly, since it fought and won the war of 1914.

To convince one, it was enough to have been a reserve officer in those years, to have had contact with the troops, alongside our career officers, and to compare our passing observations with their permanent experience. We had fewer classes, lectures, schools of theory than our comrades of 1939; we were, perhaps, less militarily educated; but we had more practical experience in subaltern commands. In accordance with the law of 1889, we had to put in some time as corporals and sergeants before becoming officers.

I recall the pleasant surprise when, during my reserve periods of 1901, 1903, and 1905, on the drill-ground, the firing-range, or on maneuvers, I noticed the difference between the army as it had evolved and the army I had known in the days when, in the same regiment, on the same drill-ground, and in the same countryside, I had performed my military duty as a private. An inflexible routine, a rigid mentality that prevails, especially where the opinion of the one who executes an order is not, and cannot be permitted, had perpetuated habits and customs dating from the days when the use of rapid-fire weapons had still not persuaded those in command to do away with close-order formations; when the longer term of service not only allowed more time for reviews, inspections, endless polishing and packing, but even made them desirable as a means of keeping the troops occupied. Performing the manual of arms in the barrack-square took precedence over instruction in the first principles of service in the field. Certain aspects of army discipline in those days, designed for barrack veterans, appeared fairly anachronistic to the young recruit called up for a length of time which the new system of generalization and equality tended to reduce.

1901, 1903, 1905 . . . Simple chronology? Or, as I am inclined to believe, a question of cause and effect? These happy changes were due to an effort to meet new requirements, affecting army regulations and the officers charged with their application, just when people were reproaching the political system for interfering in military matters and weakening the army.

That, at least, was maintained. General André was succeeded by Berteaux, patriot and republican in the best jacobin tradition. He tore up the files. But in ministerial practice, he held to the same orientation. It was he who guided through the Chamber of Deputies, then through the Senate—where a former member of the Government of National Defense, M. de Freycinet, gave him significant support—the law limiting compulsory military service to two years, which his predecessor had prepared.

It has been called one of the Republic's bad debts, a demagogic compromise, a dangerous reduction in the length of service, when Germany—which had already adopted the same plan—was gaining manpower by reason of its greater population.

One forgets that, owing to the new equality in the matter of compulsory service, the new legislation was providing as much, if not more manpower, than the three-year period of service and its accompanying exemptions.

One forgets that, along with the military preparation which

the new law instituted, and the organization of a reserve, which it promised, it was carring military training far beyond the barrack period; it really created a national army, a nation armed for its defense. We shall see later the mistakes that prevented its fulfilment.

I was to encounter Maurice Berteaux again in a few years, and sit with him in the same ministry. The skies had darkened. But he had not changed. The friendliness that bound us, since I entered the Chamber, associating myself with his projects and perturbations, enabled me to know what he wanted to accomplish, and what the army and the Republic had lost, in losing him: the Army of the Republic, as Joffre called it.

Chapter Six

THE SECOND COMING OF CLEMENCEAU

Clemenceau in power.—Picquart as Minister of War.—The Ministry of Labor.—Viviani.—Unions and strikes.—The five-day week.—The retirement law.—The speeches of Viviani.—Clemenceau and Germany.—My Parliamentary entry.—Campaign for electoral reforms.—The railroad strike.—Briand waltzes.

While these reforms were taking place in the Ministry of War, and the Ministry of Foreign Affairs recorded its successes, in the field of general politics things were not going so well. In a parliamentary regime, governments only govern if they have a homogenous and resolute majority under their control.

An uneasiness weighed upon the government that emerged from the 1902 elections. The democratic drive had expended itself in the anticlerical struggle. The Leftist Block, destroyed by the break at Amsterdam, had left an empty space. A policy that was not one of national unity, but equivocal, an attempt to strike a balance between left and right, such as had already been tried before the advent of Waldeck-Rousseau, was with us again. It demonstrated little capability of solving the problems arising from the development of trade unionism and its penetration in the affairs of government, and gave no promise of satisfying the social demands of an impatient working-class.

The Radical Party, disturbed, thrown on its own resources, though these had been somewhat improved since the last elections, was looking for a leader. It found him, or rather, refound him, for he had already led them in the party's heroic age. Against this background of grey, Clemenceau stood out. By an odd twist of parliamentary procedure, he returned by a roundabout route—in the cabinet of Sarrien.

Enforcedly absent from the National Assembly for many long years, he came back as a senator from the Mediterranean department of the Var in a local election, and promptly proceeded to allot to himself a place which, in his estimation, must necessarily be the first. No offering up of prayers, for the man had no humility; which as a matter of fact, would have been a detriment.

Included in his iconography, along with the splendid portrait by Manet, is a painting by Raffaelli, I believe, showing him in oratorical combat at a public rally in the Belleville district where his opponent Gambetta had ordered the "drunken slaves to crawl back to their lairs." Short, dark, muscular, tightly encased in the frock-coat of the period, his high collar cutting like a guillotine, wearing the tiny-knotted black string-tie he always affected, his strong-boned face turned toward the crowd, he stands alone against the tumult, like a bull that has just stepped into the arena. Yes, a bull, much more than a tiger, which was the name usually accorded him, and in which he gloried. Greying, bruised by so many adventures. this is still the way I saw him upon his tardy return to power.

The Presidents of the Republic had always been recalcitrant toward him, and even now no one wanted to give him the task of forming a government. He was made Minister of the Interior, under the lightly-wielded shepherd's-crook of M. Sarrien, who had been irreverently, and unjustly, described as "a gate-post to which one attaches the chariot of State," when he seemed uncertain of the direction to take.

One can date Clemenceau's return to power, not from October 1906, when he became Premier, but from the moment he installed himself at the Ministry of the Interior and began giving his prefects a pushing-around. For three years, like Waldeck-Rousseau, but with a marked difference of method and temperament, he was the master of the French Republic. Another example of ministerial longevity, even in a parliamentary regime which had lost its early ardor and strength, when it encounters men who, by their experience and merit, have sufficient authority to impose themselves upon it and utilize it.

None of the difficulties was spared him. By chance, or because he preferred to ride over an obstacle rather than sidestep it, he was beset by such bloody incidents as the battles over the government's attempt to take inventory of the gold and silver candlesticks and other treasure of church sacristies, a procedure strongly resisted by the parishioners and ultimately abandoned; violence in the vineyards, as the winegrowers rioted against the low price of wine; and a series of strikes, some of which were tragic. Few men have been so frequently faced with the alternative of denying their own words or ceasing to govern; because, in his long years as a member of the opposition, he had made assertions and taken stands which were difficult to adhere to when in power. He did not hesitate long; after an attempt to appeal directly to the crowd, during the strikes in the Pas-de-Calais district, in which he was not successful, he chose the way of the iron hand. Things had evolved since his young radical days, and the trade union movement, its organized power, its desire for autonomy, were incomprehensible to him.

Deeply democratic, he had always favored freedom for the worker; he had penned pages on social justice which a good many socialists wished they had written; and, in 1893, after losing his political position and his newspaper, heavily in debt, forsaken by all but a few faithful followers, he gave to the young people of all time an uncommon example of energy. A born orator, he became a writer—to support himself and serve his ideas. He even turned dramatist. Before meeting him politically, I had seen him staging a play for Gemier, another aspect of the man's multifarious talents.

He did more than write; he presented to the working-class three great reforms: the creation of a Ministry of Labor, the Retirement Law, and the Eight-Hour Day.

But the vital fact of trade unionism had no part in his earlier concept of social evolution, to which he clung with the obstinacy he displayed in everything. It required the experience of tragic years to make him realize its importance, and bring him round to remarking, in 1919, half-jokingly, half-seriously, to a delegation from the Confederation Generale du Travail, as he pointed to his ministerial chair, "You'll be sitting here soon."

It must be observed that trade unionism, in 1906, did nothing to facilitate his task. It began in violence. This was an era of multiple strikes, and the myth of a general strike had a certain vogue. It was also a period of strikes in public services, and violent union harassment of workers who had not become members. A great deal of talk about blacklists and the "sockful of nails" as weapons of persuasion, while Georges Sorel wrote his doctrinal *Eloge de la Violence*, wherein fascism later traced part of its origins.

It all seemed to prove the truth of Waldeck-Rousseau's words, in his preface to my book on trade unionism:

"To be a *gentle* man, one needs to have been a free man a long time!"

Meanwhile, we were involved in a great many of these clashes in our new Ministry of Labor, which Clemenceau had just created, and which Viviani had asked me to help him organize.

Clemenceau, already old, but younger than many of the young, had waited too long to attain power to be satisfied with merely following in the footsteps of his predecessors. He determined to startle people and politicians by the composition of his cabinet. The listing of this new Ministry, together with the name of his Minister of War, was a double surprise similar to Waldeck's teaming of Galliffet and Millerand.

An inflexible supporter of Dreyfus, cordially disliking the army's High Command until he made it an instrument of his own victory and courageously defended it against an impatient Chamber of Deputies, he deliberately sought as his Minister of War, the one man who, after Dreyfus, had been the outstanding victim of the Affair. General Picquart was an officer of merit, possessing a certain nobility of soul, and a well-cultivated mind, in a milieu pretty generally unconcerned with outside preoccupations. Galliffet, on whose staff he had served, spoke of him with esteem, but reproached him amusedly for his love of the landscape during field maneuvers.

Chief of the Second Bureau, it was Picquart who set the Dreyfus trial in motion by reporting a discovery he had made concerning the similarity of the handwriting on that famous memorandum, whereby Dreyfus had been convicted, to that of an officer of more than doubtful reputation, Major Esterhazy. Picquart was promptly shipped to a somewhat exposed post in South Tunisia to meditate on the undesirability of being a non-conformist in the secret sanctuary of the upper echelon. Following which, he was confined for sixty days in a fortress; then, discharge from the army. During the feverish days of the Zola trial, I recall seeing him in his light blue tirailleur uniform at the Palace of Justice, a witness for the defense, booed by the crowd.

Such suspicions floated around him then! He was even accused of communicating with a spy, because he had written to a friend that he planned to go to Basle to see Bocklin, a harmless reference to an art museum and an artist he admired.

He also admired Wagner—this being, to me, much more understandable—thus inspiring a very fine oratorical observation by Pressensé. A fugitive from the newspaper *Le Temps*, Pressensé, though an erudite writer, had none of the qualifications of a great orator; but on this occasion, his address to the Chamber was one of the most memorable in all my experience as a young deputy. General Picquart had seen fit to punish a group of officers from the Laon garrison for having attended some religious ceremony in uniform, and in a body. Pressensé, a socialist, and a free thinker, but also President of the League for the Rights of Man, as well as an unyielding defender of the liberty of conscience, no matter from what direction it was attacked, mounted the rostrum to protest. He moved with difficulty, suffering atrociously from rheumatism, and made his speech without gestures, both arms suspended in a sling made of two huge black silk handkerchiefs. I shall never forget the impression of a human tree-trunk, speaking in head-tones, uttering lyrical insolences, notably the one in which he upbraided Picquart, who had endured so much persecution himself, for persecuting others. "May I remind the Minister of War that there is one thing more melancholy than the Twilight of the Gods! It is the Decline of a Hero!"

In this same discourse, Pressensé, free of sectarian anti-clericalism, gave the Socialist Party a beautiful lesson in tolerance when he reminded them of the funeral of Cardinal Manning in England, "where the embroidered banners of the Church and the red flags of the proletariat were lowered in salute over the same tomb."

As for the speech itself, it was eloquent, but unjust. General Picquart, cabinet minister, had never renounced his past; but he failed to justify the gesture that had hopefully placed him in charge of the War Department. Clemenceau's choice had been more spectacular than useful.

The creation of the Ministry of Labor, a rejuvenated legacy of the 1848 Revolution, had greater importance. A new voice in our government, it supplied a real need in the relations of the State with the world of the workers, and has continued, without knowing the fall from grace that has destroyed similar creations unable to survive the subordinate combinations which caused their birth.

With one of his customary quick decisions, which were often countermanded by equally rapid reversals of judgment, Clemenceau opened wide the portals of the Republic to the unions he was soon to engage in battle. By the fact that a ministry had been created to receive them, the collaboration of unions and State became a reality, from which I tried to draw a few inferences later. In granting it legal sanction, I wanted to establish a government policy unaffected by political fluctuations. This was not too well understood.

Clemenceau's uncontested choice to head the new ministry was Viviani, long a leading figure of the Socialist Party. He had departed from it, as I was to do, but remained, as I was to remain, faithful to its ideals. Like Jaures and Millerand, he belonged to the independent socialist group, but had not been willing to abide by the pact of unity and adhere to the principles on which it was founded.

Viviani, in turn, influenced by a certain regard for my studies of unionism, and the requests of some prominent labor leaders, had chosen me as his cabinet director and chief of personnel, thus strengthening my authority in the manipulation essential to the fusion of elements drawn from several ministries. It was necessary to form a single unit out of this diversity. Our installation bordered on the picturesque. The ministry had been created, but nothing was ready. Not even the budget appropriation. We had to rush around to a bookshop in the Rue de Bellechasse to buy paper for our first official pronouncements.

But what a happy, constructive, earnest tumult animated our young group: Metin, who followed me as minister in the same ministry; Langeron, future prefect of police, until the Germans judged him undesirable; Peyronnet, later vice-president of the Senate; Candace, so beautifully black, with a heart of gold, which did not prevent him from handing President Lebrun the sacrificial knife at the time of the great Vichy hara-kiri; Coudor, Fagedet, prefects of the Republic!

The ancient archbishopric in the Rue de Grenelle, vacated under the separation law, had been made available to us; but this necessitated a complete rearranging and refurnishing. Not caring to bother with these details, Viviani gave me carte blanche. As a reporter in the Ministry of Beaux Arts, a few years earlier, I had continually called for more respect toward our historical legacies. I now had an opportunity to make a practical demonstration while turning this splendid specimen of 18th Century architecture, a replica of the neighboring Hotel Biron, into government offices without disfiguration.

Bossuet declared he needed a certain ease in his surroundings. Since the task of organizing this ministry had befallen me, I was eager to have those who worked there find, practically intact, the decor of an epoch when buildings were built with an eye to the convenience of the thinker.

It so happened that I was the principal beneficiary; for our transfer to the Rue de Grenelle just barely preceded my nomination as Minister of Labor. I loved the harmonious setting all the more, because of my personal effort to make it so. Visiting the premises on later occasions, I noted that the habitual vandalism of our government agencies had once more prevailed.

But prior to our installation in the archbishop's old palace, consecrated as we were to recently deconsecrated edifices, our temporary home was that of the now-defunct *Direction des Cultes* in the Rue de Bellechasse. M. Dumay, its head, did not long survive the separation of Church and State, which had marked the end of his function. But his ushers, modest and helpful collaborators, were still at their accustomed places, assuring the perpetuity of administrations and adding a philosophical touch to the passing of regimes. Their bewilderment was great at the sight of our offices, which in their time had known only the soft-shod tread of bishops, invaded by the clatter and the clutter of trade unionists. The usher assigned to my door, an old fellow with a name that seemed to come right out of a Russian novel, Degerine, waved his arms skyward, and lamented the lack of manners of these workers' delegations who tramped in uninterruptedly, as if aware that the house was theirs.

I can still see the ditch-diggers perpetually in a state of extreme agitation, led by Pataud, "King Pataud" as the Press called him, because he had plunged Paris into darkness during a nocturnal strike. Viviani, in a recent speech—replying to Jaures, who had complained of the governmental policy of irreligion in these words, "You have taken away the old song that soothed human misery,"—passionately maintained that social justice was being accomplished by men whose religious faith had been lost. "We have, in a magnificent gesture, extinguished lights in the sky that will never be relighted." Forain, in a cartoon depicting the leader of the band of street-light extinguishers, used this caption: Is our Minister pleased with us?"

These strikes lacked the amplitude of the miners' manifestations in the Pas-de-Calais, and more particularly the winegrowers' riots in the South, which Clemenceau had to contend with at the same time that the Catholics were spiritedly complicating the inventories of church property. But the metropolitan strikes, affecting the population of Paris in their daily routine, made the exploitation of fear relatively easy. On the eve of May 1st, 1907, there was a rush to hoard food—in those happy times, there was food to be hoarded—and Clemenceau, like Lyautey, concluded that a show of strength was necessary, if one wanted to avoid having to use it. He packed fairly dense masses of troops into the streets of Paris.

Nothing happened. But just as some officers had resigned rather than enforce the church inventories, there were some—though notably fewer—who felt a certain repugnance toward this street duty. One of them, a young lieutenant in field uniform, saber at his side, revolver at his hip, stalked into the Labor Exchange to say so. Unlike Pressensé, defending the officers who attended church ceremonies at Laon, I do not recall a single Rightist voice raised to defend this lieutenant, who had merely put into practical use the words of General Boulanger at the time of the strikes at Decazevills: "The troops will share their rations with the strikers."

If Paris, except for a few instances of fright, remained quiet, such was unhappily not true of other places. Strikes were frequent. Our ministry settled some of them. In spite of an absence of any organized and obligatory arbitration formula—there was none even in 1936—our efforts at conciliation were not unfruitful. The new ministry was playing its part well; and Clemenceau gave it his complete confidence. I often went to report to him, on behalf of Viviani, but—with this difference from 1936, for strikes were not precisely an invention of the Popular Front—the Premier did not permit himself to be swamped with conflicts of this kind which should be solved, if at all possible, outside of politics and without his direct intervention.

We did not settle them all, and the headlong speed of some of them, colliding with the stubborn strength of Clemenceau's stands, resulted in bloodshed, as was the case at Draveil.

Understandably, there were immediate repercussions in the Chamber of Deputies. That legislative body was more than reasonably busy with interrogations and with the great oratorical duels between Jaures and Clemenceau, highly interesting, but serving to dig a deep ditch between two men and two parties. Radicals and Socialists were battling in the National Assembly and throughout the nation.

This agitation, by driving quite a few republicans toward social conservatism, was obviously not of a nature to create an atmosphere favorable to the policy of reforms, which had been undertaken. The workers' organizations were gravely at fault when they would not make life any easier for a man who, all his political life, had battled for their liberty, and for a government which had given them undeniable proof of its sympathies. And now the employers were giving him a difficult time. Looking back, one can hardly believe the bitterness of the campaign unleashed by the application of the policy of a weekly day of rest. If there was one social law on which Christians and Socialists should have been in complete agreement, this would seem to be it. Yet what protests, what attempts to cripple it. Now, it is so much a part of the national life, that no reactionary force could prevail against it.

But whatever the miscalculations and the difficulties, neither Clemenceau, nor Viviani, nor those under their command, were easily discouraged. A policy of reform, of confidence in democracy, had been started. It would be continued.

With the full support of Clemenceau and the incomparable talent of Viviani, the discussion of the great Retirement Law was in progress in the Chamber and in the Senate. There, also, what incomprehension; and on both sides! But that is a story that particularly concerns me, for it was in the application of the law, which was entrusted to me, that most of the trouble started.

Up to that point, on purely parliamentary ground, so long as it was a question of voting on a law, if the battle was lively, the eloquence of Viviani, expended in numerous speeches, under Clemenceau's ministry and the ministry of Briand which succeeded it, victoriously overcame an opposition emanating from just one side of the Assembly. From the day the government finally began work on a social construction which had figured on so many programs and never materialized, all those who were on the side of democracy had the decency not to raise any objection. The obstacle came from the interested people themselves.

Those speeches of Viviani's made the days difficult for us in the ministry. Here was a man who did not compose joyously! A man of refinement, extremely sensitive, beneath a brutal exterior, with a style that bordered on the gross, he labored at his speeches with all the torment of a Flaubert. Not that he put them on paper. He wrote nothing; whereas Waldeck-Rousseau at least wrote out a few essential notes as guide-posts. But several days in advance, Viviani walked with his speeches, in his room, his office, along the quays, and sat with them at the theater, where he seemed to find in the rhythms of the music and the dialogue an aid to his own thinking. So much so that his phrases, without a word committed to paper, were completely formed in his head, and his speech somehow blended the flexibility of the unwritten line with the precision of an oft-revised text. For he was extremely thorough, and had a great admiration for Waldeck-Rousseau, frequently questioning me about him.

It had been my good fortune to work in close association with three of the greatest orators of an era that numbered many: Waldeck-Rousseau, Viviani, Briand, and to witness their methods and the state of mind in which they composed their speeches.

How varied the ways to achieve the same goal! I shall not speak of Jaures, the god; I followed him less closely; and I am not sure that one could analyse his method. The Michelangelo of the art of oratory, the perpetual flow of his genius, appearing in the splendor of the spoken word, seemed to be able to construct speeches that lived their own life, detached from him, like the sublime figures the other placed on the Sistine ceiling.

Viviani rather reminded one of those polished orators of the Restoration he knew so well, and admired so much. But where they wrote, he spoke. One can imagine the tension of mind such preparation required.

Thus, in the days preceding his appearances, he was not of a mood to meet with his collaborators and colleagues. As for the customary quantity of crashing bores demanding audience! A night or two before the speech, he shut himself in his room; and I had to use all my ingenuity in protecting his privacy.

This sometimes aroused the anger of Clemenceau.

"You hear . . . bring me your minister, dead or alive!"

The Tiger was not one to deal lightly with his ministers, even those he liked the most; and this was the case with Viviani. On one occasion, if he was not quite dead, he was seriously stricken with the grippe; and he was scheduled to appear in Parliament to reply to a difficult interrogation on the subject of the weekly rest period, with a goodly section of the governmental majority ready to give ground. Doctor Vidal, an excellent physician, though not an Aryan—today, in 1943, he would have some difficulty in practising his art—testified that Viviani should, on no account, leave his room until the hour of battle. Clemenceau consented to let him alone; and Viviani's performance before the Assembly was excellent. The Premier, whipping his majority along, after Viviani had seduced them, ended a short and energetic appeal of his own with the words, "Gentlemen of the Radical Party, I'm waiting for you!" And the Radicals voted *his* way. Then, while we were giving the profusely perspiring Viviani a rub-down in the ministers' room, Clemenceau walked in, peaceful and paternal, and said to him, "Now you can get back to bed and stay there as long as you like!" It was the same tone he had used, a few days previously, to Albert Sarraut, who had slapped the face of an insolent orator. "Bravo! You've just signed your certificate of attendance!" In order to stimulate the zeal of the deputies, and halt the abuse of voting by proxy, a list was posted at the entrance to the Chamber, and the members were supposed to sign their name upon entering. The system was not of long duration.

I seem to see the new generations shrugging their shoulders, despite the heavy burden put upon them by our surrenders, when they read these recollections of a period when eloquence was in flower. Were so many speeches necessary to get a law passed?

Obviously, with a stroke of the pen, a dictator makes a decree. And, from the number of laws, often contradictory and often corrected, which figure in the *Journal Officiel* of the new French State, we can see that it is easier, if not better. But deliberation presupposes talk. Until the totalitarians and their imitators came along to upset the established order of human values, whether the State was a monarchy or a republic, it as conceded that laws could only be voted by chosen representatives deliberating among themselves. The rest was a question of measure; eloquence only held its place by reason of a common taste for culture; and the respect in which it was held by those who were incapable of eloquence made them prefer a proper alignment of the various arguments to mere disorder, made them prefer reasoning to mere excitement, an appeal to generous sentiments instead of vicious vituperation, to which the masters of slave states have accustomed us. For they, too, speak; quite a lot; but very differently.

In the years that preceded this present war, particularly since 1932, when the new arrivals in the legislature and in business affairs were those who had grown up during the First World War and retained a little of its brutality, assailed as they were by more pressing problems, I detected a certain disdain for the eloquence their predecessors had loved. One did not speak less; but one spoke less well. Neither Jaures, nor Viviani could have recommenced their long discourses. Clemenceau, with his clipped, direct style, would have held them better. But one would not have heard the sort of discussion, between Clemenceau and Jaures, in the corridors—a discussion finally settled by the erudite Pressensé—revolving around a quotation by Jaures from a play by Aeschylus, the accuracy of which Clemenceau contested. Or, at least, the attentive circle grouped around them would have been less numerous.

This taste for eloquence in those happy years, the prestige enjoyed by the great orators, had, at least, the result that in the tragic days of 1914-1918, though Jaures was dead, a Viviani was there to emphasize the magnitude of the struggle facing France, and a Clemenceau to fanaticize the nation. The words that needed to be said, were said well. We did not hear the like in September 1939, nor in June 1940.

The victory of the Retirement Law, much more peaceful, was a triumph of Viviani's eloquence, above all in the Senate, where the resistance was tenacious, but where one was still susceptible to arguments presented in good French and capable of arousing in old republican hearts the sentiments that finally decided them.

Meanwhile, Clemenceau was "looking Germany in the eye." The phrase was Paul Deschanel's, habitually somewhat theatrical, but that evening his tone was well-suited to the event. There was a diplomatic reception at the Elysee. Clemenceau had just come from an interview with the German Ambassador, the amiable De Schoen, to whom, in 1914, fell the unpleasant duty of declaring war on us. The interview could have been dramatic; it was pleasant. The Tiger's eyes were smiling under his heavy brows, as Deschanel congratulated him. With a Minister of Foreign Affairs docile to him, M. Pichon, he had taken solid hold of our foreign policy, somewhat humiliated since Algeciras.

The diplomatic operation had been smartly conducted; France came out of it with a double benefit, certain rights in Morocco and a strengthening of the entente with Britain. Germany profited not at all from the spectacular landing at Tangier.

However, the ministerial disembarkation of Delcassé was viewed with displeasure. The sacrifice of a French minister to the protests of a foreign power hurt our pride. Since then, we have seen a lot of it. We never even waited for defeat and the armistice to place us in a position where we could not do otherwise; on several occasions, in the course of the years that brought us there, foreign pressure, and not alone that of Germany, influenced the choice or the dismissal of certain ministers.

In 1905, we were more susceptible; even the happy results did not erase the unpleasant memory.

Clemenceau tried to make us forget, and I could well understand his outbursts of anger in the halls of Parliament, when he protested that his work was being impeded by a lot of questions.

One day, Viviani had returned from a Council of ministers in a preoccupied mood. German diplomacy, which knew so well how to maintain certain points of friction, enlarging or diminishing them at will, was momentarily exploiting a slight incident: German deserters from the Foreign Legion had been apprehended at Casablanca, and the German consul, or one of his aides, who had attempted to protect them, had become involved in a brawl, was arrested momentarily, then released. Germany had protested, transforming this banal episode into a question of principle, attacking the Legion's recruiting system, among other things.

Was it permissible for a consulate to extend its protection to a foreigner engaged in the service of France? Germany proposed that the question be submitted to the Court of Arbitration at The Hague. France accepted. Was the incident closed? No, and this is what justified Viviani's preoccupation: Germany asserted that alongside the judicial question, which would be settled at The Hague, there was another aspect of the matter, and she demanded that the French authorities apologize for attacking the prerogatives of her consul.

Thus, by a political detour, any decision favorable to our thesis would be rendered vain in advance. Clemenceau had indicated to his cabinet his intention to refuse. The judgment of the Court at The Hague, and nothing more. Some of the ministers appeared to hesitate; but Clemenceau, like Waldeck-Rousseau, was not only the President of the Council, he was the head of the government. And when, in his office at the Ministry of the Interior, he replied courteously but firmly to M. de Schoen, the German Ambassador mentioned the possibility of graver consequences and threatened to leave Paris. Clemenceau quietly handed him the book of train timetables. M. de Schoen really loved Paris, where he was well liked. He remained.

When the Retirement Law was voted, early in 1910, I was no longer Viviani's assistant, but his colleague, and about to become his successor. A vacancy had occurred in the parliamentary representation of my home district, in the very section where I had been raised. It would be presumptuous to speak of destiny; but I must point out that, by a curious coincidence, it happened on the same day that I had accepted another candidacy in Paris. One of the sections of the 12th Arrondissement had as its representative an old Socialist, Paschal Grousset, who had not adhered to the party unity, and had remained independent. He had participated in the government of the Commune, and not unimportantly, since he was its Minister of Foreign Affairs; in which capacity, he boldly signed his government's notification to the representatives of the great powers. This had not gone to the head of this witty journalist, who often referred to himself as the "minister foreign to affairs." He long retained this sense of humor common to many "communards," well-known to me in my political youth, and who acted as if the years of prison and exile had merely been an interruption that failed to age them. I hope it will be the same with those of us, more or less exiled within our own country at the moment, when we rejoin the struggle.

Well-suited to the republican sentiments of an advanced type prevalent in this arrondissement, which comprised the Faubourg Saint-Antoine and the Bastille, he had maintained mastery over the district, despite the efforts of the unified party members, who resented his independence. But as he aged, and illness kept him away from the Chamber of Deputies, he made known his intention to step aside at the forthcoming elections, or even before. He had agreed to support my candidacy, especially since I had replied to the offers made me by refusing to accept unless the offer came directly from this veteran militant.

On November 20, 1908, he asked me to come and see him for the purpose of working out the details of my campaign. I found him lying on his bed in his little house near the Bois de Vincennes, very different from the alert man I knew in the days of the Waldeck-Rousseau ministry, but still meticulous about his attire, not liking sartorial demagogism any more than the other kind.

The meeting was, at first, rather melancholy. The old militant was feeling the same bitterness his teacher, Blanqui, had known on the evening when, released from his prisons, he gazed down on Paris from the top of Montmartre, at the life of the city mounting toward him, and asked himself if he had not wasted his own. Was it worth all the struggles and suffering to finally encounter this ingratitude?

But the fighter rallied quickly; he thought only of handing over to another the continuance of his task, and of helping him win a victory which would still be his own.

I returned to the Rue de Bellechasse and prepared to tell Viviani the result of this interview at the hour he habitually signed his correspondence, an administrative task of which he was not fond, and frequently interrupted with conversations on topics closer to his heart. On my desk, I found a telegram from the Loir-et-Cher, informing me of the death of M. Tassin, deputy for the second district of Blois. Their deputy since 1869, he had returned to that post after serving as Senator, losing his seat in the Senate in January, 1906. It was the following May that he was re-elected deputy, defeating the incumbent, a M. Ragot, whose earlier election he had sponsored at the time of his own arrival in the Senate. A long enmity had since arisen between them. What an imbroglio!

Nothing was more typical of the system of voting by district than these struggles which, for years, divided the countryside lying between the Loir and the Cher, created for every harmony. "Tassinists" and "Ragotards" feuded for fifteen years amid hatreds at tenacious as that of Montagu and Capulet. They penetrated right into the bosom of families, and, as in Verona, prevented or shattered marriages. Only the tomb was lacking; my compatriots have a sense of measure. But each nomination of a functionary, each grant of subsidy, each measure, small or large, taken in the interest of the district or its inhabitants, who were keenly sensitive about them, was the object of a bitter contest, and the success obtained by one faction was noisily exploited to convince the other of its impotence.

They mutually accused each other of being supported by the Rightists, a grave reproach for Republicans at that time. In one instance, it was true; to get rid of Ragot, the Right voted for Tassin who, however, in an already lengthy career, had hardly treated them gently.

Left to themselves, the two contestants, who had been

friends, and whose politics were not very different, might have become reconciled. But the debate had been further inflamed by a curious personage, journalist by profession, but honest, I believe, as honest as he was spiteful, and certainly without ambition, for he made no attempt to profit personally from the real influence given him by his newspaper articles over a period of half a century, their terms little varied, or by the number of services for which he had been the go-between, or the fear he inspired. He edited Tassin's local journal, serving him faithfully, but doing him a disservice by attacking his adversaries in a manner too injurious and low to be pardoned. His paper, an accomplice in all the vices of the system of voting by arrondissement, and the servitudes engendered by local tyrannies, was ironically named *L'Independant*. Personally, I was the object of his hatred for a number of years: precisely those that elapsed between my entrance into politics and his death.

I had been involved, rather more than I would have wished, in the Tassin-Ragot feud, of which none of the aspects were to my taste, little disposed to see the countryside I loved, its people intelligent and shrewd, from whom nothing could detach me, even some temporary ingratitude, compensated by so many enduring proofs of attachment, given over to the morality of a stagnant pool, such as Briand denounced in his speech at Perigueux.

But it happened that, warmly received by the Republicans, who had urged me to give a few lectures, I went so far as to describe *in abstracto* the potentate of the district. "He is a Moderate, an Opportunist, a Radical—and he will be a Socialist tomorrow—depending on the color of the majority ballots. As the hue is accentuated, his epithets become more full-bodied. He has served the Empire, betrayed Gambetta, overthrown Ferry. The successive ministries have had no more faithful supporter until the day when it was more to his interest to combat them. Even then, he waited for the decisive session, and, with the ministry fallen, changed his ballot after the battle. His opinions have modified, but his relations with his constituents have remained the same; at once slave and sovereign, domestic and despot; he carries out their commissions and makes them tremble. Just as he has served all ministries, all ministries have served him; as he was not very reliable, they served him in order to keep him on their side; and the services rendered have given him a solid situation. Not a road-worker who doesn't owe his job to him; not a postman who is not at his orders; not a schoolteacher he has not threatened to displace; not a ministerial detour he doesn't know; he is friendly with the ushers, haughty with the senior clerks; the ministers detest him, but let him have his way, because he has a capricious ballot and a tenacious manner of solicitation!"

This was seen as a portrait of Tassin . . . .

And as, to organize democracy and remove it from these personal battles, I had founded committees for a big Leftist union, destined to educate the electoral body, no one doubted that it was to prepare my candidacy. This was imposed upon me at the elections of the general Council of 1904, where Tassin solicited the renewal of a mandate he had held for thirty-six years. I had the feeling that, if I refused, those who had followed me in this attempt at organization would let it drop, the moment it failed to lead them to the battle they expected, and for which they had entered the fold. To battle, then! I was beaten, and, in truth, justly so; to one who knew nothing of my motives and the constraint put upon me, it must have appeared distasteful that I was trying to take his departmental mandate away from an old man who, on the local scene, and in his own manner—though it was not mine—had rendered indisputable services to the district.

I swore I would never do it again, and, while continuing my work of organization and, if possible, union in this divided district, I declined any sort of candidacy in the legislative elections of 1906.

This time, it was Tassin's friends who asked me to become a candidate, with his consent, between the two ballots, either because they were weary of these battles and were looking for a new man, or because Tassin, who had run against Ragot and had been unable to defeat him on the first ballot with the votes of his friends alone, hesitated to have the issue settled by the arbitration of the Right.

I declared that I would only run if Ragot also invited me, and if the Left would unite in my name. Which did not happen. M. Ragot was beaten.

This picture, summary and old-fashioned, of an election in 1906 will help one to understand why, when Tassin died, his friends and those of Ragot agreed to offer me the candidacy. This time, I accepted, for it was presented under the sort of conditions I had wanted.

And I quite believe—and I say it unrestrainedly, never having been a victim of this sort of phobia—that the Right, feeling the battle to be useless, and having no candidate of their own, many old friends of my parents and of the companions of my youth, though not sharing my ideas, gave me their votes. This unanimity in my own countryside, which I consider as homage to the esteem in which my family was held and to the memory my father had left, is one of the prides of my public life. I continue to be grateful to those who passed it on to me. The severe struggles I have had to endure since have not made me forget it.

Therefore it was not because I had any complaint against the system of voting by district that, as soon as I was elected, I took an active part in the campaign for electoral reform, which marked the end of the legislative session.

On the contrary, I could have been accused of ingratitude, and many friends in the district were disconcerted. The attachment to the vote by district was considerable, as in most of the districts; if the use made of it was often vexatious, the elector's preference for it was not only explained by the benefits he could draw from it, but also for reasons denoting the good sense of the community, which likes to know the one it elects, and a very honorable feeling of attachment to his person, which compensated for other errors of public life.

But the enlarging of the balloting was too closely linked to that construction of the Republican State, which was my constant preoccupation and should have been the objective of the Left after their victory of 1902, for me not to bring to it all my ardor of a newly elected deputy. Whatever attachment I had for my district, which was my own countryside, therefore more than just an electoral district, I never sacrificed my ideas for it. This was what cost me the election in 1914, my compatriots deciding that I was leading them a bit too fast down roads which they were obliged to take later, and from which they have not deviated, the natives of Touraine and Berry, slow-moving, but solid in defending.

I plunged deep into the battle for Proportional voting, less, I must confess, for the Proportional idea itself, but because I detected a breach in the citadel of District Voting. Quite rightly, the Republic had intrenched there during the days of Boulangism; it continued to hang on to it to great disadvantage, in my opinion. The Proportional method, with its mathematics, to which Painleve was to add the complications of "relationship" between the lists, was no more pleasing to the voter than to me. The voter wants to know, when he votes, what the result of his ballot will be. Difficult with these complicated calculations! They recalled to my mind that problem which the "ancients" put to their "sons," when I was preparing for the Ecole Navale: "Given the length of the ship, and the height of the mast, calculate the captain's age."

One day when we went to see Clemenceau with a delegation led by Charles Benoist, father of the Proportional system and future Monarchist, the Premier, ferociously in favor of the District method, because he believed in majority rule, gave Benoist a similar problem, but in much cruder terms.

Fundamentally, my preference would have gone to the ballot of the majority list, that of Gambetta and the Gambettists, which permits the separation of majorities that are clear, and can govern as long as universal suffrage gives them its confidence. But the Right and the Socialists were equally opposed to it. It would have been even more impossible to risse above the compact mass of District Voters with it, and they finally gained the victory by a series of maneuvers wherein they were past masters.

Rightists, Moderates, and Socialists made up the main body of the attacking troops, with Jaures contributing his great voice. Together, we went out into the country, multiplying meetings at which the diversity of the stellar attractions assured success. The Radicals played little, or no part. Those who did join were immediately somewhat suspect. My friend, Abel Ferry, sent to the Chamber of Deputies in a local election at the same time I made my entrance there, found no pardon, despite his historic surname. Aside from the Socialists —all were not enthusiastic, but Jaures was there—too many Republicans repeated the error of 1902.

Briand, Clemenceau's successor, after his Perigueux speech, could scarcely do otherwise than come over to our side. He even gave the campaign the momentary support of his government. But he experienced at his own expense, notably in the Senate, the power of resistance of those who wanted to preserve the *status quo*.

Extremely sensitive to the fluctuations of opinion, for which he really had, as he said, antennae, he never committed himself again. And upon his return, although our campaign still continued, he maneuvered to "drown the fish," something at which he excelled.

Thus, in order that a reform so bitterly contested should not succeed, the government did not even need to give a show of hostility, an air of disinterest sufficed, under the pretext that the system of elections was a matter for the Chamber to decide. There was a pretence of abstaining from the discussion; and no use was made of that *ultima ratio* of the parliamentary regime: the question of confidence. This was just about the procedure adopted by all the governments in this matter, before the war of 1914, and before the present one.

It is not surprising that it took the First World War to bring about any change; in the elections of 1919 and 1924, one saw a blend of the proportional and a premium for the majority, completely satisfying to neither. It had, however, the advantage of breaking away from a balloting system that was too restricted, and which, when re-established, appeared no better.

But already the problem had been surpassed; it should have dealt with something more than the mode of balloting. And when I set these already distant recollections alongside the more recent ones left me by these unfruitful attempts to reform the State, which an electoral reform would have aided,

I have the impression that a selfsame fatality weighed upon both, at very different and unequal periods. The reform of the State, attempted by the Doumergue ministry, after February 6, 1934, was jeopardized by the political significance given it, which ran counter to the reiterated affirmation of the Left, resulting from each appeal to universal suffrage. By their hostility or their abstention, a great number of Republicans had contributed to giving our campaign for electoral reform a less aggressive, but analogous significance. And just at the time when Briand accorded it the governmental support without which no important reform can be carried out, by a counter-blow from those same social problems that had assailed Clemenceau, the majority that supported him and his policy was not such that his intervention could suffice to republicanize a reform which the Republicans mistakenly distrusted. I apologize for this old-fashioned phraseology and outmoded classification; one writes one's recollections with the colors of the time; and these, without having kept their early freshness, had not faded; the republican sentiment, others call it "prejudice," still played a prominent part.

While our campaign continued, there were other conflicts, in a rather strained political atmosphere, more capable of retaining the attention and arousing in the Chamber something other than what the official journal calls "*mouvements divers.*"

After having overthrown so many ministries, Clemenceau had found a means of overthrowing himself. Delcassé had directed an attack against him, quite unjustifiably. The two men had no love for each other, though a mutual anglophilia should have reunited them, at least in a common foreign policy. Their characters were quite opposite; personal disagreements added to it; Clemenceau, a solitary man, but capable of exciting rare devotion, never forgave anyone who hurt his friends; Delcassé had insulted one of them, the Comte d'Aunay, who was very close to Clemenceau.

Goaded by the banderilla of his little opponent, Clemenceau bounded about the arena, evoked Algeciras, reproached his adversary for having brought France to the point of humiliation. Those who had little taste for the methods of this autocratic democrat—two complementary words which, unhappily for the Third Republic, were too rarely united—seized the occasion and exaggerated the importance of Clemenceau's angry blast. One of those parliamentary effects—and it is disquieting to see the fate of a government depend on them—brought about the fall of Clemenceau's, aided, it must be added, by the Socialists, who had endured such sharp treatment from him that they would not save him now.

Briand was called upon to form a cabinet, inaugurating his record series of eleven ministries, not counting those where he remained as Minister of Foreign Affairs. Already, he displayed a taste for conciliation and assembled a cabinet which he termed one of "relaxation." It does not appear doubtful to me that, still very close to his origins, very conscious of the power of the trade unions, and fundamentally attached to the party he had abandoned, he interpreted this conciliation in its fullest sense and not unilaterally. He intended to appease the Left as well as the Right, in the matter of church inventories and in the matter of strikes.

But men can only partly make up for the absence of institutions. Because the place of Trade Unionism in the State had not been regulated, the relations between the unions and the State were going to affect the destinies of the Republic for a long time, and leave no other choice than repression or the abandonment of certain permanent necessities of the State. The flexibility of Briand could no more avoid it than the strong-arm method of Clemenceau. In fact, during the railroad strike, Briand came even more directly in conflict with those he had meant to handle gently, and who, at the end of his career and his struggle for peace, formed the most ardent part of his following.

In the course of the debate on the mobilization order, which had broken the strike, Briand was induced to use words that roused the Extreme Left and part of the Left to tumultuous protests, of which the *Journal Officiel* gives only an attenuated impression.

"One right is superior to all the others; it is the right of a national collectivity to live in independence and in pride. But a country cannot leave its frontiers open; no, that isn't possible. And I'm going to say something, Messieurs, that will probably make you rise up in wrath; if, to defend the nation's existence, the government had been unable to find, in the law, a way to remain master of its frontiers, if it had not been able to use for that purpose its railroads, that is to say an essential instrument of national defense, well then, even if it had to resort to illegality, it would have taken that step. . . ."

When read, unless Briand altered the text in making corrections, the word "if" appears to play an important part. At the time, it went unnoticed. Many who protested with unusual violence at this blow struck, in peacetime, against the right to strike, would have been more reserved *if*, amid the dangers of war, the national defense had been threatened and the borders left unguarded.

As this was not the case, one only remembered that from the lips of the man who, at one time in his career, had been the propagandist of the General Strike, had come an appeal for "illegality." From the Left, shouts of "Dictator! Resign!" Painlevé, who had entered Parliament with me a year ago, and later became in turn one of Briand's ministers and his President of the Council, now made a maiden speech in which he impassionedly asked Briand "since when he had discovered there was a Nation!" And a former attorney-general of the High Court of Appeals, M. Cruppi, who had since become a deputy and a minister, cried out, "It's abominable!" The Leftists of that period had, in regard to the Constitution, much livelier susceptibilities than their successors of 1940.

In the uproar, Briand was unable to make himself heard. But, with more than one trick up his sleeve, as a veteran of noisy meetings, he made use of a procedure which I greatly regret was not employed recently by the colleague we delegated to bring our protest at the time of the Vichy abdication, when the National Assembly, in its haste to commit hara-kiri, prevented him from speaking. Briand leaned down toward the stenographers, finished his speech to them, without anyone else being able to hear a word, but with the whole country able to read it the next day in the journal which was still called the *Journal Officiel de la Republique*.

Then he walked out, accompanied by Laguerre, who had become calm in his old age, but had been young and full of insolence and talent in the days of Boulangism, and seemed quite enlivened by all this tumult. Perhaps he imagined it was all about to recommence. Briand had no such intention, not wanting to push his parliamentary operation that far. He was not over satisfied with this eagerness. One saw in it a symbol and one cried scandal! How far away it all seems!

It was already remote, in those Geneva years, when the freedom of our conversations authorized me to recall to Briand that turning-point in his career, when he had taken another route that brought him closer to his origins and to his heart. He spoke of it with his customary detachment and that serenity that hovered over the last years of his life.

At the time, he took it badly. One day I was riding with Viviani and Briand, from the Chamber of the Senate, in Briand's car; looking at me with a glance at once ironic and benevolent, he said to Viviani, "How young he is! And to think that he'll become, like everyone else, an old traitor, an old renegade!" Which, in my estimation, I never did. Nor did he. He merely waltzed once with Reaction. It has always had a taste for seducing and utilizing those who come from elsewhere, instead of seeking in its own ranks, where they are by no means lacking, men capable of leading it into battle, if not to victory.

It is none the less true that all this weighed heavily and long on the policy of the Socialist party. The Briand case was added to the Millerand case, to increase the difficulties encountered by those who believed in the idea of participation. By these somewhat brusque evolutions, it was readily demonstrated, some said, that a Socialist in the government had difficulty in remaining a Socialist, which is of course perfectly true, if Socialism isn't there to surround him and sustain him. And that is precisely what the Participationists hoped for.

It weighed also on politics in general, until the war of 1914 and its aftermath put things in their proper place. The Republic, deprived of Gambetta, Ferry, and Waldeck-Rousseau, did not have too many men of worth, capable of becoming leaders of government, and Briand was one. Though the opposite of Clemenceau, he was of the same class. And here was the same struggle, which had set Clemenceau against Jaures, divided the Republicans, and hindered reforms, starting again. It even took on a more personal aspect, since the Socialist party had built more hopes around Briand; and certain controversies of the rostrum between Jaures and him remain in my memory like a laceration:

"Ah, Monsieur Jaures," said Briand, "you reproach me for my policies, but I have seen you bleed from the attacks of the party!"

"True," replied Jaures, "but I never abandoned it!"

This struggle, again throwing the Socialists into the opposition, put Briand at the mercy of the conservative elements, who were not always on the right, following a somewhat summary and already obsolete geography. Quite a few radicals had become recalcitrant to social reforms. Briand was thus prevented from accomplishing them, although his comprehension of their necessary evolution seemed to point to him as the one to carry them out, and which he certainly hoped to do when he came into power. If he arrived early, it was only after 1914 that he again became himself, and gave the measure of his value.

At that time, in France, one could never hold out long against the attacks of the Left. The reduced number of those who ventured to affirm their conservatism permitted them to carry weight against the government, but not to form one and to fight under their own banner, in the English way.

Two days after the vote of confidence in the railroad strike, the cabinet resigned. Following a method he was to use frequently, and which was his way of assuring governmental stability amid changes of ministries, it was Briand who formed the new cabinet. Caillaux, at the moment rather at odds with Briand, irreverently called it the "ministry of the household." It fell, in turn, after a few months, and was replaced by the Monis-Berteaux ministry, of which I was a part, and wherein Caillaux was Minister of Finance.

Chapter Seven

FROM THE RETIREMENT LAW TO THE EVE OF WAR

I enter the government.–My friend Berteaux.–Application of the Retirement Law.–Battle in Parliament.–Propaganda in the country.–Mabilleau and the Mutuality.–Premature deaths of the Republic.–Controversy over the High Command.–Fall of the Ministry.–Agadir. Messimy, Minister of War.–The Three-Year Law.–Visit with Freycinet.–The Messimy-Boncour project. –The Berne conference.–My last interview with Jaures.

It is said that Condorcet, having developed a vast program of national education, which the Convention of 1792 was to set in motion–and which the Third Republic was to finish–met at the foot of the rostrum the Minister of War, Roland, bearing the declaration of war against Austria. This unleashed a long series of wars, which was to keep France under arms, and Europe breathing hard, until the treaties of 1815.

Apart from the grandeur of this historic encounter, it is just about what happened to me when, as a young Minister of Labor, all wrapped up in a great social work, the events that marked the end of the government of which I was a part swept me into preoccupations of quite another order, before sending me to war myself, and causing me to battle twenty years to prevent another.

The Republic was then presided over by a man of finesse, despite a fleshiness that lent itself readily to caricature and raillery at which his experience and good-nature took no offence. He had seen so much in his already long career!

M. Fallieres was one of the last representatives of a generation which had matured in opposing the Empire, gaining from this experience a measure of prudence and republican resolution. Moderate in temperament, and by political geography, he too was not moderately republican. His election in 1906, over M. Doumer, like that of President Loubet in 1899, had a clearly Leftist significance, and, in the course of his seven-year term, he never forgot it.

He was the first who ventured to call Clemenceau to power. No clear-cut indication of universal suffrage or the majority, when the ballots were counted, ever encountered the slightest hostility, open or disguised, from him. He was entirely loyal. To this was added a judicious exercising, by discreet opinions in ministerial councils, of the prerogatives given him by the Constitution, or, at least, as much as it was the custom for presidents to exercise, which is to say—excluding the principal ones. Of the various Presidents of the Republic under whom I have deliberated, I retain the impression that he was the most useful.

The fall of Briand, coming after that of Clemenceau, having shown that, even with leaders of great importance, the hostility of certain parts of the Left created a situation endangering the duration of a cabinet, Fallieres wanted to try a government which would not encounter such opposition. Thus was formed the Monis ministry, which was in reality that of Berteaux.

Radical with Socialist tendencies, as well as an ardent patriot, Berteaux, who had occupied a seat in the Chamber through several legislatures, had taken an important role in this and the preceding one. It derived from his work on committees, his constant presence at discussions, the vigor with which he always thrust himself into the forefront of battle, but also from the sympathy he exuded, and his extreme affability, always ready to go into the district of a colleague in difficulty and speak for him, or to aid with a discreet purse those to whom fortune had not been favorable. A citizen of Paris, a stockbroker, he conducted his business as competently as his political affairs and those of his constituency, which he kept in hand as no one else could. Before the automobile age, his fast horses permitted him a certain ubiquity. His activity was extreme without being haphazard.

On the one hand, people pardoned his advanced ideas in consideration of his patriotism, and the order he had restored in the Ministry of War, after the Affair of the Files. On the other, one pardoned his wealth by reason of the use he put it to, and the aid, in every form, he brought to republican propaganda.

In addition, he was dynamic and combative, physically brave, as ready to slap a parliamentary face as to explain his reasons, but above all eager to shake the hands of numerous friends, some obligated to him, but all of them faithful and profoundly attached.

I was among them. And in the first row. From the time of my entrance into the Chamber, our jacobinism had reunited us, equally advanced, equally patriotic, equally concerned with republican defense and national defense. A mutual interest in army matters was added to all the reasons we had for understanding each other.

I had made my maiden speech at a morning session, on an unimpassioned subject, since it had to do with customs-duties, but was none the less of concern to France, because it dealt with wine. The Chamber gave me a friendly reception; Berteaux in terms of particular affection. And, feeling sure of his imminent arrival in a position of power, he told me of his plans, quite unexpectedly opening perspectives for me which I had never thought would happen so fast. In Parliament, as in the Palace of Justice, the veterans had that sort of kindness toward their young colleagues. I have tried, for my part, to continue that tradition; I do not believe I received much gratitude therefrom; the young men of the war years had known a rougher youth; they were more hurried and less sentimental.

Berteaux, returning to power, simply reinstalled himself in his beloved Ministry of War. And to reassure the Senate, a bit alarmed at him, M. Fallieres, who knew so well the assembly over which he had presided, proceeded as he had with Clemenceau, when he first made him Minister of the Interior in Sarrien's cabinet; he prepared for the rise of Berteaux by forming a cabinet oriented toward the left, with

Berteaux as the activating force, but with M. Monis, former Keeper of the Seals under Waldeck-Rousseau, presiding, since he enjoyed the Senate's well-justified esteem. For, if fortune, in any of its manifestations, was never favorable to him, he was very cultivated and very sure, a Senator from the Gironde district, and Girondin in his tendencies. Injured himself, and Berteaux killed, at one of the early aviation shows, his ministry succumbed, and he returned to the ranks, silent and dignified, creating no difficulty for his successors. They proceeded to forget him when, retired from political life, and donning again his lawyer's robe, this former Premier of France accepted the humblest cases before the lowest courts. I shall always be glad that Poincaré intervened on his behalf upon becoming Premier, after his term as President of the Republic. Knowing my loyalty toward my former chief, he called me to the ministerial bench one day and asked what could be done discreetly to help this man, who had profited so little from public office.

This was rather usual with the heads of State of this corrupt Republic! Poincaré himself! And Millerand, as we used to see him at the Palace of Justice, studious as a probationer, after being President of the Republic! Others who only compromised, by their term of presidential office, more enviable situations and more fruitful employment.

I knew M. Monis quite well at the time of the Waldeck-Rousseau ministry and the preparation of the High Court trial. I lent an eager ear when the friendly Berteaux called me back from the Loir-et-Cher, where I was rusticating far from the political crisis and its preoccupations, and mentioned me to Monis as one of the collaborators he wanted to have in the new government with him. And as Viviani, after guiding the passage of the Retirement Law, wished to retire, the burden of applying the law on which we had worked together was placed on my shoulders.

And when I say "burden," I am not doing so in the manner of those who appear to be crushed when given a post they have ardently coveted. I had not sought mine; but I am not concealing my joy at joining a government thoroughly in the political line to which I was attached, alongside a man I admired, to apply a law that had been the great work of my former chief.

But, young as I was, I was not so naif as to have any illusions about the difficulties awaiting me upon my entry into the government. The parliamentary battle had been won; the social battle was about to begin. The obligatory nature of the retirement payments, and more especially the prescribed withholding by employers of the amounts due from the employed, which had already given rise to serious controversies, particularly in the Senate, was sure to encounter even more resistance in practice before it would become part of our lives. It was a whole new concept of social security, requiring an extremely complicated organization, presupposing formalities and a discipline which, for some years, had shown in Germany the happy results it could bring, but against which one had no trouble in arousing a French temperament, already only too inclined to want to evade the issue.

It was one thing to award pensions to old workers; but the question of ways and means was sharply contested. Many times, in the course of the discussion, Viviani had made the demonstration, and finally won the day. But, as often happens, more than one who voted for the law as written, made the mental reservation of softening its application, which means reducing it to nothing. And then, when would the law be applied? Once a popular vote had been taken; there would be plenty of time to wait. . . .

This demagogism was not in my temperament. When the law was voted, the promise had been that the retirement payments would be in effect by July 1911, at the latest. Having accepted the post at the head of the Ministry of Labor, which was charged with keeping that promise, I caused to be inserted in the ministerial declaration that on July 3, 1911, workers and peasants eligible for these payments would start receiving them.

And when the usual reporters who covered these ministerial arrivals in power asked me to outline for them a vast program, I replied, "To apply the Retirement Law, July 3, 1911."

This abnormally laconic response brought, from Henri de

Jouvenel, a very fine article in *Le Matin,* where he allowed his pen to run free. By joining two likenesses, my photograph and a portrait of Robespierre, he contributed to the legend of a resemblance, truer I believe, with other men of the Revolution who are nearer my heart, if I hold to the theory of the "block," like Clemenceau of the 1890's. One does not pick and choose in the French Revolution, a tremendous event, which has made a different world, and gone far beyond us.

To apply the Retirement Law. . . . First, it was necessary to obtain from the Council of State the project for the rules of public administration, without which the law, remaining on the heights, would have been practically inapplicable. I did not need the close collaboration of several months with the Council of State to convince me of its important role, one which should have been always reserved for it in legislative construction. Without being too consular, I would have seen no disadvantage—and I can see even less disadvantage today—in the role being a preliminary, instead of a posterior one; that, without binding the Chamber and the Senate, the Council of State should clarify the texts on which they were to vote. Stendhal, whose works are being reread by Leon Blum in his prison, would not have admired the style and the equilibrium of the Civil Code, if it had been born of the improvisations of the assemblies.

My first visit was to M. Coulon, a man of lofty conscience and great judicial learning, besides being a staunch Republican. From him, I obtained my office administrator, M. Tirman, a young master of petitions, from a famous administrative family, who went on to make a splendid career for himself. He was in charge of liaison. I shall always be profoundly grateful to these men and to the Council of State for enabling me to keep the promise that had been made and which had become my responsibility.

In parallel action, it had been necessary to set up new services in all departments, reaching millions of wage-earners obligatorially, and, optionally, all those artisans and small proprietors who wanted to sign up and receive the benefit of the new law.

Since direct contact with the prefects seemed essential to

me, M. Monis was kind enough to authorize me to summon them to my office. Over a three-day period, I held a series of interviews with all the prefects of the nation's eighty-six departments, to their surprise at first, and to their great interest as they received their instructions. It was the custom of the time to speak disparagingly of the prefects of the Republic, and to picture them as solely preoccupied with elections and re-elections. In various stages of my public life, I have always found them devoted to the administration and interests of their department, many of them having a taste for action and the judgment for it, which is as it should be with holders of political office, so long as the government gives them the proper orders and allows them enough initiative. No, the prefects of the Republic were not so bad. And they would have been better, if a more comprehensive system of balloting and a stronger Executive power had given them more protection from parliamentary pressure and from the local potentates. It is only regrettable that a good many, out of a habit of obedience, have continued to accomplish on behalf of the Vichy government tasks which were the opposite of those for which the Republic had assigned them.

At the time, little prepared as they were for the new preoccupations I had given them, they brought to the organization and propaganda of the Retirement Law a most useful contribution. Many had the excellent idea of enlisting the aid of their subprefects, who were abolished later, under the pretext of economy, after being retained in budget after budget for thirty years. Was it not preferable to justify their existence by making them active agents of these social laws voted by the Republic, which were overburdening the town-halls and hampering the mayors? Those dignitaries found it convenient to have someone near to inform and advise them; and it was not a matter of indifference to the Republic to have that someone a representative charged with defending it and causing it to be loved.

I took advantage of the Easter vacation to verify, by unannounced visits to the prefectures, the execution of the instructions I had given them, with the authorization of the Minister of the Interior–President of the Council.

Finally, using a propaganda procedure which has since become customary—but until then little used by the State, which left the benefit to its adversaries—posters and tracts were handed out in profusion, explaining in the simplest terms this rather complex law, marking its advantages in precise fashion, by figures and dates.

A counter-propaganda had been unleashed on the eve of the application of the law, when the ruling for public administration, taken at the advice of the Council of State, transposing into practical order, and in detail, the somewhat theoretical and general prescriptions of the legal text, brought out the reality and the mechanism of the obligations.

Part of the employer group, already imbued with social spirit, gave proof of their good will, preparing in their factories and enterprises the necessary measures to carry out the law, in advance. But another part of the proprietors protested, declaring such measures impossible. I am not aware if this group was the more numerous; it was certainly the one that made the most noise, supported by the parliamentary opponents of the law.

But it did less damage than an important section of the working-class itself, misguided as to its real interests, and upheld with extreme violence by the left-wing of the Socialist party, despite the adjurations of Jaures. As much by loyalty toward a law he had wished for and voted for, and a government that sought to apply it, as by the far-sighted views habitual with him, Jaures denounced the danger of this sabotage, and judged that the law, which already was worth a lot by itself, had even more value by reason of its future benefits.

In full agreement with Jaures, who thus brought me his inestimable aid, and strongly sustained by Millerand, to whom I owe this homage, I pointed out in the strongest terms all during the defense I was compelled to make, that this law, which guaranteed the workers against the tribulations of old age, should be widened, after this vast experience in which I was inviting them to participate, into one that would cover the other risks of a laborer's life: sickness, invalidity, unemployment, the matter of accidents having already been ruled upon by the law of 1898.

My arguments were of no avail.

Because the age of retirement was considered a bit remote, it was termed a *retirement for the dead.*

Because the amount of the pension was set a bit low, while waiting for the financial mechanism to prove itself, it was termed *a laughable retirement.*

Lastly, the law, quite justifiably, as I persist in thinking, even though recent provisions have sought to change all that, was founded on the capitalization, not on the distribution, so as to constitute a collective patrimony, which would give rise to other social works: low-cost housing, workers' gardens, sanatoria, rest homes. . . . It was therefore easy to show a disproportion between the money taken in and the pensions paid out. So it was termed *the swindling of the retired.*

And, strange to say, on these points, for once, adversaries of the right and left of socialism, the diehards of the employer group, and the extremists of trade unionism were in accord.

It was under these conditions, in a relentless cross-fire, that the debate began in the Chamber and in the Senate, provoked by multiple interrogations, for three long days in each assembly, and which I had to face alone, the Premier having been injured in the same aviation accident that had caused the death of Berteaux.

I had chosen to begin with the Senate, where the attack would be more courteous, but at the same time more perilous, in view of the opposition manifested at the time the law was voted, and which the campaign against its imminent application had evidently strengthened. If the battle could be won in the Senate, the Chamber would certainly follow suit.

It was won, but not without difficulty. The night before the balloting, it still remained uncertain. Friends in the Senate advised me to pay a call on M. Ribot, an old parliamentarian, a moderate, who had fought against the radical ministries and Waldeck-Rousseau, for which the latter reproached him in lively fashion, reminding him that he had started by overthrowing Gambetta and Ferry. Contrary to the usual procedure, when he became a senator, he also became, if not reddish, at least open-minded about social questions, and had favored the Retirement Law; his aid would be decisive, I was told. So I went to see him in his beautiful and vast apartment in the Rue de Tournan, near the Senate, after the manner of veteran barristers who lodge near the Palace of Justice to be closer to their work. He was benevolent, encouraging, without committing himself too much. On the third day of the Senate debate, he had still not intervened. After my long speech on the second day, I was compelled to return to the rostrum; this time, by certain signs that are unmistakable in an assembly, I had the impression that the cause was on the verge of victory, if it had not already won. It was then that, in the center, M. Ribot, stretched out full-length in his chair as usual, stirred his long body and raised his hand. He was ready to address the assemblage. I was much relieved. This time, the day was won. He was poised, reserved, condescending toward the young minister, but finally made it clear that he would give him his vote, thus bringing in his wake a number of moderates in the Senate, who had been impressed by the very brisk and hostile arguments of certain clever jurists and embattled industrialists, M. Touron for example, author of several dangerous amendments at the time the law was under discussion.

The cause had so clearly triumphed, that it was almost compromised when the matter of a vote of confidence became the order of the day, and two rival proponents of the vote each demanded the privilege of presenting it. Clemenceau and Combes were the pair who thus sought to befriend me, but neither wanted to give way to the other. I do not recall how I solved the dilemma without offending either of these two important figures, who both had great influence in the Senate. But it was finally arranged.

In the Chamber, the struggle was just as long, but livelier. The opposition, in the Senate, had been based on principles: for or against the obligation; for or against the obligatory withholding tax; for or against capitalization; for or against my concept of the application of principles already established by the law, but which some intended to question on the grounds of practicality. The opposition, in the Chamber, was doubled by the political intrigues arising from the virtually open succession occasioned by the death of Berteaux and the inability of the Premier to appear, following his injury.

The campaign against the retirement pensions had stirred public opinion. I had obtained from the government the assurance that it would not compromise in the matter of a law it had agreed to apply. I had, therefore, become the vulnerable point. By downing me, the hoped-for ministerial crisis would be opened. My struggle was all the more difficult, because the Left of the Socialist Party had been unleashed. Guesde was bitter. And a youthful group from the Cher and the Allier, sent up in the last elections, borne by the demands of an agrarian socialism as narrow as it was aggressive, notably a man named Brizon who, during the war, was to be one of the few *Kientahliens* and *Zimmerveldiens* of the party, cut in constantly during my argument. For quite different motives, the Center was active. For other reasons, a few urgent radicals were afire; but only a few. For the most part, this party where I had so many friends, especially among the younger members, supported me without fail, as did Jaures and other socialists who had courageously adopted a similarly favorable position in respect to this law.

By evening of the third day, the intrigues had accentuated. Although, in a long discourse, I had refuted, point by point, the slogans circulating against the retirement pensions, in spite of the future perspectives I had opened, in spite of the powerful aid Jaures had brought me, it was going badly. I was made aware of it by the fact that many of my colleagues of the cabinet had absented themselves; I was quite alone on the ministerial bench; if the government was to fall, better not share the responsibility. This enraged me; young and impetuous, I rushed to the rostrum. And it must have been that my very attitude showed an energetic will to win, because there was a storm of applause before I said a word. Those who wanted to save me, and save the cabinet, recomforted, displayed their determination not to be played with at this point. Without consulting anyone, since it had been decided at the Council, I put forward the question of a vote of confidence for the entire ministry!

I won. And I prepared to apply, without weakness, a law thus doubly consecrated by the will of Parliament, and to take action, as I had announced, against employers or workers who resisted deciding to defer to the lofty impartiality of the Court of Appeals any points that might seem doubtful in application.

I was not allowed the time.

A few days later, on quite another question which already demonstrated our preoccupation over our relations with Germany, and served as a pretext to finish off our ministry enfeebled by the death of its guiding spirit, we were overthrown. I was not a part of the new team; and they, without absolutely abandoning the application of the law, seemed more disposed to let time take care of its entrance into our habits and customs.

However, I did not believe that my departure should interrupt the campaign I had begun. I was convinced, I repeat, that this reform, already important of itself, was a necessary experiment for more important ones to come. I already saw it being enlarged into a law of social insurance similar to that which had given the German worker and, as a result, German industry a security such as we needed in our country at this time.

While the forces of reaction and demagogism had formed an alliance against me, I had found efficacious support among the mutual aid societies. Too often disdained by socialism, in my opinion, and too timid so far in their objectives, which they usually restricted to insurance against sickness, they were—by reason of their deep penetration even into small towns and rural districts, and the importance of their resources, amassed by high assessments, subsidies, and numerous gifts—quite capable of serving as a strong ally of the new law. I had wanted the ruling on public administration, deliberated by the Council of State, to exploit thoroughly the possibilities opened by the text of the law to the autonomy of the various treasuries, regional, trade union, and mutual aid. If the obligation to participate was the basis, there was nothing governmental in the organization I had conceived; that was to remain flexible, thus doing away with the red-tape and bureaucracy too frequent in social laws, and which have not aided in their popularity.

In the great majority, the mutual aid societies understood this quite well. At that time, they had at the head of their federation, an outstanding man possessed of a dynamic quality which he passed along to them. A schoolmate of Jaures at the Ecole Normale, and of Monseigneur Baudrillart also, Leopold Mabilleau had been a professor at the University of Toulouse and that of Caen before coming to work in that Social Museum founded by M. de Chambrun, a relative of Savorgnan de Brazza, the great humanitarian who gave us the Congo. Mabilleau's astonishingly varied and rich intelligence—for he spoke well and with equal ardor on art, philosophy, literature, and social sciences—soon enabled him to grasp what a powerful factor in starting a social organization among the habitually refractory peasants and middle classes, these mutual aid societies could become. Generally prosperous, reassuring by reason of their capable handling of the funds in their possession, they spanned the nation with a vast network of groups already formed.

With a broader concept and an incessant propaganda, holding up well, like a good citizen of Touraine, whether at the banquets of which the mutual aid societies were so prodigal, or at those educational reunions of which he gave them the habit, Mabilleau made of Mutual Aid a real social force, which his understanding and friendship placed entirely at my disposal, at a time when so many others dodged the issue, for the application of the Retirement Law.

It was on him then and on Mutual Aid that I leaned during my own propaganda campaign, for I had not considered my work at an end simply because I had gone from the charming setting of the ministry in the Rue de Grenelle. It was all the more necessary since—under political pressure, or more correctly, corridor emotionalism—the legislators seemed disposed to let the principle of obligation rest, and not demand the compulsory withholding of wages on which the entire mechanism of the law was based. One had to convince, since one did not dare demand, and use persuasion because, after all that agitation to obtain the law, one drew back before the first difficulties of its application.

I undertook to "do the provinces." In the joyous company of Mabilleau, who, in sampling the wine of honor or approaching the banquet table, gave a performance compared to which mine was admittedly inferior, we appeared at Roubaix, Bordeaux, Saint-Etienne, Nantes, and elsewhere.

Neighbors in Touraine, how many evenings we spent, until the twilight of his life, in his ancient abbey of Villeloin—which he had had restored, and where he had gathered together his treasures of the France and Italy of the Middle Ages and the Renaissance—talking by the light of the lamps, for he refused to put in electricity or central heating, in front of the huge fireplace where the first fires of autumn were burning, as we lived over those tours of ours in 1911 and 1912.

We recalled how, surrounded by the presidents of the great "Mutuals," we tried to persuade their organizations what an outstanding part they could play within the framework of the legal obligation, today for retirement, tomorrow for invalidity, not to mention sick benefits, which they were so well equipped to handle. The collective patrimony of the treasuries, added to what they had already gathered by way of assessments, would permit the construction and maintenance of sanatoria, vacation camps, rest-homes . . . everything that the trade unions should have understood and undertaken, but which, for the most part, they had ignored.

Better carried out, better aided, if there had been stronger insistence on the principle of obligation, while developing the financial autonomy of the individual treasuries, here was, I am convinced, a work that would have contributed a profit when the Retirement Law, neglected before the war and paralyzed after it, was enlarged, as I had foreseen, into a Law of Social

Security. It raised more difficulties of organization, because it had not been preceded by sufficient experimenting with the Retirement Law and social autonomy.

Over almost every line of these last preceding pages, where I have allowed myself to relate, at perhaps unreasonable length, my recollections of a period on which I like to dwell, because they are those of a time when I was full of happiness and hope for the social task confided to me, hovers that of the death of Berteaux.

There would be a chapter to write of melancholy considerations on the premature passings which deprived the Third Republic of men whose statesman-like qualities or their popularity would have permitted them to play a role they never finished.

Gambetta, dead at forty-four, of the after-effects of a bullet wound from a revolver, under circumstances some still describe as mysterious.

Waldeck-Rousseau, dead at fifty-eight, under the scalpel of a German surgeon, who had consented to operate after French surgeons had refused the risk.

Berteaux, laid low in the midst of a rising career, on the aviation field at Issy-les-Moulineaux, his head crushed by a plane which, with improbable imprudence, had been allowed to fly over the spectators.

Jaures, assassinated on the eve of mobilization, the first victim of the great hecatomb, depriving French Socialism during and after the war of a guide such as it never could replace.

I admit that it requires more careful study, a personal knowledge of the projects we had planned, to evaluate the consequences—less widespread, but certain—of the death of Berteaux. The fall of our cabinet was the least of these. But if it had lasted—and it would have, if Berteaux had lived, supported as he was by a leftist majority, including the Socialists, who had returned to the governmental usages practised from 1899 to 1905—no one doubted that, as Clemenceau had succeeded Sarrien, Berteaux would have replaced Monis, played his hand personally, with every chance of winning.

And already, among republicans of foresight, with an eye to the passing from power of M. Fallieres, a candidacy was shaping up, having the backing of the Left and a certain amount of favor from the Right, which assured its presentation under the best conditions. Then what? Continuing to ride the hypothesis, but not the chimera, with his temperament and his unquestionable republicanism, could it not be imagined that Berteaux, without giving rise to too much distrust, could have lifted the mortgage which, since MacMahon, weighed upon presidential prerogatives? Clearly defined by the Constitution, bearing the right of message and the right of dissolution, handled by a courageous president who was above suspicion, here were the efficacious means of correcting, at least partially, the weakness of the Executive and introducing into French politics an element of continuity that was lacking.

Such were the reflections we exchanged with several colleagues, as we walked behind the gun-carriage which bore the body of our friend to the cemetery of Chatou. We had spent the night beside the casket in that same office of the Minister of War where I had sat with him most of the evening, a short time before his death. He had given me his last Sunday; he had come to preside at a banquet tendered me at Saint-Aignan by my compatriots of the Loir-et-Cher. The previous evening, I had visited him to go over the details of the occasion; then we conversed at length. He spoke of the preoccupations that assailed him, which the Agadir incident was so soon to justify, and the care he was giving our army; he discussed a new invention which was to give the artillery, a branch of the service in which he was a reserve officer, a serious advantage.

Although generally distrustful of civilian ministers mingling in its affairs, the army had confidence in him. He, so impassioned in political combat, had given undeniable proof of his objectivity in these matters. He had re-established things after the Affair of the Files, and, at our first council of ministers, had brought in two symbolic nominations, confiding two army corps, simultaneously and in the same decree, to Sarrail and Lyautey. This binominal made it clear that neither politics, nor conformist principles would dictate the selections made by the head of the army.

He gave every attention to the march on Fez, in regard to which M. Fallieres, with his good sense and the experience of a man who had lived through the colonial expansion of the Republic, mistrusting the military somewhat, said to us at the Council that care must be taken not to be drawn into a position where we would not have the means of holding on.

One might even write that the march on Fez was the work of Berteaux, not only in execution but in its decision. If memory serves, it was taken at his instigation, in accord with the Minister of Foreign Affairs and the Premier. The Council was only informed of it later. Some of our colleagues displayed a good deal of discontent, and I believe I was one of them. I had not yet undergone, during fourteen months, the inconvenience of submitting my negotiations in progress to weekly discussions, where divergent points of view on foreign policy were mingled with unequal wishes for the success of the minister entrusted with it. I profited by that experience when I began the negotiations that were to lead to the Franco-Soviet pact, informing no one but my President of the Council. But in 1911, I still had illusions about ministerial solidarity.

My solidarity with Berteaux was complete: I am quite sure I never raised the slightest objection to any move that he, with his keen sense of the interests of France, had decided, and which he guided for the best. Which did not prevent the newspaper *Le Temps* from printing in an article attributed to my comrade of the Waldeck-Rousseau cabinet, André Tardieu: "The Council of Ministers sought some satisfaction to give Messieurs Paul-Boncour and Dumont. It gave them the humiliation of France in Morocco."

Dumont and I, along with Berteaux, were considered the left wing of the cabinet. Thus we were tossed overboard together, when the succeeding ministry steered its majority more toward the center.

Thank God, we had not needed to ask, they had not needed to give us any, and there was no humiliation. France had affirmed her rights, and her troops had entered Fez on the eve of the day we buried the man who had sent them there.

But it was also the eve of a rather serious debate, the import of which was not immediately apparent. There was to be a discussion in the Senate regarding the organization of the High Command in time of war. And by the unexpected counter-blow this debate gave to the duration of an already enfeebled cabinet, one may consider that, among the hypotheses induced by the premature death of Berteaux, there is at least one which would be certainly verified: if Berteaux had lived, if he had had to stand up to that interrogation in the Senate, subsequently repeated in the Chamber, things would have happened differently. I knew his views on the subject; their presentation would have satisfied the preoccupations and, at the same time, stopped the intrigues of which they were the pretext.

It was significant that such a question arose in Parliament.

Since the great basic laws on the constitution of the army, it had hardly ever been asked: practically the only discussion had been the duration of service and the resultant reorganization. The question raised, it stirred up sufficient commotion for politics to take a hand; and nothing better reveals the already heavy atmosphere and the tension existing between France and Germany since Tangier and the German discomfiture, which that country wanted to avenge.

That explains the attention Jaures gave the Moroccan situation, his repeated interventions in Parliament, which could be interpreted as a systematic hostility to our penetration. I do not think so. A talk I had with him at the time of that march on Fez, which our ministry had favored and ordered, persuaded me that, while speaking out against possible risks and the exploitation of the natives, he did not view our colonial expansion with the uncompromising attitude of Clemenceau and the Radicals of 1887 against Ferry, nor that of the Socialists who later were to exclude Varenne from the party, because he had accepted the governorship of Indo-China.

Jaures divulged his sentiments in a little-known and quite remarkable political page: his own preface to the first edition of his *Discours*, published in 1904, and interrupted until such time as a young professor, M. Bonnafous, then our companion in the struggle and Jaures' disciple, later a regional prefect in the Petain government, Minister of Agriculture and Food, would again take up its integral publication. Doubtless, it will not be continued, at least by him.

In Moroccan matters, Jaures appears to me to be primarily preoccupied with the tension they were causing between France and Germany and the risk of war they entailed. He would have wished a preliminary accord to the enlarging of our own rights. In his way, he anticipated the idea of a common exploitation by a united Europe, that "Eurafrica" extolled today by a goodly number of those who decried it then. He retained the illusion, more understandable than it is today, that Germany was preoccupied with economy, not hegemony.

The atmosphere created by the landing of the Emperor of Germany at Tangier, and which was to become even heavier with the Agadir incident, made it necessary for Parliament and public opinion to come to grips with a problem hitherto left to the technicians. The lectures given at the War College by Colonel de Grandmaison, quickly seized upon by the Press after the rather lively incident resulting from them, brought to our attention in the Council of Ministers, were the relatively little-known starting-point of events and changes that re-echoed well beyond the closed circle for which they were destined. Here is what happened:

A strong advocate of the all-out offensive, Colonel de Grandmaison, who was to pay bravely with his life in trying out the theories he taught, had used this terrifying phrase—I cite it from memory, but it had so impressed me, I do not believe I am misquoting him—"I will have summed up my message in these words, only seemingly paradoxical, by saying that in the matter of attack, *imprudence is the best security!*"

General Michel, eventual generalissimo, who favored a

more cautious doctrine, and had foreseen with considerable clairvoyance the German march through Belgium, was very disturbed, and walked out of the room in protest.

Shortly thereafter, M. Provost de Launay, Senator from the Manche, a very ardent rightist, with whom I occasionally evoked memories of my Norman side of the family, registered an interpellation. Was it expressly directed at the General Michel incident? I do not have the text before me, and, detained at the Ministry of Labor by my Retirement Law problems, I was not present at the discussion. But it certainly resulted from it, and I can remember quite well the report we received at the Council of Ministers, for it caused considerable agitation during our last days. Answering the very direct and embarrassing questions of Provost de Launay, touching not only the subject of the high command in time of war, and the choice of a generalissimo, but also the fashions in which the government understood its relations with him, General Goirand, who had been brought from Nice, where he commanded an army corps, to replace Berteaux as Minister of War, and whose first contact with Parliament this was, spoke without nuances, and with the frankness of a soldier, but a soldier respectful of civic authority: "in time of war, the Generalissimo is the Council of Ministers; whoever held that rank was merely, in peacetime, the inspector general of the army, and in wartime, the commander of the armies of the North and the East."

This rigorously conformed to the legislation then existing, at the same time underscoring the resultant deficiency. It was only filled, legally if not practically, much later, after the war of 1914, by the law which became mine by reason of all the attacks it brought me, concerning the Organization of the Nation in wartime.

But, confusing the conduct of the war with the conduct of operations, people believed, or feigned to believe, the General's reply was a matter of thoughtlessness or sycophancy. What the *Journal Officiel* designates as "*mouvements divers*" greeted this unexpected declaration from Berteaux' substitute.

A clarification would have sufficed. With the President of the Council bedded with injuries, the Vice-President, M.

Perrier, said nothing. He was a very dignified man, an esteemed barrister from Chambery, white-haired, bearded in the fashion of Napoleon III which gave him something of the look of Victor Emmanuel, under whose reign he had studied law at the University of Turin, when Savoy was still Italian. At the time our ministry was formed, in the apartment M. Monis occupied at the Hotel Continental, he had been summoned in the middle of the night to take over the Ministry of Justice. He himself was astonished at the choice, for he was a very simple man, incapable of intrigue, even though the selection was perfectly justified by his judicial career and the high opinion in which he was held. But no one remembered that, by uninterrupted tradition since the beginnings of the Third Republic, the Keeper of the Seals was automatically Vice-President of the Council. Above all, no one had foreseen the horrible accident at Issy-les-Moulineaux, which necessitated his becoming chief of the cabinet during the unavailability of the Premier.

Perrier was obviously swamped by his task; during the long discussions on the debates I had to face regarding the Retirement Law, he held his hands to his head and complained to me about the heavy and unexpected responsibilities that had descended upon him.

His silence, after the incident, augmented the confusion. Next day, at the cabinet meeting, most of my colleagues showed great severity toward the Minister of War, who had put them in this embarrassing position. It seemed to me that a few of them were more concerned with the succeeding ministry than with the difficulties of our own. I am not aware by what signs M. Fallieres, who followed the discussion with great attention, noticed that I was not in accord. He called on me to speak. I tried to point out that the question was far removed from those in my charge. M. Fallieres insisted. "The question is grave. I want each one to give his opinion."

Thus pressed, I explained my viewpoint.

When I turn over in my memory the arguments with which I, a young minister, maintained that, in spite of its somewhat summary form, our colleague, the Minister of War, said nothing so very extraordinary, it appears to me that my ideas, in which the war of 1914 further convinced me, were just about the same as those I succeeded in getting adopted seventeen years later in the Law for the Organization of the Nation in Wartime. No one will accuse me of being changeable.

I advanced the argument that there would be not only a Northern and an Eastern Front, with the generalissimo-delegate in command; there would perhaps be an Alpine Front. The foreign policy of 1900 and the happy effort of M. Barrere, inspired by Waldeck-Rousseau, and later by Delcassé, had not yet produced their full effect. Despite the accord of 1902, Italy remained judicially and diplomatically bound by the ties of the Triple Alliance. And there might even be a Pyrenees Front, for Spain, at that moment, was creating rather serious difficulties for us in Morocco. There would be a Maritime Front and a naval war. Even though military aviation was in its infancy, it opened perspectives of its own.

Who would regulate all this?

The very conception and attributions of the commander-in-chief required modification. Would the government yield all control over him? Leaving in his hands, understandably, the direction of operations, would the government have no say in running the war?

And the co-ordination of military operations and diplomacy would be left to whose discretion? The war aims? Who would determine them?

Finally, who would assure the recruiting of these armies, these fleets, this manpower, and the manufacture of their equipment? What of internal security, the morale of the nation? The maintenance in good condition of the vast reservoir where the nation's armies could be fed in the course of a war that might be a long one? And, long or short, would it be waged without enthusiasm? Who would stimulate the effort, if not the men in whom the sovereign nation will have placed its trust?

And I concluded: if, in wartime, the Generalissimo could not be the entire Council of Ministers, as our colleague of the War Ministry had put it a bit, it was the Council that would have to direct the war effort even if, to effectively carry out its task, it would have to be less numerous—it was not then the plethora it became during the 1914-1939 period—modify its structure, unify its prerogatives, become a true Committee of Public Safety, not merely in name, but in action, a successor of The Other, which had not done badly during the Revolution.

It appeared to me that, during this explanation which the President of the Republic had drawn from me, and in which I poured out all my thoughts on the problem, Messimy was making signals of assent, and Fallieres did not disapprove. These veteran Moderate Republicans and patriots firmly upheld the idea of civilian supremacy; men of good sense, if they had no thought of interfering in matters of strategy, in war or in peace, they felt that the government should govern.

On the other hand, and I do not know why, these ideas aroused in M. Caillaux, who already loomed as the likely successor to our enfeebled ministry, a vehement protest in such violent terms that our friendly relations gave me the right to lead him aside, after the Council meeting, and demand—not reason, but his reasons! He mentioned the esteem in which he held me, but objected that I had allowed myself to be led astray by the ideas of Jaures. It was true that I was an admirer and a follower of Jaures; but in this case, my arguments had nothing to do with Jaures or Socialism; they were inspired by the eventualities of a modern war. And if, in the conviction with which I presented them, a certain ideology appeared, it was strictly jacobin and along lines which the great bourgeois, who, at several times in his career, showed himself to be a foresighted democrat, had not always resisted.

I believe this divergence had a great deal to do with my absence from the cabinet he assembled a few days later. But after several years, when the war came—that war on the conduct of which we had deliberated—many things happened that brought our viewpoints nearer together. At a critical moment—I had come to see him, on one of my leaves, curious to know what were the conjectures of his ever-alert and non-conformist turn of mind—he gave me a rare token of his probity and friendship. As I recalled our disagreement, he interrupted me.

". . . I'd like to say one thing to you. I don't believe I have often been mistaken. But I was mistaken that day. You were right. And you were right, too, in admiring Jaures. He saw clearly and far. . . ."

After being vigorously supported by them, when his own followers had deserted him, disagreements on financial questions separated Caillaux from the Socialists, who wanted no part of the great penitence his wisdom prescribed to slow down the postwar deficit, just as they rejected the offers of their former comrade, when I proposed in 1933 that we should re-establish together a balanced budget to free our policy from subservience to powerful financial interests and foreign countries. Caillaux seemed to be angrier with the Socialists than I was, while continuing to regard Jaures in the manner he had expressed to me.

If he reads these Recollections, he will not mind my recalling our conversation. It dates from a time when, under the influence of tragic events, an underlying truth expressed itself, free of the minor conflicts of politics.*

As a matter of fact, before those tragic years, during one of the events that preceded them, in which he played a leading role, one I still believe was useful, Caillaux had been able to ascertain that Jaures "saw clearly and far."

Our ministry had fallen, while the march on Fez, which it had prepared and ordered, had succeeded, considerably strengthening militarily our situation in Morocco. If one had taken into account a communication, made known to us by our Minister of Foreign Affairs, Cruppi, at one of our last council meetings, one would have believed that our diplomatic situation had also brightened. A dispatch from our ambassador to Germany, Cambon, stated that, standing alongside the Crown Prince at an official ceremony, a funeral, if I

* (1944) Caillaux died in the house where he was born at Mamers. In the tumult of events, it would seem that the disappearance of a man who was a statesman in the fullest sense of the word, has been received with excessive indifference.

remember correctly, the heir to the throne had said familiarly:

"So, you are in Fez. A great success. I suppose you'll stay?"

Cambon maintained a diplomatic reserve regarding the intentions of the French government.

"Yes, yes, you'll stay," continued the Crown Prince. And I believe he added, "You'd be perfectly right."

I do not think that any of us accepted, without distrust, this tacit encouragement from the Crown Prince, who had already begun putting himself forward, to his father's detriment, as the champion of the military party. To keep us watchful, we had the precedent of the Congress of Berlin.

At the Congress of Berlin, speaking privately with the representatives of France, Bismarck had pointed out Tunisia as a conquest worthy of ambition and the necessary complement to our Algerian possessions. "Go in that direction, and you won't run into me." In point of fact, we did not run into him. But Germany made capital of the move with Italy.

As for Morocco, Bismarck, before his dismissal, was finally unwilling to come to an agreeemnt. Von Hohenlohe, his ambassador in Paris, having sent a report on our projects, the Chancellor expressed to him the opinion that Germany could only rejoice if France awarded herself Morocco, for "she'll have plenty to do when she goes in." He is even said to have added, "We could afford to concede her this African expansion in compensation for Alsace-Lorraine." But when the ambassador asked if he should convey these words to Freycinet, Bismarck replied, "No, that's going too far. . . ."

With Bismarck gone, the Kaiser, throwing aside his policy, turned toward another, maritime and colonial, which brought him into direct opposition with England. There was little chance that he would allow us a free hand in Morocco without strong compensation for such an aggrandizement of our African Empire. Caillaux was sure of this, and it determined the direction of the infinitely difficult negotiations in which he was about to be engaged. Tangier had forewarned us. The gunboat *Panther* at Agadir was about to refute the words—whether a trap or a thoughtless remark—of the Crown Prince.

This time, war was only just averted. And everything that

could be said, before or since, to crush Caillaux does not hide the fact that, thanks to him, and without going to war, we were given enough a free hand in Morocco for Lyautey to build his empire. Even at the expense of a slice of territory in the Congo, it was worth while.

When, at the trial of the assassin of Jaures, I subpoenaed Messimy, who had previously made the same statement to me in a friendly discussion, he confirmed the fact that, meeting Jaures, a strong supporter of the government in its negotiations over Morocco, he had remarked, "Well, Jaures, we avoided war. We did all we could to avoid it. But if, despite our action, Germany had forced us into it, what would you have done?" And Jaures answered gravely, "Just what Gambetta did. I would have toured the country to activate the national defense."

While events were unfolding, heavy with a future that promised war, there was one that would only have moved the admirers of her smile, if public opinion had not found in the theft of the Mona Lisa from the Louvre in broad daylight evidence of a certain disorder in the Ministry of Beaux Arts.

The excellent Dujardin-Baumetz, who was in charge there and handled its affairs with so much pleasure that he should have been most successful, was even threatened in his subsecretariat. As I had been designated, the previous year, by the Budget Commission as a reporter for the Beaux Arts, I had made a voluminous report, which attracted some attention, and was published in book form under the significant title, *Art et Democratie*. Caillaux, who had already ceased to be hard on me for our divergence in the matter of the High Command, and desired to have me in his government, instructed Malvy, Under-Secretary of State in the Ministry of the Interior, to ask me if I would not consent to return to a cabinet post by taking over the Beaux Arts, there to accomplish the reforms I had recommended.

I do not know if the excellent Dujardin-Baumetz had wind of it, but from then on he was cold toward me. I had enjoyed the best of relations with him, when he was my neighbor in the Council of Ministers and drew, during the deliberations, some very lovely pen sketches, which he presented to me. They inevitably represented battle scenes, for he was a former militiaman and readily chauvinistic.

My friend and neighbor had no cause for anxiety. I had told Malvy that, while the reforms I had recommended in my Beaux Arts report were close to my heart—they still are, and a few of them have been accomplished—this was purely a hobby with me, an interlude between my supervisory work in the office of the Ministry of Labor and my own ministry, and that I desired to continue, from my seat in Parliament as a deputy, and in my free propaganda, to serve the ideas I had defended there.

And new preoccupations were presenting themselves to me.

Toward the end of the preceding legislature, Jaures had said in the presence of a group of deputies who, like myself, were rather astonished at his words: "The next session will be one of military questions."

Once more, he was far-sighted. After the debate on the High Command, which had disturbed the final days of our ministry, the election of Poincare to the presidency of the Republic was promptly followed by the presentation of a project for a law to limit military service to three years, which itself preceded a realignment of manpower and reinforcements, particularly in the covering units.

The era of armed waiting had begun.

It was Messimy who started it. Because Millerand had ordered the resumption of frequent military parades and Barthou had established the three-year law, one forgot that, since 1911, during the Caillaux ministry, Messimy reorganized the High Command and placed Joffre in charge.

Caillaux had selected Messimy to head the War Ministry. With Berteaux gone, the choice was excellent. Having served in the light infantry, and retained a good deal of its dash, a former staff-officer, he was sufficiently well-versed in military technique so that the generals could not silence him, sufficiently Republican to impose a respect for the Republic upon them. A man of great bravery, as he demonstrated when, in August 1914, he was let go rather cruelly for being too much of a jacobin. He acquitted himself admirably as commander of a light infantry group, then took command of a division, his military record bearing comparison with the best. It was a great joy to me, as Minister of War, on July 14th, 1932, to place upon his old uniform, kept since his war days, the "*cordon de grand officier de la Legion d'Honneur*."

Our friendship, formed during the ministry of 1911, and my increasing interest in these questions, made me a witness and confidant of the seriousness and consideration with which, in spite of a somewhat impulsive but always generous ardor, he viewed the delicate problem of the High Command in wartime.

Delicate, because it was necessary for the eventual leader of our armies to be able to choose his immediate subordinates, commanders of army groups, armies, and large units. Also, it was necessary for the General Staff to work under his direction. On the other hand, it meant reversing the decision to suppress the classification committees as Waldeck-Rousseau and Galliffet had ordered, thereby reducing, on a touchy point, the powers of the minister. And it meant interfering with the minister's direct collaboration with the Chief of Staff, who had been under his orders, but would now have to take them also from the Inspector-General, eventual Generalissimo.

Everything depended on the choice of this Commander-in-Chief and the guarantees of loyalty he offered. And what provision could be made to allow the minister some margin of valuation among the choice of collaborators the Commander-in-Chief wanted about him. This point was settled with the adoption of a rule whereby the Inspector-General would submit *three* names as his top aides, from which the minister could choose freely. It was a great mistake to allow this to fall into disuse, as I observed when I became Minister of War in 1932; and I hastened to put it into effect again, despite some opposition from General Weygand.

As for the choice of a leader, Messimy wavered between Gallieni and Joffre. I believe he preferred the former, rating him highly, as had Waldeck-Rousseau. But Gallieni was nearing the retirement age. Messimy chose Joffre, whose military merit, after The Marne, it would be presumptuous to dwell upon; but it can be said that he also possessed a Republican firmness indispensable for such an important collaborator of a government that still extolled its Republican origin. This was Joffre's reputation in army circles; and it helped considerably. His close friend Huc, of the newspaper *La Depeche de Toulouse*, has related to me many significant traits of Joffre's republicanism, and the tone of the general's proclamations amply indicates it.

Taking into account the strong currents carrying our High Command toward a policy of an all-out offensive, Joffre, who must have been a little distrustful of it, perhaps wanting to satisfy other tendencies, more specifically political and religious, took as his aide General de Castelnau, whose reputation on these two points satisfied Joffre's preoccupation. The solid good sense I observed in General de Castelnau, when I came to know him, first as a leader, later as a parliamentary colleague, makes me doubt that he ever condoned the imprudences that were the fashion early in the 1914 war, with Colonel de Grandmaison setting himself up as their protagonist. "Let's attack, attack . . . like the moon," protested General Lanrezac, and was subsequently removed from his command.

But it was the dynamic support given by the partisans of the all-out offensive that influenced the preparations, already under way, for the clash which the initiated, informed by the increasingly pessimistic reports of Cambon, felt was inevitable. It was that, and not the refusal of funds, for which Parliament was not to blame, that determined the direction of these preparations, meaning that all the necessary care was not given to the materiel, heavy artillery, permanent fortifications and field works, and the organization of reserves. And, after the fall of the Caillaux cabinet, Millerand, who replaced Messimy, put all his good will, which was considerable, and his stubbornness, not less considerable, into following the directives of the General Staff, without seeking to control them, or to correct anything erroneous, in spite of warnings from minds more clairvoyant and less conformist, in the very heart of the army. It required a certain amount of experience and a great number of casualties to repair these mistakes.

And I quite believe that the memory of this resulted in the extreme timidity we displayed during eight months of the war of 1939, when the fighting conditions were vastly modified by the use of mechanized equipment.

These controversies finally passed from military circles to parliamentary groups, or at least to those who, among the politicians, followed such questions. They prolonged the echo of the great debate on the three-year law, which absorbed a good part of the third year of the legislature, and in which I took an active interest.

It was logical that those who saw in a swift, lightning-like attack the one way to bring success to our arms, would give all their attention to the training of our regular army and its manpower. It was no less logical that those who remained faithful to a more prudent strategy were more concerned with organizing masses of reserves and, before throwing them against the enemy, waiting till that enemy had worn itself out attacking solidly entrenched troops resolutely committed to defensive tactics.

I can hear the objection: "Do both! Augment the effectives of the standing army and organize the reserves!" Obviously! But, along with the fact that the intentions of the High Command, which the government followed, were not headed in that direction, there were material obstacles: finances, cadres, armament. One could not simultaneously augment and strengthen the regiments already in service, including the first reserve classes, and equip, absorb, and train the mass of the other classes so as to make of them an instrument of war capable of being readied rapidly. In fact, it was not done; when the hopes the High Command had placed in the initial attack were frustrated, our reserve regiments, sent into action much earlier than had been anticipated, could not hold their ground. It took all Joffre's stomach to absorb the blow, repair the damage, and, by retreating, gather strength for the counter-attack.

It was not so much a question of electoral considerations

and the thought of sparing the country a sacrifice, but a certain concept, true or false, or rebuilding our army—a task everyone judged indispensable—which grouped a good part of the Left in opposition to the three-year law.

Jaures favored a counter-project for which his party, hesitant about committing itself, allowed him to assume full responsibility. He backed to the extreme limit the idea of the Nation under arms, extolling the militia system, reducing the time spent in the barracks to a few months, but arming the entire citizenry and training them, from youth to old age, in periodic exercises, in pre-military and post-military organizations. This was intended primarily for the future, and presupposed an international understanding among the workers, able to impose in their respective countries the same type of army of which Switzerland, a neutral nation, had given the example and had carried to a high point of defensive capability, but which encountered, in our case, and in view of the reasons for which the legislation was being prepared, the menace of the great permanent armies of our neighboring countries. It was a preview of how things might have been if the League of Nations had been a success, and if an international armed force had been there to parry the first effects of an aggression.

Furthermore, it was less a vote that Jaures sought, but a propaganda victory; and, first of all, in the bosom of his own party, so as to draw from it a positive affirmation of national defense and thus strike a blow against antimilitarism, which had become more virulent since the Dreyfus Affair, as a reaction against the savage nationalism that had sprung up, willing to keep an innocent man in prison under the pretext of safeguarding the honor and interests of the army. The intellectuals, brought to Socialism by the Dreyfus Affair, were much more easily led into antimilitarism than the older party-members, among them Guesde, who was pitilessly opposed to this deviation. It was all the more dangerous because it was now reaching the very sources of a patriotism, still living in the heart of militant workers of the past, who were not prevented by antimilitarism from joining in the protest of the people of Paris against the first capitulation of

Bordeaux. At least one might well fear its present effect. 1914 proved such fears to be groundless. But Jaures was apprehensive too, and that is why he wrote *L'Armee Nouvelle*, his last book before his death, a sort of testament of his political thought, a magnificent fresco of the French Army through the ages, at the same time full of extremely ingenious and new military ideas, some of which found complete justification in our miscalculations in the early days of the war. The book went much farther than the counter-project, somewhat schematic and premature, being little more than an attempt to set down his conclusions in legislative text.

The real battle—and it was thereupon that Jaures directed his efforts in his speech and in the course of the discussion—was conducted, not on the question of new reductions in the term of military service, but for or against the maintenance of the two-year period, and the use that should be made of it, by bringing to the maximum the organization of reserves.

Meanwhile, Messimy and I, and some friends who signed with us, had presented another counter-project. We had decided that under the present circumstances, a transitory measure was needed. In the thesis of the partisans of the three-year law, there was one grave argument—the gap in manpower between the discharge of the old class and the time when the new class had received sufficient instruction to be ready for use. The authors of the two-year law had realized this, and it was quite wrongly that, in the debates in progress, they were accused of short-sightedness and demagogism. For, as could be expected, the politicians were making capital of questions that should have remained exclusively military. It was argued that the three-year law was a condemnation of what had been accomplished in another climate of thinking and with another political majority.

The authors of the two-year law, supplying the army with the same number of effectives as the three-year law of 1899—by cancelling a large number of dispensations, whereby certain recruits had their term of service reduced to one year, either for family reasons or studies—were in favor of a pre-military education which would give the recruits a foretaste of army training before their actual term of service, thus reducing the gap in manpower previously mentioned.

Unfortunately, nothing was done about it. The military had no faith in it; the deputies had not given it much thought. Some contended that no one could receive adequate military instruction outside of the barracks; others felt it was unnecessary to require of the young men in their electoral districts an obligation and an inconvenience which the military authorities had not demanded.

This obligation, this discipline, Messimy and I expressly wrote into our counter-project.

A visit to M. de Freycinet strengthened me in these considerations. The young men of our generation had not the same offhanded way with their elders that the young men of today have with us. We conceded that experience had its uses. For quite some time, M. de Freycinet had abandoned the center of the stage, but continued to play his part in the wings; and Paris kept him in his seat in the Senate, grateful for his services of the past. To me, his slender figure and white hair still retained the image of the government of National Defense, which had not only saved our country's honor, but made the enemy uneasy. Having made a conscientious study of military textbooks before drawing up the project, I had been impressed by the writings of Von der Goltz, where one could judge to what point certain operations of our Army of the East, in 1870, threatening the rear and the communications of the German armies, could have resulted unfortunately for them, if the generals of our Second Empire had had more confidence in the weapon Gambetta had furnished them by his "nation in arms." Or if Gambetta had instilled this confidence in them by the somewhat rude processes the Committee of Public Safety had used against timid generals in the Revolution.

I chanced to attend a session in the Senate, after 1905, when M. de Freycinet, who had supported the two-year program of Berteaux, fought against an absurd proposition, originating in the Chamber of Deputies and aiming at a reduction in the training periods for the reserves. He was logical. And so was I when, as Minister of War, I battled against similar propositions, despite a press campaign inspired by the military camarilla opposing me. M. de Freycinet had ended his speech, which had been listened to religiously, by saying in his soft tones: "Upon the scales where the destinies of my country are weighed, I should not care to have the light weight of my ballot chance to tip them unfavorably."

M. de Freycinet listened to the outline of the counter-project that Messimy, for whom he mentioned his esteem, and I were getting ready to present. I cannot say that he was sharply appreciative; to affirm, was to compromise oneself; but he displayed little enthusiasm for the three-year law and the use the High Command planned to make of it, in view of the tendencies he knew so well and which alarmed him, fearing that the High Command would proceed to neglect the organization of the reserves.

We submitted our counter-project.

Faithful to the principles set down by the authors of the two-year law, we recommended a firm maintenance and a more judicious arrangement of the term of service demanded of the reserve, which the parliamentarians tended to lessen, and the military authorites to discard. We organized military preparation. But this effort regarding preparation and periods of training would take a little time to accomplish. Until these measures were able to produce their results, we estimated that a six-month extension of the term of military service in the regular army was necessary; the class just trained would not be discharged until the recently incorporated class had been instructed. This was known as the "thirty-month" project.

It answered the principal argument whereby the government and the General Staff sought to justify the necessity of the three-year law. And although this was not our sole preoccupation, which remained fundamentally military, it appeared to offer parliamentarily a possible transaction, capable of rallying a majority large enough to impress public opinion abroad. Those who were going to vote for the maintenance, pure and simple, of the two-year law had decided in advance to vote next for our counter-project. And they did, including Jaures and the Socialists, which was what the government and the General Staff had dreaded the most.

Joffre's good nature brought me proof of this later, in a quite unexpected manner. In the spring of 1915, I was a staff-officer from the detachment of the army of Lorraine, when the Commander-in-Chief came to visit us. Before moving up to the lines, he inspected us. Stopping in front of me, he appeared surprised:

"Aha, it's Monsieur Boncour. I didn't know you were here. Glad to see you. Are you happy here?"

"Yes, General."

Then we broke ranks to go to lunch. Joffre was having lunch with General Humbert, our commander; I, at the mess. At the end of our repast, an officer arrived, breathless:

"The Commander-in-Chief wants to see you!"

"The devil he does!"

Here is what had happened, as I discovered later. Upon arriving at the table, Joffre said:

"I didn't know Monsieur Boncour was here." And he added this delightful reflection, "Nobody tells me anything."

Gamelin, his chief aide, and very important to him, replied, "I didn't realize you were so interested in Boncour."

"I beg your pardon," said Joffre. "Very interested. You don't seem to know that he almost defeated our three-year law. That idea of his was very well-presented; it held up. Also, he was extremely courteous, very patriotic. I'd like to see him again before I go."

Thus it was that I was sent for, to the great surprise of my comrades and myself. When I arrived at the house where General Humbert made his headquarters, the Commander-in-Chief was descending the front steps with his heavy tread.

"Monsieur Boncour, I wanted to see you again before leaving your army. I have a very high regard for you . . . and yet, you nearly beat me in the matter of that three-year law."

I thought of an answer.

"General, it would have been the only time you were defeated."

He smiled and added:

"That was a very interesting project you submitted. It would have worked under other circumstances. But, you see, we didn't have the time."

While we conversed, Joffre, rotund and good-humored, posed on the steps, I at the foot of them, slim and respectful, hands at the side seams of my trousers, a photograph was taken of us. Later, when I had again become a deputy and Joffre had been retired, he outdid himself in graciousness by autographing it, as a souvenir of our double encounter, in the Chamber and at the front.

". . . We didn't have the time. . . ." In these simple, direct words, Joffre had made the sole valid criticism of a project which he recognized as potentially effectual. As he said, "It held up." War was a lot closer than we supposed, Messimy and I, and, with us, those who had confidence in our project. Perhaps, if we had known the proximity of peril, if we had been aware of those dispatches from Cambon, the one of November 22nd, 1913 particularly accentuating the gravity of the situation, we would have hesitated to present and defend this counter-project which we took seriously enough to want it to meet exactly the realities of the problem.

Perhaps it was because *he* knew, from the mouth of Poincaré, that Clemenceau voted for the three-year law.

For he had hesitated at first. In his opening articles, he had declared that he wanted, as did everyone, a strengthening of our military power, but stated that he had no particular preference among the systems proposed. I am convinced that if, from the beginning, he had made a choice, he would not have failed to warn me against mine with all the brutal frankness habitual with him and the benevolent interest he had shown toward me.

There was a good deal of talk at the time of an interview to which Poincaré had invited him, forgetful of past wounds, and following which Clemenceau came out in favor of the government's project, thus making a far from minor contribution to its success. This support was all the more significant, and of a nature to startle public opinion, because on all other points Clemenceau was in opposition to the government, not to mention Poincaré, against whom he fought violently at the time of Poincaré's election to the Presidency of the Republic, and treated roughly during the war.

Whereupon the question arose . . . whether to go to Berne, or not to go to Berne?

For my part, I went. Although Clemenceau grumbled under his moustache and shrugged his shoulders, when I came to take leave of him and his *Homme Libre*, to which Mandel, Buré, and Francois Albert all contributed at the same time.

If I were tempted to forget, a poster pasted on the walls of my district, during the 1914 elections, and which I kept for its artistic merit, was there to remind me.

It was the reproduction of a drawing by Hansi, the Alsatian artist, who held out firmly all through the German annexation of his province, and had specialized in devastating caricatures of the invaders. But this time, he had pictured Frenchmen: the parliamentarians who had taken part in the Berne Conference of May, 1913. He depicted them, dressed as choir-boys, placing palm branches at the feet of a plump Germania, her hair heavily-braided. Behind her stood two tall grenadiers of the French Revolution, who pointed at us, and said, according to the caption: "In our time, we talked differently to her." The drawing was well done; Hansi had talent: I have since spent some good moments in that pretty museum at Colmar, of which he was the curator, and which sheltered within its red brick walls the paintings of Grunewald with their lovely greens, and many souvenirs of Old Alsace. The grenadiers of the Revolution were certainly not displeasing to me, though the caption was unfair. But my adversaries at home had improved on Hansi's work; they pasted my photograph over the face of the choir-boy nearest Germania.

That was but one of the episodes in the war waged against me by some I recognize today among the few of our region who were willing to collaborate with the Germans. They criticized my journey to Berne with a hundred-and-twenty-three other members of Parliament, belonging to all the parties of the Left, and including Franklin-Bouillon, alongside Jaures and Sembat. Quite understandably, there was M. d'Estournelles de Constant, a descendant of Benjamin, who had constituted himself an early and obstinate defender of arbitration and peace.* At Berne, we were to meet members of the German parliament to talk of peace and the means of maintaining it. Doubtless, it was already quite sick; but it is not when one is well that one needs care.

Unfortunately, on the German side, the doctors were less numerous; the sampling less rich. The Socialists, be it said in their honor, comprised almost the entire German delegation; twenty-nine, out of the forty-five members the Reichstag had laboriously assembled to carry on the conversation. However, as they were men of good will, all went fairly well at first. Cordial exchanges of viewpoints took place. I was particularly friendly with a young Socialist deputy, Frank, from Frankfort, I think, who looked like Lassalle, and who was killed in Lorraine, in the same sector where I myself was fighting, on the other side. Gustave Hervé, almost ready for his conversion, but still the incarnation of the noisiest sort of antimilitarism, asked one of our German colleagues, "What is the most striking thing about this meeting, in your opinion?" And the German, respectful of authority, replied, "Having some of your former ministers here." There were, indeed, some of us present who had wielded governmental powers. It was only too clear that, on the German side, those who had come to the conference were merely members of the opposition, without real influence on the German government, and who, unfortunately, supported it, when it came to a decision of peace or war.

Trouble commenced when it became necessary to approach the question of Alsace-Lorraine. There had been some talk of not bringing it up, but how could it be avoided, when it was the very root of the debate? The brutal annexation, like all annexations, when not consecrated by the clearly expressed will of the countries involved, had raised a problem which, without an international organization to judge it—and we were far from that premise—could only be resolved by force. This was readily seen when an attempt was made to find a formula

* Caillaux, his colleague of the Sarthe, pays homage in his Memoirs to this fine man, often laughed at, but always esteemed, and who was ahead of his time.

acceptable to both parties. Even Jaures lost his fire, his ingenuity as well, for this most lyrical of orators had, upon occasion, the wiles of a peasant of the Tarn. But no formula could circumvent this: we Frenchmen must go on demanding something which Germany had no intention of returning to us, and our German colleagues would have been cut to pieces if they had consented to return it.

And while the train, carrying us home, traversed, between Basle and Delle, part of that Alsace, on a beautiful German Sunday, which so greatly resembled a beautiful French Sunday, I watched the strolling couples, the soldiers on leave, walking through the hop-fields, doubtless giving not a thought to what we had been deliberating, of the war that was coming, and which we were trying to avoid. I swore to devote a life, which then stretched a long way before me, to the establishment of an international order capable of protecting peoples against such calamities.

To quote from a tragedy of Corneille:
"*Pharsale a decidé ce qu'ils n'osaient trancher* . . ."

The pistol shot of Sarajevo, which was to touch off the powder accumulated all over Europe, had already been fired when, on July 12, 1914, I paid a visit to Jaures before leaving Paris for my vacation. He was also getting ready to depart, planning to celebrate Bastille Day in his constituency of Carmaux, which I was to represent later on.

Jaures lived in a quiet little house in the Passy Quarter, in the Square La Tour. During the last two years preceding the war, I lived in the Square du Ranelagh. I often used to accompany Jaures, who was an excellent walker and loved to go on foot to the Chamber of Deputies. The furnishings of his dwelling were unremarkable and bourgeois; his particular domain was a rather large study, situated on the second floor, and it was there that our last interview took place. How it remains in my memory! He was surrounded by books, the only ornaments in the room. I do not recall a single engraving, a painting, a print, or a statuette. He had no need of them, for all art was within him. Vandervelde told me that, on the occasion of a Socialist Congress in Dresden, he and Jaures had visited the Museum, and there, in front of the Sistine Madonna, Jaures had delivered a verbal improvisation of such magnificence, one would have liked to jot it down. But as they were leaving, Jaures stopped at the guardian's office, then rejoined Vandervelde. "See, I'm taking it with me," he announced joyously, displaying an atrocious painted plate with a traitorous reproduction of Raphael's masterpiece. Painting and sculpture provided a sort of springboard for his genius, rather than a repose for his eyes.

Yet I have heard him speak with great emotion of sunsets on the red soil of the Tarn, and the word-painting would have been the envy of a landscape artist. One day, at the Chamber, during a discussion of the budget of the Ministry of Beaux Arts, he gave an incomparable lecture on a mediocre sculptor he somehow admired, from whom came the busts we inaugurated later. A pity that such a head could not have been "caught" by a Rodin or a Bourdelle.

As I entered his room for what was to be our last meeting, Jaures said to me in his beautiful, trumpet-like tones:

"Well, Boncour, if you had belonged to the Party, as you should–and will–you still would have been against me at the Paris Congress."

A great Socialist convention had just been held in Paris, and Jaures had spoken in defense of a general strike in the event of war–not *any* war, according to the caricature some people made of his proposition, but only a war where no effort to maintain peace had been attempted by the government responsible, and where arbitration had been refused.

I replied, "It's true, Jaures. You know the respect and the admiration I have for you, but this time I should have been against you. Do everything possible to avert war . . . yes, one must demand that of governments. But if in spite of that, war breaks out? One's first duty is self-defense; one must try to win. The calling of a general strike, unless there is an absolute certainty that the same thing will happen to the enemy, could imperil national defense at an hour when every minute counts, Which is why," I added smilingly, "I would side with Guesde, rather than with you."

Guesde was very hostile to the proposition of Jaures, set

in terms to which these conventions had become accustomed.

Jaures replied to me:

"My friend, I know your preoccupation with national defense. And it is exactly for that reason I am so insistent on having you join us; those ideas must be defended within the Party; you are quite qualified to do it."

Then, returning to our friendly controversy, he said:

"Yes, I know well the risks involved. But, you see, one must do everything, follow through to the end a desperate effort to prevent war. It would be a dreadful thing!"

Pausing briefly, he added—and I shall never forget these words, uttered with prophetic seriousness:

"*They'll kill us first . . . maybe they'll regret it, after . . . It will be too late!*"

I turned to go, and said to him, replying to his invitation, so pressing, so affectionate:

"Jaures, I promise you I'll join the Party, when I can belong to it and still vote funds for the war and the fleet."

Two weeks later . . . war . . . and the assassination of Jaures.

Eighteen months later, on the Lorraine front, I kept the promise I had made to him.

Chapter Eight

THE REPUBLIC WINS THE WAR

Gallieni.—The Workers' Exchange in the trenches.—The victor of the Marne?—Gallieni and the Near East.—On the Lorraine front.—I adhere to the Socialist Party.—Petain in 1917.—What would Jaures have done?—Clemenceau's hour.—"Lafayette, we are here!"—"We bring you the Republic!"—"Allons, enfants de la Patrie!"—The chimes of the Armistice.—For what peace?

The declaration of war caught me bedded down in the Loir-et-Cher with an abscessed larynx, following the bitter fight I had had to put up in the last elections. A losing fight. It irked me not to be able to honor my stripes as a lieutenant of the territorials, which I had never asked for, not wanting the political rank I had occupied to have anything to do with the accomplishment of my military duties.

From the 10th of August, not completely cured, I decided to join up. Rail traffic being heavily encumbered, a garage worker drove me to Paris. Along the road, I passsed regiments moving up in perfect order; the same road where the flood flowing in the opposite direction in 1940 made me unhappily conscious of the contrast.

Upon my arrival in Paris, I went to see Messimy who, with hair disordered, very much the Revolutionary dignitary, faced the crushing responsibility of the mobilization. After our greeting, I said: "Give me a job."

A very dapper general, with moustache like that of an old Gaul, was waiting. Messimy had him come in, and introduced us.

"General Hirschauer . . . Paul-Boncour, former Minister of Labor." And, to the general, he added, "Here's your man."

Hirschauer was a general of the Engineer Corps, in consequence, one of the two chiefs of staff of the troops defending the Paris area. He was personally charged with putting it in a state of defense.

I did not at first understand what I, an infantryman, could do in the engineer arm, a branch of the service I quickly learned to appreciate for its science and its seriousness, just as I appreciated and admired this chief, who later became a senator for liberated Alsace.

After Charleroi, I understood.

General Michel, then in command of the Paris area, has been accused of negligence in organizing its defense. He was strictly following the mobilization schedule which, conforming to the great expectations of the all-out offensive so paramount in military circles these last years, was to require *forty* days for its completion. It was thought that it would not have to be accomplished; it had been planned that the artillery of the forts and the siege guns the capital had available—that it *should* have had available, for there was not much of it—would be transported as soon as possible to positions before Metz and Thionville!

Events decided otherwise.

One afternoon, as I awaited General Hirschauer and General Michel at the Invalides, to go with them on an inspection of the defenses, I could read in their faces the disaster of Charleroi.

Next day, without giving me the details, General Hirschauer, aware of the close relationship between Messimy and myself, and not wanting to give an account of the disaster over his chief's head, asked me to explain the exact situation to Messimy as a personal friend, and point out how reality was going to necessitate a change in plan.

Messimy, who had retained all his esteem for Gallieni, and had long pondered whether to use him or Joffre, when it was a question of choosing a commander-in-chief, readily understood the importance of Paris in the present status, and saw that a man was needed there who would work at full speed and make good use of the slender means at his disposal. He appointed Gallieni Governor of Paris and commander-in-chief of the outlying defenses. At the same time, he made these effective by putting pressure on the Grand Headquarters to constitute an army for that purpose. It was this army, placed under the command of General Manoury, that was to play a decisive role in the Battle of the Marne.

Forty-eight hours after General Gallieni took over, General Hirschauer called me into his office.

"The Governor," he said, "is very concerned about the situation. He considers it imposssible to get the defensive organizations, even the lightest of them, set up in the short period of time unfortunately imposed on us, with just the engineer units available and the territorials. He sees no other alternative than to call upon civilian labor. There are workers who are unemployed; it doesn't appear to be impossible; you were the Minister of Labor; would you take charge of it?"

"Gladly."

"Then the mission is yours. Where will you start?"

"At the employment center, the Workers' Exchange."

Hirschauer was stunned. "You can't mean it."

The Workers' Exchange, the Federation of Exchanges, the Confederation of Labor, had all been wildly antimilitaristic these last years, recommending direct action, the rifle reversed, etc.

"Let me handle it, General; something tells me a lot of ideas have changed. And then, as you say, there's unemployment, more of it than you imagine. It'll be arranged."

For, anticipating a short war, the moratorium, the almost complete stoppage of all enterprises except the manufacture of munitions—which had not yet begun to any great degree—had put tens of thousands of workers out of work.

I added, "If it goes, the Governor can sanction my hiring terms. If it fails, he can cancel them."

And I left for the Workers' Exchange.

It was, I can well believe, the first time an officer in field uniform crossed the threshold since that May Day in 1907, when a young lieutenant came to proclaim his solidarity with the workers on their festival day. I asked the Secretary of the Exchange to call together the Administrative Commission for an urgent communication. And I came face to face with the most talked-about representatives of Trade Unionism, whose tendencies I have mentioned before. I explained the situation to them.

"Your comrades are out of work. The enemy is approaching Paris. You need the work, we need the hands. The defenses have to be put in shape quickly. Will you send out a call for workers?"

They exchanged glances.

"Why not? What are you paying?"

"Union rates."

"Food?"

"The regular rations furnished by the commissariat."

"Sleeping quarters?"

"Either billeted among the inhabitants or in barracks to be built. Each man had better bring a blanket."

They consulted one another again.

"It's agreed."

"For when?" I asked. "And how many can you promise me?"

They reflected.

"Oh . . . a thousand . . . in a few days."

"That's way off. We want two thousand in three days . . . and up to twenty thousand at three-day intervals."

"We'll do our best. *Au revoir*, Lieutenant."

I must confess that I said as I left:

"And you can say to yourselves, if the shells fall, that's no reason to run out on the job. After all, it's the Paris of the Commune you're going to defend."

All went very well; three days later, at dawn, I was sent to check the first departure. The men were to assemble at the Hotel de Ville where M. Delanney, prefect of the Seine, gave us his active assistance.

When I arrived, my two thousand workmen were already in line, haversack over the shoulder, blanket rolled and slung across the back. And the column moved off at the command of a large lad, a sort of General Henriot in a work-blouse, who shouted, "The first one who gets out of line is going to have trouble with me." He was the secretary of the ditch-diggers' union, Hubert, who had lost an arm in the riots at Draveil.

The promised speed was just about maintained and the poor earthworks, hitherto lagging, Gallieni aiding and we seconding, began to take on an aspect already disproportionate with the weapons of the time, and even more so with those of today, but, nevertheless, constituting a battlefield organized in advance, on which one could put up a defense. Only the owners of fine domains in the environs of Paris had anything to say against us. If the discipline was perfect during working hours, if the engineer officers supervising the work informed us that all was going well, we received a number of complaints about the state of the game-preserves and poultry-yards.

To M. Doumer, ex-cabinet minister, ex-governor-general of Indo-China, ex-president of the Chamber of Deputies, who was humbly serving as chief of Gallieni's civil cabinet, and transmitted these complaints to me, I replied:

"Which would you prefer? Should we annoy these people, or get the work done?"

M. Doumer did not hesitate.

This battle, Gallieni had decided, would be fought to the end. Before the government departed for Bordeaux, he had been to see Millerand, who had replaced Messimy as Minister of War. This is their conversation, as reported to me, and I have reason to believe it exact:

"It is understood, Mr. Minister, that I shall give battle when the enemy reaches the limits of our entrenchments."

"Yes, General."

"And if the enemy breaks through, I fight on the outskirts of Paris?"

"Yes, General."

"And then I fight inside Paris?"

"Yes, General."

If I regretted Millerand's later complacencies toward the High Command, abdicating certain governmental prerogatives which I had defended in the Council of Ministers and later had them passed into law, he was under these present circumstances irreproachable in his audacity and cold resolve.

This gave its full meaning to the few lines of the proclamation Gallieni caused to be posted on the walls of Paris, when the government had gone—and gave me a copy as a souvenir.

Fortunately, there was no need to go to this extremity. The afternoon of September 3, in a corridor of the Invalides, still our headquarters before being moved—I do not know why, as very few bombs fell, and the Invalides had more of an air—to the Lycee Victor Duruy, I met a cavalry officer, who asked the way to the office of the Chief of Staff. "I've been sent by the general commanding the cavalry in the Paris area. We expect to be attacked early tomorrow."

Indeed, the swift advance of Von Kluck, commanding the German right wing, moving from north to south, seemed to indicate it. Already our outermost forts and advanced posts had seen the first patrols of the usual Uhlans. The night before, Lieutenant Jean de Castellane and I had delivered the order to set fire to the bridges over the Oise and the Marne nearest to Paris.

But at the same time, our limited air force observed a slackening movement of Von Kluck's army toward Meaux and the southwest, and reported it to Gallieni.

At a glance, the glance of a great leader, he saw the possibilities open to him. He decided to hurl against the right flank of Von Kluck the army of Manoury which, at the insistence of Messimy—as one is too apt to forget—though part of the forces at Joffre's disposal, had been given to Gallieni for the defense of Paris.

Next day, at one p.m., after making all preparations for the attack, Gallieni climbed into his car, a fast one driven by an ace of the steering-wheel. "Don't run over the soldiers," Gallieni used to say. Following the method he had adopted in Madagascar—as I was told by General Gerard, who had been his chief-of-staff there—his decision was to act first, report later. He was now ready to report to Joffre.

It was this that caused Von Kluck, a disconcerted conformist, to write—in an attempt to excuse his defeat—that what happened was without precedent in military instruction, the commander of a fortified place sending the troops designated to defend it into battle beyond the defense perimeter.

It is certain that the initiative was audacious; Gallieni would have been roundly reproached if it had failed. It is also certain that it touched off the Battle of the Marne.

Not that the battle was not a part of Joffre's plan. There have been many attempts to picture the two men as opposing each other; and their entourages have contributed considerably to it. Under the circumstances here involved, their temperaments were complementary, their views mutually helpful. Joffre? A 1914 Koutousoff! Nothing could be closer to the unforgettable portrait Tolstoy paints of the Russian general in *War and Peace* than this fat, placid man, taking the blow of Charleroi, retreating in good order right up to the outskirts of Paris, and who might have withdrawn further and waited some days before again taking the offensive had Gallieni not gone into action. This would appear to be indicated in a prudent dispatch sent by Joffre to Bordeaux, where the government had taken refuge; a message in which he covered Gallieni and yielded to his reasons.

But it was also necessary to convince Field-Marshal French. This was a little more difficult; there was no single command; that only came later; and French seemed to favor further withdrawal. I had even been sent to Melun, on the Seine, the night before, to recruit civilian manpower destined for the organization of a bridgehead. But Joffre was tenacious and Gallieni importunate. That evening an accord was reached; Galliene returned to the Invalides to give his orders, while Joffre issued his famous proclamation: "No further retreat . . . die where we stand . . . etc. . . ."

The rest is history.

Also the anxiety, which ended with the second day of the battle. Von Kluck had been able to extricate his army, thanks to the over-prolonged retreat of the British, which had continued during the talks at which the offensive was decided; he even threatened in turn the left wing of Manoury. It has become a legend—though a part of history as I saw it and lived it—that the blow was parried by the units sent by Lyautey—who stripped Morocco to do so, holding that territory from then on by his personal prestige alone—and rushed in taxis to the danger point of the battle, there being little or no motorized transport in those days.

Meanwhile, at the extreme right of the front, Sarrail, general of the extreme left, almost disobedient, refused to abandon Verdun and held this supporting-point in readiness for the over-all movement. Strict discipline is a beautiful thing. So is initiative. The Miracle of the Marne was made of these convergent wills, this French unanimity.

And I speak only of what I actually witnessed, or knew by personal means; there are many other glories to be noted in the common glory.

The Victor of the Marne? As in speaking of the builders of cathedrals, one must use the plural, and, above all, not forget the mass of soldiery, the living and the dead.

Paris saved, and the front stabilized, the great talents of Gallieni had nothing more to do. He suffered because he was not better utilized. But his leisures were fruitful; the projects he conceived in long meditations in his office would doubtless have shortened our martyrdom. I had gone to see him, one day, about a service matter. He was there in his bright study, a former classroom where the young girls of the Lycee Victor Duruy, after those of the Sacred Heart, had listened to their professors, and which gave on to the beautiful and quiet garden of this old convent. Seated sedately at his work-table, dressed in his tunic and long trousers, his eyes keenly alert behind his glasses, reminiscent of the spectacles of Faidherbe, he did not remotely resemble that statue you see of him today, on the road to Meaux, or the one on the Esplanade, or any of the paintings of battle scenes in which he is depicted. The iconography of modern wars and their generals in heavy boots, draped in the folds of a greatcoat whipped by the wind, an arm indicating the direction of the enemy, are quite misleading.

This extreme simplicity, this unwarlike apparel, were well-liked by those who knew that it was thus he had planned and executed his Battle of the Ourcq. Times have changed since, as in Bossuet's funeral oration, the great Condé found in his battlefield reflexes the inspirations of his genius. And it is thus that I remember Gallieni, in a photograph he gave me, and in that copy of his celebrated proclamation. The words he inscribed on the photograph were the joy of Gustave Tery, when he came to consult me in my law office: "To Lieutenant Paul-Boncour, in memory of Waldeck-Rousseau, and of the *interesting days* we spent together in Paris . . . September, 1914."

For, as soon as service questions were disposed of, the memory of Waldeck-Rousseau gave to our conversation a less hierarchic turn. He knew that I had served under Waldeck and the esteem I had for him. The two men were well-suited to a mutual understanding; taciturn, both of them; both loving order and method; their instructions were equally laconic, but such that the responsibility of those executing them was involved. When Gallieni directed the Grand Maneuvers, as Inspector of the Army, before his retirement, he was able to write out three days' instructions in an order of five lines. And General Gerard, in our evening talks in Lorraine, told me that in Madagascar he frequently gave an administrator or an officer, about to go up-country, brief instructions, but so precise and outlining so thoroughly the activity of his subordinate, that he could add, "I'll come and see you in a year, to judge how well you've executed your orders." Traits of character that Waldeck would have loved, they were so like his own. And Gallieni remained grateful to him for the unreserved support Waldeck gave him, at a time when the general distrusted government offices and ministers; when he had something in mind that was very important to him, he took care that the instructions he had to ask for would arrive after he had succeeded.

That brought us to a talk, not about politics, but about the useful role Parliament and its committees could play in shaking off the inertia into which the heavy armature of the Grand Headquarters had a tendency to slip. And, not without reason, he felt a certain bitterness toward Grand Headquarters.

He did not appear particularly convinced. Military men, even the best of them, are always a little distrustful of politicians; all that talk, inseparable from assemblies, clashes with their desire for action, when they have any such desire, as was the case with Gallieni. But, in 1916, at the end of my holiday of convalescence, before rejoining the front, I went to see him at the Hotel Trianon at Versailles, where he was resting between two stages of the prostate operation which was to carry him off. He had just had a ministerial experience, and it had been no more successful than the one Lyautey tried; the Ministry of War had been stripped of just about all its powers by the Grand Headquarters; men of action were finding themselves paralyzed there. His colleagues—and, if one is to believe the *Memoirs* of M. Poincaré, his President of the Council—had not helped him much. But he had known how to see and judge. He said to me. "Monsieur Boncour, you were right. I could tell there's a lot to be done with Parliament."

That day, at the end of 1914, maps interested him more. There was the map of the front, of course, marked with tiny flags, which barely moved any more. There was another: that of Greece and the Balkans, striped with arrows of different colors. Several days later, Gheusi, director of the Opera Comique in civil life, now a reserve captain of artillery, and a very trusted friend of Gallieni, who had made him his aide-de-camp, came looking for me. He knew of our conversation—he had even arranged it—for he was as gracious with his friends as he was devoted to his chief, with a useful, very useful devotion; this shrewd fellow from Languedoc, who had become quite Parisian, and the intimate of a number of political figures and journalists, cleared up a good many misunderstandings to the benefit of his chief, misunderstandings created by the great popularity enjoyed by the Savior of Paris—to the annoyance of some. He explained to me the general's views: Gallieni believed it was all but impossible to break through the German front in France, where the respective forces, solidly entrenched, were about equal; one must look afar for a suitable place for a break-through or a passage that would enable us to take the enemy in the rear. The front no longer extended from the North Sea to Switzerland, but from the North Sea to the Dardanelles; which is what the Grand Headquarters appeared not to see. An operation by way of Salonika or any other port of this region would merely be, widened to the extent of the immense front, the application of an old strategic rule: attack at the weakest point and where the exploitation of success can give the maximum results.

I have never played at being a strategist. Nor am I hypocritical enough to say that strategy is a domain forbidden to governments, who are ultimately charged with the responsibilities of the war, and that they cannot judge strategy on its major outlines. There is no need to be a physician to understand the *Introduction à la Medicine Experimentale* by Claude Bernard, any more than you have to be a mathematician to read Einstein. On a given level, certain simple ideas are accessible even to non-specialists. Particularly these of Gallieni's. I accepted the suggestion Gheusi made, my impression being that Gallieni was not a stranger to it. Gheusi knew of my friendly relations with Briand, and judged that to go himself would involve Gallieni too much, and too publicly.

Briand, at that time, was merely Keeper of the Seals; but he was, in the government, the one most likely to understand the plan, being of an open mind, while Millerand, the Minister of War, would see and hear no suggestions but those of the High Command. So I went to see Briand. He was interested; he even sent for a map, so he could follow better. After which, I heard nothing. And Gallieni remained in Paris.

But Briand, who knew how to wait, and liked to let ideas ripen over a long period, with no particular haste to put them into execution, took advantage of an occasion, at the Council of Ministers, when someone was deploring the useless offensives and the resultant stagnation of the front, to remark that there might be another solution. Perhaps Joffre could be summoned to discuss it.

"Impossible," said Poincaré, speaking as a jurist, "the Constitution is opposed to having the Commander-in-Chief sit in on the deliberations of the Council of Ministers."

(It would appear that this rule was not followed in June, 1940).

"That doesn't matter," said Briand, ingeniously. "Invite Joffre to luncheon, and the Council can simply continue its deliberations in the dining-room."

Which was done. But as often happens at political luncheons organized to discuss one thing, the talk veered to another subject. Joffre ate well; he slept well; even before a battle, like Condé, but in his bed, where no one wanted to wake him. It was only when the coffee was served, and he was busy stirring it, that he was asked:

"What would you think, General, of an expeditionary force being sent to Salonika, or some other port, to attack the Austro-German army in the rear?"

To ask any commander, or any functionary, to detach part of his manpower and resources for an enterprise beyond his immediate needs, is asking a lot. General Joffre was unenthusiastic. No one insisted.

And Briand waited once more to resubmit his idea.

Politics, and it was not the politicians who took the initiative this time, gave him the opportunity. Grand Headquarters, very unjust toward Sarrail, had relieved him of his command in the Argonne; he was in Paris, unemployed, and his friends of the Left began to agitate on his behalf, protesting a removal which seemed to have politics as its basis. Furthermore, Gallieni's idea, adopted by Briand, whether it had made its way in people's minds, or whether its evident clarity had imposed it, was gaining ground. A decision was arrived at, to send Sarrail to Salonika and to assemble an army which, as long as Sarrail remained there, was too deficient in numbers and armament to successfully carry out the large-scale operation. Later, it was strengthened, under General Guillaumat's command, and further increased when General Franchet d'Esperey was in charge. The use made of it is well-known, and how it was this army, together with the battering-ram blows of Foch in the west, that began the enemy's debacle.

Franchet d'Esperey was promoted to Marshal, which he merited. But when, in 1932, as Minister of War, I presented the baton, as a posthumous honor, to the son of my former chief, I was thinking not only of Paris and the Ourcq.

I only saw Gallieni again, before my visit on the eve of his death, to take leave of him. Paris was then quite quiet under the protection of the trenches of the Aisne, where I had often walked, as inviolate as those of the enemy across the way. I considered it unseemly for a man of politics to parade his uniform when there was fighting elsewhere; and I made reiterated requests to be sent to the front. Getting no reply, I decided on the one approach possible, at least for me, in wartime: I went to call on Millerand. He understood, but said gruffly, "In any case, there are two generals I wouldn't send you to, Sarrail and Gerard." Two notorious Republicans. Was Millerand distrustful of politicians, more than one of whom was shuttling between army headquarters and the Chamber of Deputies, either to undermine or build up such and such a general, according to their own interests or those of their party? This was not the case with me. In addition to the fact that I was no longer a member of Parliament, I always try to perform the duty assigned to me to the best of my ability, and to do nothing else. At the moment, there was a war on. I told Millerand I would be very much obliged to him, no matter where I should be assigned, so long as I could serve. I was sent to the Second Bureau of Detachment of the army of Lorraine, commanded by General Humbert, a splendid soldier, a leader of value, but with whom there was certainly no Republican collusion to fear. This did not prevent him from displaying toward me, when he came to know me, a benevolence which outlasted his transfer to another command. He continued to keep up the best relations with me, even asking me to rejoin him. Ironically, he was replaced by one of the very generals from whom Millerand tried to preserve me: General Gerard. I stayed with him until the armistice, following him in his successive commands, with the First Army, and the Eighth, and was even, at certain periods, his intimate collaborator.

In my memory, as on a film screen, the dates roll by in huge numerals . . . 1915 . . . 1916 . . . 1917 . . . . Years heavy with so many sacrifices, with no weakening of the spirit of abnegation of that admirable army Joffre addressed as, "Soldiers of the Republic!"

For, after all, it was the Republic that had made it. The

same institutions, the same regime, accursed today under the weight of defeat.

1915

Perthes, Les Eparges, Vauquois, Carency, Les Hurlus. . . . Names that, until then, were only a mark on a map, a remote corner in the chalk-land of Champagne or the mud of Flanders, passed into a page of history all too forgotten today, since one now speaks against so many things for which so many men have died, and one accepts so easily, collaborating with the invader, the occupation of a territory of which it had been said that one inch was worth all those deaths.

We received the still vibrant impressions of these battles from our comrades of the units participating in them, many of them sent to recuperate on the Lorraine front, where the vigil never slackened, but calmness prevailed after the first combats of 1914. The High Command could have had its reasons for engaging in those repeated offensives, where the permanence and the extent of sacrifices only equalled the ineffectuality of the efforts to break the equilibrium established after the Marne. The principal reason was the necessity for removing the pressure from the Russian front. The Russian army had assured us the victory of the Marne, obliging Von Moltke to weaken his right wing despite the deathbed plea of Schlieffen. Since then, the Russian lack of preparation, undoing the sacrifices of their soldiers, caused us considerable disappointment. And from what we heard from those engaged in the offensives of ours, the outstanding impression was their futility.

Even the great Battle of Champagne, in September—which left deep impressions in my mind, and a rather vile memory regarding my health—though the fighting was preceded by artillery preparation of an as yet unprecedented duration and intensity, achieved no result, in spite of the high hopes of the first day, and the dispatch credited to General de Castelnau, in which the old Catholic intoned the words of the psalm:

> "*Non nobis, Domine, non nobis . . . Sed gloria tibi Domine. . . .*"

From the command post, where I had been in liaison, I saw three regiments of young boys of the 1915 class mowed down by machine-guns like wheat in harvest-time. The enemy positions had been churned up by our artillery-fire; but its duration had, as always, sufficiently forewarned them, so that they withdrew from their first lines, set up their machine-guns on the far slope, and shattered our assault.

1916

Verdun! For months, hecatombs scattered over the ground ravaged by shellfire and wet with blood, thousands of young men seeking to block the brutal German attack, which had flung its own youth into the butchery for an objective more symbolic than strategic. But even if Verdun had fallen, the general plan of the French armies would not have been dislocated; trenches would have been dug farther back; barbed-wire would have been added to barbed-wire. Since we had dug in, and until the day when Foch, possessing the numerical superiority given him by the American effort, multiplied his battering-ram assaults on a German army already exhausted by its perpetual shuttling between the battle in the east and the battle in the west, and now despairing of victory, no advance was decisive.

If the Battle of Verdun testified to the courage of the German troops, sometimes marching to the sacrifice in close order, its conception hardly does honor to the strategic imagination of their leaders. And when, at the end of the battle, sent in liaison with a group of staff-officers from our neighboring armies, I contemplated those demolished forts, under which we had hollowed others, that landscape, so churned, so furrowed that it looked like an imaginative impression of a depopulated planet, out of which protruded, along with the twisted metal, the debris of human bodies, legs driven into the ground, arms upraised as for a supreme appeal, I asked myself: why? As for us, we had to defend ourselves, our soil. But those across the way? What profit, in relationship to such sacrifices, would they have gained, if they had succeeded?

The lesson bore fruit. At least, on their side. During the years from 1914 to 1939, the German staff worked its imagination tirelessly to find a formula which, by its suddenness and audacity, as soon as the necessary materiel was available, would dispense with these useless slaughters and give an ample and immediate result.

Since the war of the trenches, work was accomplished in Germany.

In 1916, the procedure still involved the more or less classic line attacks and long preparation, which we still expected in 1940, and which produced nothing, except a lot of corpses.

The army adjoining us, with its headquarters at Toul, occupying a quiet front, had the duty of gathering the debris of divisions arriving decimated from the horrible and heroic battle. They sojourned a short time with us, regrouped, and returned to the struggle. General Gerard, who commanded the army, was an infantryman and a colonial veteran, which doubly qualified him for the task. By the care he bestowed upon the soldier, by the material benefits of all sorts brought to these unfortunates, who arrived from Hell, he accomplished what Petain was able to do later, over the entire front, when he took command of the French army after the reverses and rebellions of 1917.

Small causes, great effects. It was touching to watch these brave fellows, arriving discouraged, battered, their soul torn and their greatcoat in shreds, having passed the limit of the possibility of suffering, regaining their courage and confidence little by little. And, rested, reconditioned, they went back to the front by that road from Bar-le-Duc to Verdun, incessantly used, in both directions, by trucks filled with men and materiel. This road, carefully kept in repair all day long, thanks to the foresight of Petain, who had taken over the command after the initial shock, which had had us wavering, it was the umbilical cord that bound the battlefield to the rest of France; the Sacred Way, where no Frenchman should travel without kissing the soil trod by so many soldiers climbing toward the place of sacrifice.

What sadness in writing these things when the occupying

army is there, facing us, in the heart of France! And it is the same Petain who signed the shameful armistice!

It was at that time, under the influence of the drama which, for months, was played alongside us, and from which we received immediate impressions day by day, through the frantic heartbeats of those arriving from it, that, long a Socialist, but kept apart from the Party for reasons I have mentioned, I decided to become a member.

I no longer doubted that this long war—of which the drama of Verdun, though a holocaust, was not going to be a catastrophe like 1870—was a revolution as well as a war. The blood-letting it imposed upon the country, the fearful expenditure of men, material, and wealth, the moral upheaval in the soul of the combatants, like the material upheavals in economy, would bring counter-blows which would continue beyond the war and its conclusion.

A deep conviction was rooted within me, and has never left me, that Europe would perish, the world would be shaken, the human values acquired through civilization would be threatened, if an organization of Europe and the world did not prevent the return of war. And when I glanced over the parties, here or elsewhere, which would be called upon to take part in such organizing, I saw only the Socialist Party, which was sufficiently new and possessed of an ideal vast enough to attempt it. All the others were going to be more or less emptied of their substance, despoiled of their reasons for existing, by the political, economic, social, and moral results of such an event.

Imperfect as it was, and it has shown itself much feebler than one could have supposed, the International, meeting-point of all socialist parties of the different countries, belligerent or neutral, seemed to me to be alone capable of taking charge and animating the new order, after the peace. In any political construction, a party is needed, as a starting-point and as a basis. This is what was well understood by the bolshevist, fascist, and nazi regimes, which quickly shot past democratic socialism, too entangled in the old formulae, and established their order, which the latter two are today trying to impose on others.

So, I no longer had reason for not keeping the promise I made Jaures on July 12, 1914, to which his death added a certain solemnity. "When the party votes funds for the war and the navy, I'll be one of you."

The Party did better than vote them. It was a fundamental factor in the national defense. It kept it animated. Not only had it given its young, like everyone, but its leaders were in the war governments or aided their work, fanatically organizing the defense in the parliamentary group and in the party organizations. In the name of the Confederation Generale du Travail, beside the tomb of Jaures, Jouhaux had answered, "Present!" to the mobilization call. In the government councils, Guesde was among the firmest. Vaillant, in the Chamber of Deputies, found again the patriotic ardor of his youth during the Commune. In September 1914, he could be seen coming down the halls of the Palais Bourbon at the head of a delegation of veterans of the Commune, to urge the government to defend Paris. Albert Thomas organized war production in the factories and promised them the full assistance of labor groups. And those socialists, militant in the Party, working in the factories, dying at the front, did all this—not in spite of being socialists, but because they were socialists, because they had the certitude that the victory of the Allies would be that of democracy and socialism—and with it, the end of wars.

I have long carried on me these verses, written by a socialist schoolteacher, on the eve of battle, from which he was destined not to return:

> "*Matins joyeux, soirs embaumés,*
> *Jardin en fleurs, maison cherie,*
> *Tous mes amis, tous mes aimés,*
> *Mon paradis: c'est ma Patrie.*

O France, si je vous donne tout,
Votre grande oeuvre de lumiere,
L'accomplirez-vous jusqu'au bout?

Je vais mourir pour vous, o France,
Vous vivres pour l'humanité.

These humble words, blood-stained, express what thousands of socialists, in the government, in Parliament, in the factories, at the front, were thinking, after they had received, imposed by war, the great baptism of "La Patrie."

One evening, while from the belfries of the cathedral of the old fortified town of Toul, the bells tolled for the dead of Verdun, I sent my membership application to the socialist party of my native city, where the various stages of my political life had unfolded.

For fifteen years, I remained a member. Not always disciplined but always loyal, I believe. Battling ceaselessly to obtain a revision of certain positions which seemed to me to have been bypassed by events, so that a party, in which I had placed my hopes for the necessary renovations of the post-war period, would be able to accomplish them. I only departed from it when a case of conscience arose for me, the same one that had long deferred my joining it. At the Congress of Tours in 1931, the majority had returned to their ancient errors. I had to choose between party loyalty and the refusal of military expenditures, when the defeat of the Social-Democrats in Germany was a warning to prepare for a possible future war.

1917

A year which, perhaps, a more alert diplomacy, a keener sense of great historical events in the process of accomplishment, could have rendered favorable to peace. It was one of the blackest. Less because of the course of military happenings which, uniformly murderous, did not seriously modify a situation that had reached a sort of bloody equilibrium, than because of what was stirring within our armies.

The peak was reached with the Spring Drive of April, led by General Nivelle. It has been argued that he was hampered by governmental interference, not sufficient to prevent the offensive, but enough to shackle it and shake the confidence of the generals charged with its execution, of whom more than one had denounced its folly.

One, in any case, who was neither general, nor colonel, but a mere major, had not failed to protest; my comrade De Bourbon-Busset, transferred from the army of Lorraine, where we had served together, to the First Army, as chief of the Second Bureau. A great nobleman, somewhat addicted to irony, and who, outside of duty, loved to mystify people. But perspicacious, and not at all afraid to tell his superiors the truth.

By the usual analyses: interrogating prisoners, checking the listening posts, reading letters found on the dead or the wounded, interspersed with information sent along by our observatories and our aviation, he had become convinced that the enemy, aware of our intentions, had taken the necessary measures to paralyze them.

There has been much shouting of betrayal. As if, with the vast preparations necessary for any offensive—battery emplacements, roads of access, munitions depots—until the last months of 1918, there was ever an attack the adversary had not foreseen. This was precisely what rendered them inefficacious, the enemy having long prepared his withdrawals or his reenforcements.

This time, getting ready to shorten his front in the west, and to pull back to the Hindenburg Line, so as to be able to strike heavier blows against the Russians, he had not waited for us to attack. Bourbon had the conviction that the enemy had already pulled out; our offensive would break against prepared positions behind those we would have taken great trouble to destroy.

He told this to his chief, General Debeney, who told Grand Headquarters about it. Grand Headquarters listened, but did not believe. Bourbon insisted. The Commander-in-Chief, Nivelle, came in person to the headquarters of the First Army at Verberie, on the Oise—where I had been stationed a few weeks before, with General Gerard, before leaving with him for the Eighth Army in Lorraine.

Bourbon stated the case with all the clarity he knew how to put into it. He told me he received only this response, which can be interpreted in various ways, unequally indulgent: "Are you aware, Major, of the responsibility you take in affirming information that upsets the plans of the Commander-in-Chief?"

Bourbon, not easily intimidated, went right on affirming it. Was the offensive modified? I do not know. The positive fact is that it took place, and that the result was a complete and murderous failure which profoundly affected the morale of our troops. A British officer—the British were to attack on the left of the First Army—was present at Bourbon's meeting with Nivelle; convinced by Bourbon's presentation, he hastened to let his superiors profit therefrom. Bourbon, meeting him later, just before the end of the war, after the Britisher had become a young general, congratulated him on his rapid advancement. The Britisher responded, "My dear chap, our people know how to reward correct information."

After this disastrous offensive, following others, less important but equally unsuccessful, military uprisings occurred at various places along the front, among regiments that had been particularly decimated. These mutinies were rigorously repressed.

Returning together from a reunion in the Ain, after the war, Painlevé, who had become the parliamentary representative of the district, confided to me what qualms of conscience were unleashed within him, when he had to choose between his human heart and the Commander-in-Chief, who demanded executions.

But repressive measures would not have sufficed to reestablish the morale. The evil was deeper. Few had mutinied; many no longer had confidence. Politics sought to exploit this movement of insubordination after it was over.

Certainly, the Germany of old already knew, though not as well as the Germany of today, how to break down morale before destroying armies. I am not sure in what measure, in

1917, it had succeeded in the interior of the country. The knowledge I had of part of the dossier when, after having commanded a battalion, I became chief of the Service of Information of the Eighth Army, caused me to judge that, among the troops, shielded from these propaganda attempts by their isolation at the front, the mutinies came from purely military motives, the ones I have just indicated.

I had the occasion to explain this before the High Court, where I was called as a witness in the trial of Malvy.

It was, in this instance, that I was able to verify to what a degree, in these affairs, deviations and superpositions of memory occur, and are afterward considered as added truths.*

The great service Petain rendered was not so much the saving of Verdun, for he was not alone in that; it was the

* In 1915, in the Second Bureau of the detachment of the Army of Lorraine, we had a woman agent, remarkably audacious, Madame L . . ., wife of an adjutant, who had entered our service, and, with the aid of one of our best men, N . . ., an inspector of the Surete and an old hand at shadowing suspects on the Lorraine frontier, we were frequently able to get her through our lines. She brought us, from Metz, information all the more interesting because she had been able to make contact with the Information Service of the other side.

In July 1915, if I am not mistaken, she returned from one of her voyages bringing a sensational revelation, even a bit too sensational not to be viewed with caution. The chief of the German Information Service had said to her, "On your next trip, we'll entrust you with a mission to a member of the French government, who is working for us!"

The chief of our Second Bureau, Major de Thomason, whose benevolence toward me, his Socialist subordinate, former Minister of Labor in a Leftist cabinet, I shall never forget, was not too favorably disposed toward our government. He said to me one day, "People are afraid of being called reactionary? If I founded a newspaper, I'd like to call it '*La Reaction!*' " But he was a man with a conscience, a man of loyalty. Rather reserved in manner. His aide, Captain Bourbon-Busset, the same one who demonstrated his perspicacity before the 1917 offensive, did not believe a word of our woman agent's story. However, we turned in the information. Grand Headquarters and the Ministry of War must have checked it by means we did not have at our disposal, and let the affair drop, for we heard no more about it.

But Madame L . . . made no more trips. Grand Headquarters

rebuilding of the morale of an army, profoundly shaken by too many bloody attacks, the only utility of which was to hold down more German forces on our front, thus relieving the hard-pressed Russians, an indirect and faraway goal, its benefit not too clearly apparent to the victims, to whom there was no attempt to explain it.

Petain, now Commander-in-Chief, understood the real

---

doubtless considered that certain information she had supplied, having brought about the execution of German agents, notably two women in Lorraine, would result in her own execution if she returned there. Courageously, she wanted to continue her service. Her request went unheeded. Insufficiently recompensed—we are rather parsimonious in paying for services of this sort—she lived quietly, operating a canteen we had presented to her as an ample reward.

But when the trial before the High Court began, her imagination took flight and she wrote to the newspaper, *L'Action Francaise*, her account of the happenings, what the chief of the German service had confided to her, and that, despite her requests, we had not permitted her to return to Germany, where she would have obtained the name of the traitor-minister. One can imagine how *L'Action Francaise* took up the story.

It did such a job that Madame L . . . was subpoenaed to appear before the High Court and testified in that sense.

Curious to get this clear when I returned to the front, after my appearance before the High Court, I sent for Inspector N . . . and asked him:

"Do you recall exactly what Madame L . . . told you when she got off the train at the frontier station where you were waiting for her? It was on the Swiss border, wasn't it? She'd crossed Switzerland, coming from Metz?"

"Yes, major. Lieutenant P . . ., chief of the German Information Service at Metz, had told her that on her next trip, he would give her a mission to someone who could *approach* the French government and was in their service."

Notice the superposition!

The information could still be grave, if it had to do with a personage of importance; which was not to be excluded, for the Fifth Column, though not called that as yet, was already functioning.

But it could also point to one of those adventurers who swarm in the backwaters of politics, and who, to get more money, was boasting of his connections.

In any case, nothing, in reality, to justify the monstrous suspicion which, for a moment, appeared to apply to the accused before the High Court.

motives for these military seditions. A great leader, he was not afraid to act like an infantry colonel again, to study the needs of the soldier, his comfort, his morale. By a series of very simple prescriptions, containing a goodly amount of good sense and concern for his men, he reduced the fever.

Chief of the Information Service of the Eighth Army, and as such, charged with these questions, I was able to verify how each of these measures prescribed by the Commander-in-Chief had immediate repercussions on the morale of the divisions. Many of them continued to pass along our route in turn, coming from various sectors of the front, to rest at ours, which remained calm, although each year we prepared to repulse conscientiously the offensive announced as coming our way, but which never arrived.

With a more comprehensive glance, Petain had appraised the situation as a whole, and knew what it required. Often, at the mess, my commissioned comrades testified that, at the War College, he had been the first to measure the effects of fire-power, the result of the rapid-fire rifle, itself surpassed by automatic weapons, and the modifications that would bring to tactics and strategy. In the same way, he measured, after the experience of three years of war, the enormous quantity of artillery, munitions, and materiel of all sorts needed for a successful offensive. He decided not to order another offensive until our war-plants were in a position to furnish the weapons and munitions. Painlevé, who had confidence in him, made the government accept this decision, which prolonged the war by many months, but was full of wisdom and a comprehension of realities that should have been seen sooner.

Another consideration made this waiting role advisable; on April 6, 1917, America entered the war. By the end of the year, her troops began to disembark. Why use up our men and kill them off in limited and isolated attacks, when, in a year's time, one would have available, with the uninterrupted flow of American manpower and production, the effectives and material necessary for extended operations on all sectors of the front?

It seems very simple. Nevertheless, at the time, amid the

lassitude of a war that had already lasted so long, it needed clairvoyance and courage to have it accepted.

Often, in our personal or public life, when we have lost someone dear to us, or who was our guiding star, we ask ourselves, "What would he have done?"

How many times, during the year of 1917, in the cell of the former convent which served as my office, or in my dugouts in the forests of Champenoux or Parroy, where I commanded my battalion, I would ask myself, "What would Jaures have done?"

From a military viewpoint, a soldier's glance made this long waiting seem necessary.

But from the political point of view? And that of propaganda? And diplomacy? It seemed that there was undue timidity in not exploiting, for a just and possible peace, one or the other of two great events that marked that year, and which strengthened each other mutually.

America entered the war. She entered without any direct and material interest necessitating it. It would have even been an advantage to her to keep out of it, to continue to supply the belligerents, and to make money. Yet, she came in; laugh if you like; so much the worse for those who deny the role of ideological and moral factors in History; never was the decision to enter a war determined by loftier motives.

These were the ones defined by the high conscience of her responsible leader, holder of the title of President in the American way, where the president presides, where the president governs. In the name of a great Republic of which he was the chief, elected, controlled, but still the chief, Wilson defined the fourteen points which were to be the basis of the armistice, and which should have been the basis of the Peace, the statute of a new order.

But at that moment, at the other end of Europe, riding over into Asia, a revolution rocked a great Empire and substituted for imperialist Russia a government which declared it wanted peace without annexation or contribution.

What dialogue, across two continents!

One voice, that should have been raised on behalf of the Allies, was missing. Jaures had been killed.

One evening, during discussions of the Treaty of November 4, 1911—the treaty between France and Germany, which settled the Agadir affair and gave us Morocco—at the end of a long discourse, rising above the Franco-German problem and encompassing the entire forces of war and the forces of peace, which were vying for the world, Jaures had foreseen the power represented by the great Republic beyond the seas. He had pointed out, in magnificent terms, what deep roots of idealism existed in a people whose material success would lead one to suppose, if one did not know them well, that they were given over to the preoccupation of obtaining it.* And he had invited faraway America to the pacification of a world in peril. With what joy would he have hailed the realization of that evening's dream!

And if one considers that at the moment when American intervention and the promise of their infinite resources sent a

* ". . . and there is a third peaceful force . . . the renaissance of Angle-Saxon America, of the old ideal of the Puritans . . . Messieurs, we do not know, or we only know in its most brutal period, the life of the great American people and the American conscience. We only see in them men of dollars, of millions, of business, of the obsession for gold. From certain signs, one would say they are beginning to pass that crisis, that the millionaires, from the summit of their magnificent fortunes, perceive the emptiness of horizons filled only with the reflection of gold, and seek, before dying, a nobler food for thought, and for their soul.

"One would say that they are surfeited with a fortune that surpasses their faculties of enjoyment and direction, and that they resemble an enormous, tired sun seeking at what spot in the ocean it should extinguish itself.

"Hence these words of melancholy and this cry of lassitude; hence these nostalgic appeals to the fine culture of Latin traditions; hence the regretful phrase of a dying millionaire, 'I'd give all my millions to be able to read Virgil and Homer in the original!' Hence this awakening of idealism, which is not on the surface, because it goes deep, past the dollar period, the period of mercantile materialism, down to the sources of English and American life, to the soul of those Puritans filled with the enthusiasm of the biblical prophets and dreaming in their fashion of a society living in liberty and justice . . ."

shudder of inevitable defeat into the German soul, the Russian revolution gave hope of a possible peace, does it not seem that a better utilization of these two events by statesmen capable of grasping their amplitude and presenting them to public opinion would have hastened the hour when peace could be concluded?

Not among the chiefs, nor with the Kaiser—who, incidentally, carried little weight in the decisions of the two dictators, Hindenburg and Ludendorf—nor with those still haunted by their imperialist dream, but with the rank and file of the German army, the fact of the Russian revolution had repercussions, as I was able to convince myself. The interrogation of prisoners, the reading of letters, the reports of our agents, lastly the usual information-gathering apparatus had permitted the measuring of its importance. In 1914, the German people had been made to believe they were menaced by Czarist Russia. Revolutionary Russia proclaimed it had nothing to demand. Then why continue to fight? I remember quite well conversations with officer prisoners which confirmed that state of mind.

It was only momentary. But it existed. If we had seized it, if we had utilized the maneuver against the morale of the enemy, as the totalitarian states were to give us such cruel lessons later, is it not likely that Germany, who had its own revolution a year later, would have done so a year earlier?

Right at that moment, a rare opportunity for propaganda was given us. An international socialist conference was to meet at Stockholm. Who knows, if French and British Socialists would go there to bring word from their countries and peace proposals such as Wilson in America and Kerensky in Russia had outlined, would they not awaken ideas and arouse movements of unforseeable importance? So much discontent and so many sufferings were already fermenting among the peoples of the Central Powers in that year of 1917!

But we were afraid. Going to Stockholm was forbidden. Then it was authorized; but the reunion was made difficult. The conference was held anyway; but the Socialist patriots, not wanting to attend without the express consent of their government—and quite rightly—it was the other kind who went. Not defeatists; in that war, except for a handful of "Kientaliens" and "Zimmervaldiens," there were none; but there were pacifists-at-any-price, still retaining excessive confidence in a somewhat dismembered Internationale. So the German and Austrian Socialists heard none of the sort of talk that would have precipitated it. It was only a danger now, instead of a hope.

Jaures would have prevented that.

As for the Russian revolution, we demanded of it, and of that unhappy Kerensky, incapable of saying no, immediate offensives, which were impossible in the state of disorganization and demoralization in which the Russian army found itself. They contributed to the downfall of the first revolution, and the success of the Bolshevist revolution of October, which led to the peace of Brest-Litowsk, creating the difficult and dangerous situation wherein we were to find ourselves in the spring of 1918, before the American troops were ready to go to the front.

Since we are in the domain of hypotheses, who knows if the little emperor, Charles, the first to talk sincerely of peace, would not have discovered in the socialist Jaures—who had announced the coming resurrection of oppressed nations, but knew that they were hot-beds of war unless integrated in a new order—a man of greater understanding than those statesmen who believed themselves to be realists, but went ahead with the dismembering of Austria without asking themselves what they would put in its place?

I know the element of fantasy in such second-guessing, which has all the inconvenience of future predictions. But who can tell? When events have taken a certain turn, it is permissible to ask what would have happened if they had taken a different direction. I believe there was, in 1917, a collection of possibilities which more audacious statesmen, with longer vision, backed by less unstable majorities and better determined currents of opinion, could have used to better advantage.

Was this not what Caillaux saw, and which determined him to make rather vague contacts, until he found himself charged with a crime? I am willing to believe so. But, a parliamentarian of high quality, he also had the limitations thereof. He had neither the inclination nor the means of arousing mass movements in the Central Powers, a preliminary to any useful negotiation. It would have required Jaures and his influence over the Socialists of all countries, for they alone could crystallize the discontent and channel the anger, as they did one year later.

It was perhaps from a realization of this that Caillaux spoke of Jaures with such admiration, during a conversation I had with him a short time before his arrest, and which I mentioned in Chapter Seven.

Since these possibilities had not been grasped, it was necessary to play the game out to the end, and let the force of arms decide. The hour was one for energy without nuances.

That meant Clemenceau.

Of the two great events that had marked 1917, one had turned out very badly. The peace of Brest-Litowsk had sent almost the entire strength of the German forces rolling toward us, and the offensive of Ludendorf, then at the peak of his career, a true war-lord, under cover of Hindenburg, made us relive the worst days of the struggle.

But it seems that France, unable to find, in the war of 1939, either the government leaders or the military chiefs so badly needed, was luckier in 1914, or more vigorous. In the most dramatic moments, the men of the hour, military or political, were ready.

The 1914 Koutousoff, with his imperturbable calm and his deliberate retreat almost right up to the outer defenses of Paris, had transformed into the victory of the Marne the defeats of Charleroi and Lorraine. The wisdom of Petain, aided by the confidence Painlevé had in him, had saved the French army, exhausted and demoralized by murderous and finally inefficacious offensives into which the High Command had gradually slipped. Petain rested his army, strengthened it, took it in hand. But if his wisdom had preserved our soldiers, it would still not have sufficed to bring us victory. It needed Foch and his audacity. And it required his becoming the Supreme Commander of all the allied armies.

But also, providentially—if Providence can be mentioned in connection with an unbeliever—there was in the government a man with an energy accumulated during more than a half-century of ferocious opposition. For, except for three years in power, which had not impaired him—others have become debilitated in less time—since the Empire and prison, Clemenceau was always more or less in opposition.

The war found him all the more vehement because he stood alone, or almost alone. So alone that a misadventure happened to him, rather unusual for an ex-Premier, even more so for a man with such a past as a leader accustomed to be followed.

Since the beginning of the war, he had abstained from ascending to the rostrum. He had been made president of one of those parliamentary committees of which Gallieni said to me, a few days before his death, that they were of considerable support in getting things done, and played a more active and effective role in the 1914 conflict than those of today, when it seems that everything has become enfeebled, military command, government, and Parliament. For months, Clemenceau animated with his fighting vigor the Senatorial Army Committee, to which a great deal was owed in the effort pursued and the reforms realized in our army organization and the speeding-up of manufacture.

Pitilessly, he brought the ministers before him, and would not permit them to hide behind their subordinates when they had not been doing their work, which was to supply the army's needs, and to see to it that the High Command did not settle down too comfortably to the business of war, but went at it with the energy such as he himself displayed.

The day came, however, when he decided to develop before the Senate the searching criticism which, each day since the war began, he had tirelessly presented in the columns of his newspaper, *L'Homme Libre*, or as he renamed it, after the censors got through with it, *L'Homme Enchainé*. He took to task Poincaré, the government, and the High Command, which he accused of uncertainty, weakness, and lack of imagination. "The Germans are still at Noyon." He found again, in this campaign, along with his customary injustices, all the ardor of his youth and that mastery of attack that had cost the governments of the 1880's so dearly, as it had those of the Dreyfus Affair.

His patriotism and his pride, the one incontestable, the other legitimate, had convinced him that he alone was capable of winning the war for us. Which is indeed what happened.

But the Senate, respectful of the presidency, the government, and the High Command, would hear nothing. It inflicted upon him the cruel disappointment of giving him only three votes at the conclusion of his appeal. Three votes for him . . . Clemenceau . . . once the dreaded leader of the Extreme Left, the energetic chief of the 1906 government, the man who overthrew Briand and Caillaux in this same Senate, the man so long respected and feared by most of these timid souls who voted against him.

I was in Paris at the time, convalescing from an operation. The affectionately friendly relations I had with him since I had been a collaborator of his *Homme Libre*, and during the 1906 ministry, when I ran the office for Viviani, the Minister of Labor, authorized me to go and see him. He had not held it against me when, favoring my trade union ideas over my friendship for him, I had voted against him in 1909, at the time of the postal strike. My adversaries having made capital of this during the 1914 elections, he had written me a letter, as affectionate as it was ironical, in his usual style, saying in substance: "When one is lucky enough to have a deputy sufficiently independent to vote according to his conscience, one retains him." The Old Opponent had these indulgences for his young successors.

A meeting at Toul, during the war, had brought us still closer together.

In the spring of 1916, a typical Lorraine springtime, cutting and cold, he had obtained authorization to come and get a little of the air at the front, which he liked so much, and, as chief of the government and of the army, for it was his understanding that he was both, he was to indulge in frequently. Grand Headquarters had not dared refuse, but "to do him honor," as Louis XI says of the Duke of Burgundy in Casimir Delavigne's tragedy, they had him accompanied by an officer to watch over what he said at the same time he watched over him.

This did not bother him much, and after he had been to the most advanced section of our front line—for he was not one of those tourists who huddle at headquarters after a vague excursion at the back of the front—we were lunching together at the table of General Gerard, the army commander when, half mocking, half serious, he spoke of the High Command, the government, and the Chief of State in terms alluding to the most energetic decisions of the Revolution, the unity of which he praised. "Too bad he can't be locked up in the Temple," he said of a very important personage. The principal one, in fact.

I was not in the best shape, suffering from an extremely painful and purulent sinusitis, brought on by tear-gas inhaled during the fighting in Champagne in September 1915. It had resisted the entire series of rather disagreeable treatments, even those of the eminent rhino-laryngologist, my friend Doctor Le Mee. It was necessary to resort to the radical cure, under chloroform, at the hospital in Nancy, a few months later.

However, I had not wanted to leave the front and my job. Clemenceau did not care much for political figures, of an age to serve, who remained in civil life. He told me so in his own way. When he took leave of us, after a disagreeable word for the officer from Headquarters, whose presence had irked him, I moved toward Clemenceau, held out my hand. "No, both!" he said. And, taking my two hands, he gripped them hard, with a show of emotion.

The day after his resounding defeat in the Senate, I was with him. His anteroom was not crowded that morning. Under his heavy brows, his mocking eyes were almost tender for this eccentric who had come to visit him. He was seated in his armchair, at that great horseshoe-shaped table which interviewers have described, in a setting adorned with marbles and casts of Greece—which, along with France, was his religion—a room well-known to pilgrims who journey to his home, now transformed into a museum, thanks to the piety of

Jeanneney and the Friends of Clemenceau. He was a sick man, suffering too from a sinus condition, on his head the triple-pointed cap, which became legendary when glory returned to him with victory and vengeance.

He was already thinking about "*La Revanche*." Ill, beaten, crushed as no parliamentarian had ever been on the occasion of an interpellation, he still thought only of revenge. What a lesson of energy I learned that morning! I had learned another in his empty antechamber; ingratitude, the extent of which he was to measure a few years later, after having been at the peak of popularity, is the lot of public figures. However, it took the horror of that defeat to point to what depths ingratitude can descend.

He remained very mysterious about the manner in which he would gain this revenge.

"Well, *Monsieur le President*, what will you do now?" I asked.

"Rest a bit . . . let them blow."

By "them," he meant all those who refused to learn, the wilfully blind, the timorous, the hesitant, those he had spent his life trying to jolt–with unequal success.

". . . and then resume the struggle . . . but on other grounds," Clemenceau added.

"On what grounds?"

"Ah, my dear fellow, permit me not to answer that . . . yet." And, his eyes blinking, ferocious again, he said, "I have my own idea!"

A few months later, still attacking the President of the Republic, the government, and the High Command, he began another campaign, remounted to the rostrum, to make a quite different speech to the Senate, denouncing the defeatists and the treasons.

This time, he stepped down, a victor. Disappointments had been aggravated in the meantime; the year 1917, marked by the disastrous April offensive, had been one of the worst of the war; not a few of his criticisms of the High Command had been verified; the Germans were still at Noyon. To palliate these displeasures–there must always be a scape-goat–it was no longer the President of the Republic, the government, and the High Command, respect for whom had paralyzed his listeners in November 1916, but those he now designated as traitors and defeatists, thus making himself the rallying-point for all those who want a change. A new ministerial crisis having developed, the Painlevé ministry overthrown after the Ribot ministry, which had succeeded the Briand ministry, Poincaré, despite the repugnance he might have felt, sacrificed it to his sense of duty and patroitism—in no way less than that of Clemenceau—and called on his old enemy to form a cabinet. In time of war, there remained but one enemy, the one who occupied our territory.

The rest is well-known; how, without ever disavowing parliamentary control or trampling on our institutions, Clemenceau made our government one of authority, awakened the energy of the High Command, gave confidence to the Nation, and guided us to victory, borne to the clouds by those who, like the *Action Francaise*, had dragged him in the dirt a short time before.

I am not sure, but the idea persists that it was that means of turning public opinion in his favor he had in mind, in the rather mysterious finish of our conversation, immediately after his parliamentary defeat.

A beautiful revenge indeed, if he had been capable of planning any other revenge than that of France! But that was all he thought of. Across the tumult of an exceptionally unequal and tormented life, one constant, dominating idea; France, brought low in 1870, would rise to victory. Even his anticolonial errors came from a fear that the conquest of distant territories could distract, and lead us to accept something that is, for any people—no matter with what fine words it is coated—a permanent diminution; the acceptance of defeat.

Without these tumults, where his steel was tested, would he have been the man we needed when we had to end the war and win it by straining all our springs?

He had conquered, in a grim struggle, the place he coveted in order to accomplish that for which he had lived. He found his plan, and he was worthy of it. He had his proper climate. And this old man blossomed in an astonishing flowering, in the evening of his life. Certainly, he did things in a way I then considered a bit brutal. Except for his treatment of Caillaux, which was clearly unjust, and of that against Malvy, where the ferocity surpassed the fault Malvy may have committed, I confess that I would have welcomed such measures before and during the war. I have observed too frequently the ravages effected among us by the Fifth Column and by the complacency with which politicians, writers, journalists, and various functionaries prepared our defeat, opening the way to ideas in the name of which we were to be crushed.

But for those who fought the war, his hardness was tempered with humanity. Under his thick moustache, emotion sometimes made his lip tremble when he came in contact with the troops, whose dangers he shared. In his little residence in the Rue Franklin, which has remained intact, just as he left it on the day of his death, a vase containing a handful of earth from the front, a dried flower picked in the trenches, give a rather unexpected impression of Clemenceau. One is reminded of the sensibilities of a shopgirl, or, better yet, one thinks of those words of Ferry, against whom Clemenceau had fought so often: "My roses grow within."

Prejudices vanished; injustices were appeased; even those he had attacked the most, the military leaders, when he saw their work, felt their anguish, similar to his own, at the time of our hard blows, found in him a loyal defender. Some have forgotten rather quickly. Foch, who sought to quarrel with him; their dispute over the shreds of victory was atrocious. What evil counsellors had passed by there?

And it needed all his authority, his republican prestige, the blend of fear and devotion that went with him. The last quarter-hour was the most painful. And it was his to win or lose. Who else could have surmounted the unrest of a Chamber, reflecting an opinion, that four years of war had badly prepared to continue to endure the alternatives of 1918, where we were tossed in turn from the heights to the depths, almost without transition, from the German break-through on the Marne, to Mangin's break-through in the forest of Villers-Cotterets, beginning that series of attacks, struck in turn by Foch all along the front, each one pushing the adversary further back and liberating more French soil? Offensive, everywhere.

This would not have been possible if, in the spring of 1917, from that Pointe de Grave, scene of Lafayette's departure, we had not seen, coming toward us, the first American troopships. The helmeted Minerva of Bourdelle, still scanning the horizon, unless the Germans have destroyed her, is a symbol and a splendor. And General Pershing's "Lafayette, we are here!", whether he said it or not—as is the case with so many phrases of history—answered a profound reality, and, whatever one thinks of it, a sentimental one. It sounded a death-knell to the German High Command. They knew that the mastery of the sea, the manpower and materiel arriving, were going to tip the scales where our destiny is weighed.

The fierce energy of Clemenceau could not have been used, the military talents of Foch could not have displayed themselves, and the armies would have long continued to be immobilized, face to face, in a war of position, intercut with costly and useless offensives, if, in the summer of 1918, a major event had not taken place, finally shattering the equilibrium of the fighting forces: *the arrival in battle of the American troops.*

And how they were welcomed! In the interior, to begin with! My old house, transformed today into a Kommandantur, had the honor of sheltering a number of officers belonging to units which, coming from Saint Nazaire, were trained in our Touraine before going up to the front. I was up there myself, and could not act as host. I know how the officers and soldiers mixed with the local population, who acclaimed them as saviors, and profited largely from their prodigality. War, in those days, was not one of restrictions.

They found our ancient dwellings a little old. They put them to rather rigorous tests, leaving the windows wide open in winter, then building great fires, which was all very healthy for the vigorous chests of our friends, but rather hard on the woodwork, which had aged.

"Quite a few rats," observed an American comrade, when I had come home on leave.

"But quite a few memories," I replied.

I am sure that, having lived in our homes, where our past is read in the objects, pictures, decor, in the atmosphere which became receptive and familiar for them, because things have a certain sensibility and knew we loved them, a new bond of sentiment was created between us and our guests of the difficult years, who became our comrades of victory, and have remained our friends.

Perhaps this memory, passed along from the veterans of yesterday to the youth of today, has helped their great President to get their country to accept so resolutely the idea of aiding Britain, in a struggle where France is no longer participating, but on which depends our liberation.

If such was their reception in the interior, what must it have been when the first American contingents arrived in our lines? It meant the certainty of getting out of the trenches and marching to victory.

We were fortunate, in the Eighth Army, to have several American divisions on our left flank, facing the plain of the Woevre where, for thirty years, during the between-war period, our strategists believed the first engagements would be fought. All our eventual Commanders-in-Chief successively studied the terrain. General Gerard, pointing it out to me on one of our inspection tours, said that Gallieni had paid it the usual visit.

All the activity took place elsewhere. But in the summer of 1918, with the general offensive, for which Foch now had the manpower and equipment, it regained its importance. At the end of it lay Metz. The American generals, without gold braid and stars, real soldiers of democracy, barely distinguishable from their men, could feel what Metz meant to us. One question went straight to our hearts. It happened at Marbache, at the end of our sector, adjoining the one where the Americans had just moved in. A conference had been held between the staffs of the two armies: General Gerard was explaining to the American generals the places and direction of attack assigned to them. One of them, I believe it was General Liggett, asked, "Will we be with the advance on Metz?" Perhaps, it was only a request for information. Perhaps the operation, which had been the object of so many kriegspiels with us, had reached the military schools of the great Republic? We saw in it the fraternal accord of preoccupations similar to ours, the magnetism of Metz which, with Strasbourg, was one of the two poles of attraction for the between-war generations, still patriotic. Even more so for us, officers of the army of Lorraine, who, for three years, saw it through our field-glasses every day.

It was not only the generals who knew how to find the right thing to say. I cannot forget that of one of the first American officers to arrive on our front. I met him at Nancy. I knew little English; he, not much French; but we understood one another quite well.

"*Alors,*" I said, "*what do you think of France?*"

"Oh," he said, with a very pronounced accent, "little country, little cities, little rivers, little bridges, but. . ." And he lifted his hand high over his head, ". . . the French soldier . . . le poilu francais . . . very big. . . ."

What fine comrades! And what a young army, full of enthusiasm and go! They found us a bit meticulous, when they came to us, these officers, civilians yesterday, with so few generations separating them from the horizons of the Far West and the days of the wide, open spaces, business-men accustomed to seeing far and fast, farmers used to vaster fields than the small ones of Europe. But they were full of consideration for our staff officers, whose imagination was sometimes short, but whose habits of precision and method had mellowed in the hard school of three-and-a-half years of war. The collaboration was cordial, the results excellent. The first action, led with heroic dash by the American army on another section of the front, had caused it to pay dearly for its inexperience. On the other hand, they were able to win back Saint-Mihiel and Thiaucourt for us without too much damage. The first liberated towns of French Lorraine were liberated by the Americans.

In liaison with them, I followed the second of these operations. While I was on the way to Thiaucourt, leaving the Bois-le-Pretre, where the woods now consisted of nothing but calcinated tree-trunks left from the bombardments in the first years of the war, a column of prisoners passed the advancing American soldiers, who were happily noisy, taking little precautions. The Germans, already demoralized, showed little reaction. And I heard the soldiers of the young America, shouting benevolently to the conquered, "We're bringing you the Republic!"

Yes, that is what these people from across the Atlantic imagined they were bringing to a Germany, delivered from its masters, which would then re-enter the free community of democracies.

It was that which had been repeated to the soldiers of France, to sustain their sacrifice. "Soldiers of the Republic," Joffre had said at the start of his proclamations. "*Allons, enfants de la Patrie*," cried Clemenceau, at the end, from the rostrum of the Chamber of Deputies. Words we have not heard very much in this present war. And one already heard less of them right after the armistice.

The armistice! That November 11, 1918! Dear and glorious phantom rising before me on this, its anniversary, as I write this page of recollections! It has been the companion of my public life these twenty years, the reason for my struggles, the inspiration for my acts.

Already the trumpeter of the First Army, commanded by General Debeney, through whose lines the German plenipotentiaries were to pass, had sounded, "Cease Fire!"

Major de Bourbon-Busset, chief of the Second Bureau, my comrade on the staff of the army of Lorraine, then with this same First Army, where I had been assigned for a few months before returning to Lorraine, had been ordered to receive the Germans. If the official discussions and their results belong to history, many picturesque details which preceded or followed the interview in the railroad car at Rethondes are known only to him and to a few comrades of the army of Lorraine, when he related them at our post-war reunions. He has never cared to write them, despite my insistence. What a pity! It would have persuaded people what an important part the German revolution played, with such little help from the Allies later, in the enemy's decisions. Talking with Bourbon, distant but courteous toward the conquered enemy, one of them, M. de Winterfeld, former military attaché at the German Embassy in Paris—a fall from his horse during our grand maneuvers at that time had given him the opportunity to appreciate French hospitality—and now a member of the armistice delegation, remarked, "We are prepared to sign one of the most shameful capitulations in History. We are obliged to, because of the revolution. We don't even know if there will be a Germany tomorrow."

It was signed; the terms were hard, but not shameful; for the German army had fought well, as Foch declared, and he firmly opposed, at least in form, any stiffening of the armistice terms, though he actually held out for the left bank of the Rhine. Let us be thankful to him; we know now the cost of being conquered, and we are being made to walk by the same road to Calvary.

It was signed; and all the trumpets of all the armies, and all the bells of all the churches sent out the great news, so long awaited.

Since the evening before, assured of the imminent armistice by the broadcasts of the German radio, heard by our staffs, I was no longer with my unit. Once more, I was a guest at the Bon-Secours Hospital in Nancy, haven for wounded or sick officers, under the direction of Sister Louise, well-known to all who served with the armies of Lorraine. A saintly woman as well as a diplomat, the care she dispensed in her hospital did not prevent her from exercising her influence on army commanders who came by. Even the most notorious anti-clericals and free-masons—I could, in fact, speak in the singular—after holding out at first, surrendered to it, for the greater good of all, for her kindness was clairvoyant.

It was there I had been operated on in 1916. While the war was on, I had not wanted to be returned to civilian life, as my condition would have warranted; either in the line, or on the staff, I carried out my service duties to the end. Now the war was over; no reason for remaining.

Since our army had been designated for the occupation of the Palatinate, and, as Chief of the Information Service, I would no longer have anything but a civilian and political task, I had no liking for it. A Socialist patriot, having stayed in the war till the last quarter-hour and shared in the victory, like the galley-slave on the last bench in Kipling's story, I foresaw that our armies' penetration into Germany would be quite unlike the advance of our armies of the revolution over the same territory, freed by them from feudal servitude. Nor like that of the armies of the Consulate, those grenadiers who sang the *Carmagnole*, returning from Saint-Cloud, the night of Brumaire, still appeared to the foreigner like propagandists of the Revolution.

They founded clubs and fraternized with jacobins in the occupied cities. It was not quite the same as what we were about to do now. The instructions, as I saw them passed along, were enough to convince me.

There were no more clubs, but there were committees of workers and soldiers, which had sprung up spontaneously along with the defeat, and we would encounter their proclamations as we advanced. They proved, however, that even when it stages a revolution, the German people retains its liking for organization and discipline.

But it was all rather reminiscent of the Russian revolution. And it sounded bad to the ears of most of our military leaders, men who loved order, having no liking for this revolution that had, however, rendered them a great service, and to which, not without some protests, I had proposed a toast, at our mess, during the luncheon that followed the great news.

Incontestable patriots, faithful servants of the country, remarkable technicians, their war experience rectifying their early errors, they were, together with our magnificent soldiers, the artisans of victory. Silent and disciplined, in my place, during four years, I had watched them at work and esteemed them highly. But it was no longer a question of military technique; it was about to become a political question. The future would depend on the orientation we would give to our victory, on the aid we would bring to the German revolution.

For it existed. That it was insufficient, ephemeral, that is possible; we did hardly anything to make it otherwise. But it was there. We saw it through our field-glasses in the trenches across the way. In the days preceding the armistice, we could see German officers molested by their soldiers, weary of the slaughter, stripping off the officers' insignia. A bad example, anyway. What was happening inside Germany was more serious. The spirit of our Commune, of September 4, 1870, had crossed the Rhine. The Republic had been exported to Berlin. There was a movement there which, better supported by the victors, could have gone deeper, shaking the foundations of a disabled Germany, seeking to find itself after its defeat, and where, once the inevitable disorder that comes with all transformation had passed, there were points of support for a German democracy, a requisite for a peaceful Europe.

At least, such was my conviction. And I was in a hurry to help in this conception of victory and its results. For that, I needed to regain my freedom, my speech, my pen.

This I did, after a short sojourn in the hospital, and the convalescence that preceded my demobilization.

That is why I was at the Bon-Secours Hospital, when I heard the bells of November 11th. It was at Nancy, plunged into the blackout for long months, that I saw the lights and the celebrations of a population that had earned the right to let its joy overflow after so much sacrifice and danger.

Next day, returning to the army to bid farewell to General Gerard, whose affectionate confidence in me had often permitted me to join in the preoccupations of his command. And to take leave of my comrades of the staff. Here, better than at Nancy, I could share the joy of our troops. Ah, the beautiful day! If these soldiers had been told, while they sang, after all that fighting, and suffering, that it would be useless. . . . Thank God, for their recompense, they did not give it a thought!

And then, all at once, at a turn in the road, between Nancy and Flavigny, a column of artillery appeared. Going up into the line? To take up position? But the guns were wreathed in foliage and the gunners were singing. A great offensive had been ordered for our front, and, following the traditional army joke, always good for a laugh in the mess, "before carrying out an order, wait for the counter-order," the counter-order never came. So, one moved up. But on the road they had learned of the armistice and decorated the guns with greenery. Thus discipline and sentiment were equally satisfied.

It was in regard to this offensive that General Mangin has been credited with a remark which even if inexact, must have said what he was thinking, and points up rather well his character and his warlike ardor, which brought us—and him—some successes. It was he who had been put in charge of the attack. The chances were serious; the aim was to push through to Strasbourg, where, at the beginning of the war, the fate of our army in the annexed territory took an unfortunate turn. The preparations were far advanced, undertaken for a long time by our own army, with which Mangin's troops were to be integrated. Mangin's men had been superbly trained by their preceding victories, including that of Villers-Cotterets, which had been decisive in the renewal of the general offensive.

Mangin had set up his headquarters in a suburb of Nancy, and his residence in a house surrounded by a park. The day of the armistice, the elderly lady who owned it, met him as he was taking a walk.

"Ah, General, what a lovely day!" she observed.

And he replied, crossly, "I don't think so!"

Si non e vero, e bene trovato.

As a matter of fact, the question has been seriously debated since, whether the operation should have been carried out, and the anticipated victory exploited in Germany. Those who believe that only force will convince people not to make war, claim that we were wrong in not showing the German people, who had not had a taste of it since Jena, what invasion is like, and what it means to have the war brought home to you.

A problem of politics and conscience, which our military leaders solved in its most human sense. But Mangin would not have been Mangin, if he had felt otherwise. In later meetings of the Commission on Studies for the Higher Council of National Defense, over which I presided, I have heard him express opinions which prove that the remark attributed to him, if true, was not merely a retort.

To this thesis, Foch always answered: "From the moment the goals set for me had been attained, not another drop of blood should be shed." Words as sensible as they are humane. One is reminded of Joffre's remark, after the Marne. Someone proposed putting up lanterns in celebration, and Joffre replied, "No, too many men have died. . . ." Such words testify to the state of mind of the conquerors in that war.

But if a sense of measure and of humanity dissuaded us from continuing the fight, it was all the more necessary to carry it into Germany, all the more reason to help Germany consolidate its revolution, and to found a regime, the structure of which would be a safeguard against these warlike enterprises, whereof she had known only the success, never the horror.

It would seem that not much thought was given to it, as our armies advanced in the recaptured provinces, whose joy was the clearest of plebiscites, then in the territories on the left bank of the Rhine which, by the armistice terms, were to be occupied.

After all, that was a government matter. It would have depended on those of our Allies to give directives, to which, with more or less good humor, our generals would have complied. It was not sufficient to make a pilgrimage to the tomb of Hoche and Marceau; it is the memory of what these two had done on this same soil, before they fell, that needed to be reanimated. It is their example that should have been followed. And to let the German Socialists and Republicans know clearly where our sympathies and our support were directed.

What did our own government think about it? What role would our Socialist Party play on this post-victory day, when it was the duty of the victors to fashion the New Europe?

This is what, as I strapped my luggage for the return to Paris, I was in such a hurry to find out. Not being a soldier any longer, I became a militant. . . . Still the struggle. . . . But this was more difficult, morally . . . the good comradeship, the deep-rooted unity of the men at the front. Frenchmen, united during the war, were to find themselves divided on the aims of peace, even sometimes finding themselves in opposition to their allies.

"For each thing, there exists but a moment in human affairs. . . . Later, one no longer has the choice between two ways, and necessity guides. . . ." So said my poor, great Lamennais.

An hour was about to pass . . . that one had not known how to hold.

END, VOLUME ONE

INDEX